# SEBASTIAN WILLIAMS

# SEND THEM TO

# HELL

## The Brutal Horrors of Bangkok's Nightmare Jails

# SEND THEM TO HELL

Sebastian Williams now lives in Spain in semi-retirement with his family, where he is working on his next book.

# SEND THEM TO HELL

## The Brutal Horrors of Bangkok's Nightmare Jails

### SEBASTIAN WILLIAMS

MAINSTREAM
PUBLISHING

EDINBURGH AND LONDON

*To all those throughout the world who don't*
*get a fair crack of the whip*

This edition, 2012

First published in Great Britain in 2009 by
MAINSTREAM PUBLISHING COMPANY
(EDINBURGH) LTD
7 Albany Street
Edinburgh EH1 3UG

ISBN 9781845965815

A catalogue record for this book is available
from the British Library

Typeset in Badhouse and Palatino

Printed and bound by
CPI Group (UK) Ltd, Croydon, CR0 4YY

3 5 7 9 10 8 6 4 2

# Acknowledgements

My personal heartfelt thanks go to Barbara for her dedication and patience while editing this work. Without her help, it would have been a shambles.

It is not prudent or even possible to name all of those inmates, prison officials and others who provided details that have been included in this story; nevertheless, I offer them all my sincere appreciation for their contributions.

*Sebastian Williams*

# CONTENTS

# Author's Note

I FIRST BECAME INTERESTED IN THE CASE OF THE MAIN CHARACTER OF this story, whom I'm going to call Sly, after being introduced to him and a friend of his, a chap I have named Brent, by a mutual friend of mine and Brent's, whom I've named Willie.

Sly was a British fellow, whose claim to eventual mini-fame was that he spent a total of 17 years imprisoned in several of the infamous calabooses in Thailand and survived to talk about it. His crime, at least as far as the Thai authorities presented it, was possession and sale of around six kilos of heroin. His own version of events, however, was that he was an innocent victim of extortionist cops and their cohorts – not an unheard of possibility in that country – whom he said were bent on extracting a large amount of his hard-earned cash in exchange for his freedom; when he refused to play the game their way, they made certain that he paid heavily for his imprudence.

It was a written analysis that had been prepared by Sly of what he said was presented to the courts by the prosecutor during the first 12 months of his trial that triggered my initial interest and got me a bit wound up, because it seemed on the surface to be grossly unfair treatment. This began an illumination spanning one and a half decades, and which I can only say was at times an intense and staggering experience for me, one that gave me a clear understanding of the ingrained corruption and other malfeasance that appears to be par for the course within the Thai criminal justice, penal and political worlds. Over the years, I became privy to a vast amount of information, a lot of which simply beggared belief, and as a result I became determined to use as much of it as I could, partly in the hope that exposing it might encourage positive reform.

Although I was unaware of it until after his release, Sly was not a stranger to the inside of courtrooms or the confines of prison walls prior to his arrest in Thailand; he had a history of arrests and convictions for petty crimes that spanned two decades. Nevertheless, he professed his innocence in regard to the drug charges in Thailand for the duration of his incarceration there, and there's no denying that his trial through the three Thai courts was nothing short of nonsensical.

I decided in the end, mainly because Sly was the only one of those with whom I had become acquainted who had in fact experienced it all himself in one form or another, the only one who had stayed the course and survived for longer than the full period of my involvement, that the story should be approached as being seen through his eyes and as if being told by him, in his own voice. *Send Them to Hell* is the culmination of that effort. It begins about a year before Sly's arrest and concludes with his eventual release 17 years later. I hope you enjoy it, but be warned – it is quite unsettling in places.

*Sebastian Williams*

# Prologue

'SLY, LOOK! OVER THERE, BY THE WALL! WHAT THE HELL?!'

I turned my head and followed Fred's wide-eyed gape of horror. It was then I realised that the muffled thumping sound I had heard as we entered the prison yard was in fact the result of the repeated blows being administered to a prisoner by one of the uniformed guards.

The prisoner, a short, thin Asian man with a large blue tattoo of some kind of Buddhist symbol in the centre of his back, was tied to a tree with his hands pulled above his head and fastened tightly to the trunk. Though the prisoner was limp and appeared to be unconscious, the guard continued to swing his baton haphazardly across his back and arms, as if possessed by some enraged demon that had rendered him totally out of control of his senses, not seeming to care, or even to be aware, that there was no longer any response from his victim. He continued until he himself was exhausted and had to stop to rest, handing the blood-stained stick – which was similar in length to, but not as thick as, a baseball bat – to a trusty, with orders for him to clean it.

I couldn't believe what I had seen. The cloud of apprehension that had engulfed me up to that point faded into insignificance as the enormity of my predicament slammed into focus. With the thwack of his gavel, the magistrate I had faced the previous day had surely sent me to hell.

# PART 1

## Slipping into a Quicksand of Circumstance and Entrapment

It is dangerous to give the benefit of
your compassion to a fool.

*Anonymous*

# CHAPTER 1

# I Swallowed It Hook,
# Line and Sinker

I HAVE ALWAYS BEEN A BIT OF A SUCKER FOR THE UNDERDOG – THERE were lots of them where I spent quite a bit of my adult life in the UK, and I got to know some of them pretty well – and generally don't mind handing out a few pennies here and there if asked for a little help. However, had I been able to foresee that this concession to the less fortunate would lead to the annihilation of another large chunk of my life and all of the unimaginable things that I experienced and was made to suffer during the next 17 years, I would surely have been a trifle less accommodating and this story would in all likelihood not have been written.

I first came into contact with a middle-aged German fellow – who I'm going to call Hansel – about a year before my nightmare began. I was in a small café on Sukhumvit Road in Bangkok having a cup of coffee with a mate of mine who had just arrived from the USA. Sukhumvit Road is the capital's longest road: an endless parade of hotels, bars and restaurants that extends north from almost the city centre to way out past the city limits. Everything that's hip and trendy generally makes an appearance there first. Certainly for food, drink and entertainment, Sukhumvit Road and the lanes and alleys running off it are unrivalled. Never one for the bright lights and boozy crowds myself, however, I frequented just a few favourite old-style cafés, where the staff knew me by name. Most of them were located near a little office that I had rented close to the city end of the road.

I noticed Hansel initially because he was walking in a peculiar way, but when he spoke to one of the waiters in Thai, I took a closer interest in him. It's fairly uncommon for a *farang* (Western foreigner) to be able to speak Thai; at least it was then. The best that most foreigners can manage is a kind of pidgin-Thai – half-Thai, half-English – myself included. Hansel cast a practised eye around the room and, seeing that I was watching him, made a beeline for the table. Speaking in German, he offered us his services as a guide, believing, I suppose, that we were German tourists.

You see a lot of guys like him in Bangkok, hanging around places where tourists tend to circulate, surviving on their wits and a bit of luck, but mostly by using practised tricks and scams to fleece their targets. Speaking no German myself and having no interest in his presence or his service – which he clarified in broken English in response to my blank expression – I thanked him, telling him that we were residents and didn't want a tour guide. Once he knew we weren't tourists, he lost interest, nodded his head and shuffled off to try his luck elsewhere.

I saw him again about a month later, once again in the same part of town. The reason I spoke to him on this occasion was because, as we approached one another, I could see that he was in pain. When I asked him what the problem was, he complained loudly that he was on his way to the hospital because some 'idiot street vendor' had scalded his leg with boiling oil. We exchanged only a few words, and he stumbled on, cursing and mumbling under his breath, causing heads to turn in his wake.

A few months after that, we crossed paths again. This time he approached me as I was walking down Soi Nana, one of the lanes running off Sukhumvit Road. We'd had a little off-season rain that morning and, though it had stopped after a couple of hours, as is usually the case in Bangkok at that time of year, the incessant heat and resulting humidity turned the city into one gigantic Turkish bath. I wasn't feeling too comfortable that day, because I had a touch of the flu and was in a hurry to get home, so I was a little impatient with him when he started telling me how he had just been robbed and had lost all of the money he had in the world, pulling his pockets out of his trousers to emphasise his destitution. The predictable entreaty followed, with a request for a 5,000-baht loan. (At that time, 60 baht was the equivalent of about £1, so 5,000 baht worked out as approximately £85.)

Well, I'd seen it all numerous times since arriving in Thailand, though it was usually a Thai doing the begging. But even though I didn't believe him – figuring that it was probably nothing more than one of his panhandling lines – he did look a bit desperate and was still wobbling on his legs as he walked, so I gave him the benefit of the doubt. I mean, it wasn't such a lot of money to me at that time because I was doing pretty well with a small business I was involved in, and I would hardly miss it if I didn't get it back. But not having that much spare cash on me. I gave him a cheque made out to cash.

It was at that very moment, with that stroke of my pen, that I made the biggest mistake of my life, and I have kicked myself ever since for not telling him to get lost right there and then, because had I done that . . . Well, what's the point in moaning about it now? While I really didn't expect to be repaid, just before I rushed off I fished a business card out of my wallet and gave it to him, telling him he could pay me back when he was able to do so.

That was my second mistake, because a little over a month later my secretary popped into my office and told me there was a farang waiting at reception to see me. Well, there he was again. I was quite surprised to see him, naively thinking that he had come to repay the 5,000 baht, an expectation that was shattered the moment he opened his mouth and began to recount another sad story that ended with him wanting to borrow another couple of thousand baht.

Just as he got through the punchline, I had to take a phone call, and while he stood there waiting for me to finish, I noticed that he was paying particular attention to the books I had open on my desk. They were manuals relating to my business, written in German. I was in the process of having them translated to Thai as was required by the Thai authorities to conform to local regulations.

After I hung up, I was more than a little surprised when Hansel explained that he was an engineer and, after an explanation of what I was doing with them, suggested that he might be able to assist me with those translations. I tested him on some of the illustrations, and he was able to accurately identify them. Recognising then that he could possibly be of assistance to me, I told him that if he would like to help the lass I had doing the job with the technical names and terms, I would allow him to work off his debt and would also pay him extra on top. Of course he accepted, and he'd come to my office several times a week to work on the manuals. I wouldn't say that we became friends during that time, but he was capable of the job and he was cheap. It was a win–win situation as far as I was concerned.

It wasn't such a long time after he started that he came hobbling into my office all excited and told me that he knew a rich Arab who was looking for a buyer for a standby letter of credit. He asked me if I knew how to go about finding one, probably assuming I did because I had told him during a casual conversation – even though it was complete bollocks – that I had been employed by a bank in Switzerland for years. However, I did know all about letters of credit – documents allowing banks to act as intermediaries between buyers and sellers, usually companies involved in the import and export trade. The bank undertakes to pay the seller on the buyer's behalf, on the condition that specified documents are produced and certain conditions are fulfilled. It's a sort of safety mechanism for both sides.

I was interested because I could see that, if handled properly, a quick profit could be made on the exchange. I told him that I could possibly do the deal myself, which was more bollocks, of course. I couldn't have raised sufficient cash to do so, but I have never been slow to hear opportunity knocking at my door. I told him that I would need him to give me a copy of the document before I could make a decision. Accordingly, a few days later he arrived at my office with a photocopy of the letter, telling me that he had told the Arab that I was a 'Swiss banker' and definitely the man to handle the deal.

Well, that was a nice touch, I guess, and made me look like a big wheel, so I let it pass without comment. I inspected the document and saw that it was drawn on the Chase Manhattan Bank in New York, with a face value of $5 million. The goods were specified as coffee and agricultural produce, destination Yemen. It looked genuine enough, so I told him I would see what I could do.

Later, after Hansel had left my office, I made a dozen or so copies of that photocopy and then began talking to some of my contacts in Thailand to see if I could get a good deal on a discount basis.

There was a lot of chasing around involved here, but, to cut a long story short for the present, I eventually made an agreement with the manager of the representative office of a large British bank in Bangkok and was assured that they would discount the letter through their Singapore office, leaving me with about $150,000 net and the seller 87 per cent of face value.

Hansel first introduced me by phone to a Kuwaiti Arab fellow named Fahad, who was supposed to be the go-between, just a couple of days after he had given me the photocopy, and I met him in person for the first time shortly after that at a hotel in Bangkok. He told me that he was brokering the deal and wanted a chop of the cherry. We finally agreed on a fair split of the proceeds, to be paid when the deal was completed. However, I made it a condition that I meet face to face with the seller and that I was to see and be permitted to authenticate the original letter of credit and have certified copies made before proceeding.

I'd really like to be able to say that I distrusted Fahad the moment I set eyes on him, but, in truth, that wasn't the case at all. He was well presented, spoke like an educated and cultured gentleman and didn't exhibit any outward signs of the devil he really was. In short, he was the epitome of an experienced and successful con man, and I swallowed the illusion hook, line and sinker. You'd think I would have been a bit wiser, all previous experience considered.

Around lunchtime two weeks later, I was in my office, finishing off some translations with Hansel, when Fahad phoned and asked me to go to the Bangkok Bank head office to meet his client, who, he told me, was already there waiting to see me. Hansel and I jumped in my car more or less straight away and headed for the bank. When we arrived, Fahad was there waiting for us, but the seller wasn't with him. When I asked him where the seller was, he said he hadn't arrived yet but that he was on his way. That didn't impress me much, but after he assured me that he would be there very soon, I agreed to wait for a short time, took a seat in the banking hall and left Hansel and Fahad together. About five minutes later, Hansel walked over to the front door of the bank and disappeared outside. When he returned, both he and Fahad came over to where I was sitting, and Fahad told me that the seller was not able to make it.

Now, having a ton of work to do, I didn't appreciate it one bit that this guy was wasting my time, and I told him so as I left in a rather cranky frame of mind. I decided then that Fahad was a moron and that Hansel was in good company with him, and I told myself that I had probably wasted my energy finding a buyer for something that more than likely wasn't there to sell.

A couple of days later, though, I received a phone call from Hansel. He told me that Fahad was very sorry for the inconvenience that I had been put to but needed to meet me again to arrange an appointment for the sale. Well, at that point I didn't give a damn what Fahad needed to do and had no intention of allowing him to muck me around again. Making that quite clear to Hansel, I added that if Fahad wanted to talk to me, he would have to do it in person at my office. He arrived that same afternoon, all apologies again, putting the blame squarely on the seller. After a short discussion, I agreed to proceed with the sale. He left, promising to get back to me soon.

I heard nothing at all from him until late in the evening two weeks later when he phoned and told me that he would be at the Prince Hotel in New Petchaburi Road with his seller at 11 a.m. the following day and asked if I would mind going there to meet them. I took my motorbike this time because I was alone and it's a lot quicker – though a little unnerving in the traffic – and got there about 20 minutes early to find that Fahad was already there. Hansel was with him, but there was no seller. Nevertheless, believing that he would arrive at the appointed time, I accepted Fahad's offer to sit in the lobby lounge and have a cup of coffee.

We had only been chatting a few minutes when, quite out of the blue, Fahad asked me if I would like to go for a few days' holiday with him to Phuket, an island off the south-west coast of the mainland. He explained that he had already arranged the plane tickets for himself and a girlfriend but that the girlfriend was unable to go, leaving him with a spare booking. The trip would cost me nothing, he assured me.

I was somewhat taken aback; in fact, I was a little embarrassed. I mean, I hardly knew the guy and here he was offering to take me for a free holiday. I decided to treat it as a joke and replied that I only accept free holidays if they are first class all the way, five-star penthouse accommodation and with a harem of pretty girls thrown in just for fun. But when he persisted, I told him that I was far too busy and didn't have the time. Hansel, however, wasn't too busy. We'd finished the technical side of the translations by then, and, saying as much to Fahad, I hinted that he would surely be more than happy to fill the vacancy if it was for free.

To my utter astonishment, Fahad then hit me with the news that the seller was not going to be able to make it at such an early hour because he liked – of all things – to *sleep late*. After almost choking on my coffee, instantly very annoyed to be hearing this nonsense again, I said, caustically, 'Why the hell didn't you just phone me this morning and tell me that? Why was it necessary for me to come all the way over here to hear it?' I mean, I had risked my bleedin' life travelling there in the traffic to meet this guy, and once again he was nowhere to be seen. I also had an appointment to meet a friend of mine – let's call him Fred – at my apartment at midday, leaving little time for playing silly buggers.

'No, Sly, I promise you we will see him today for certain. I have arranged to meet him at the Bangkok Bank at one o'clock and thought that we could have some lunch together and then go to the bank from there,' he replied.

'Well, you thought wrong, didn't you? And I don't appreciate it one iota that you have made arrangements that include me without consulting me first.' Splashing coffee as I dropped my cup onto the saucer, I got up to leave, telling him that I would be at the bank at one o'clock and that if the seller didn't show up this time, I would go no further with the deal; I had better things to do.

'All right, Sly, I'm sorry. No need to be so angry,' Fahad replied, totally unperturbed. 'I have to be at the airport myself no later than four o'clock, so that I can leave for Phuket at five. I just figured that if we arrived at the bank at one o'clock, it would give you about an hour to inspect the letter of credit and to get the bank to provide you with the authentications you need, as well as time for you to have a talk with the seller as to a settlement date and so on. Why don't Hansel and I meet you at your apartment in, say, an hour, then we can all go there together?'

I left the Prince that morning a little after 11 a.m., agreeing, God only knows why, to give them one last chance to come up with the goods. Fahad walked out of the hotel with me, saying that he was going home to pack an overnight bag – his house was no more than 200 metres away. Hansel stayed in the lobby waiting for him to return so they could travel to my place together.

I had known Fred for some time. We had become acquainted during one of his previous trips to Thailand, and we occasionally met for coffee or to have some dinner together when he was in town. A Croat of Muslim faith, he had been a refugee from the war-stricken Balkans, escaping the region via the Italian camps to seek sanctuary in Australia, where he had later become nationalised. He married and lived there for many years in reasonable contentment. Though now in his mid-50s, he carried his years very well, and one could be excused for presuming him to be mid-40s at most. His full crop of sandy, wavy hair, slightly greying at the temples, crystal-clear blue eyes and excellent posture gave him an air of aristocracy. He also had a strong and sinewy, though not large, physique that he kept in good shape. He was almost passive by nature and tolerant to a fault, traits that were to serve him well over the following several years and that also became a much-needed cushion between me and Hansel.

Fred's god was that day clearly working in one of those 'mysterious ways' we often hear about, because he had only been with me so we could go apartment hunting together. He had been staying at the Park-Inn Hotel way out near the river in Nonthaburi Province and, apart from it being a bit expensive for him, it was not at all convenient – the taxi fares were costing him a small fortune. He had been in Thailand for some months, doing some trading business with timber firms in Bangkok and in the south of the country, and as this business had begun to show a lot of promise, he needed to get a more permanent residence.

A few days earlier, he had joined my wife – let's call her Jaidow – and me for some dinner to welcome in what we hoped would be a prosperous new year for us all. That was when I'd offered to help him find a new place, and we made the arrangement to meet at my apartment and go from there. I arrived on time, after meeting Fahad, to find Fred waiting for me in the foyer. It wasn't until I apologised that our hunting expedition would have to be delayed for a few hours while I took care of some business at the bank that he knew anything about the letter of credit, but, having set the day aside anyhow, he said he was happy to accompany me and wait until I had finished.

Jaidow had made us some chicken-salad sandwiches and coffee for lunch, and we were still sitting in the living room finishing that off when Hansel showed up at around 12.30 p.m. He was alone and carrying a white suitcase.

'Ah, so you're off to Phuket, too? Fahad's a very generous fellow, isn't he?' I said as I showed him in. 'I mean, to be taking you along just like that and all at his own expense. Didn't take you long to get ready. But where's the man himself?'

Hansel shuffled past me and entered the apartment, his eyes quickly scanning the room, lingering disrespectfully on my wife as he did so. 'He had to go to the airline office to change the plane tickets. This is his case not mine. He asked if we could take it to the bank for him because we are going straight to the airport from there. But, Sly, I didn't have time to go home to pack anything. Would you lend me a couple of shirts, please?'

Now, I don't consider myself to be a naive person by any means. You can't afford to be when doing business – legitimate or otherwise – particularly in Thailand. But while I couldn't have put my hand over my heart and said that I fully trusted Fahad or Hansel, I also couldn't say that I didn't trust them, at least not in what we were involved in together. I mean, there was nothing that either of them could have done to get at me with regard to the letter of credit, and there was nothing that Hansel could do to cheat me as far as the manuals were concerned. I realised, of course, that Hansel was little more than an opportunist who lived on his wits and whatever he could get for free, but that was of no importance to me at all. I'm a bit of an opportunist myself, in truth, and needed to have the translation work done. He was able to help me do that, and at a low cost. That's all that concerned me.

Fahad was a different kettle of fish, though; he was certainly a smooth character and more of a mystery. But this was business and nothing more. I merely had to weigh up the advantages against the disadvantages and decide what would be best in the end as far as my bank balance was concerned. In this case, I needed only to authenticate the letter of credit; I had a buyer for it, it was legal business and there was a good return for the effort. That's all that mattered. My feelings with regard to Hansel and Fahad were more or less irrelevant.

Fred had never met Hansel before I introduced them that day. I'm sure he must have wondered what I was thinking as I proceeded to give Hansel several shirts and a few pairs of new underpants that were still in their packaging, all of which I put into a used brown-paper shopping bag for him. As we set off, I couldn't help wondering if this fellow's gall had any limits.

The traffic was reasonably light that afternoon, and we got to the bank in good time. We went in my new car, which I was keen to take for a spin, having only had it since the day before. Fred sat beside me in the front, and Hansel sat in the rear with the suitcase beside him on the seat. As we entered the bank driveway, Fred asked me to let him out so that he could buy some cigarettes and told me that he would wait for us outside the front of the bank in the garden area. I dropped him off and continued on up to the fifth-floor car park.

As we were getting out of the car, Hansel asked me if he could put the suitcase in the boot for safe keeping, and I pulled the catch on the floor to the right of my seat to open it for him. We then took the lift down to the ground floor, where we found Fahad waiting for us. Once again, he was alone, and my hackles began to rise, but before I had time to blow a fuse, he said that the seller was already there, waiting in the banking hall. He then asked Hansel where his suitcase was, explaining that he needed to get some documents from it to show to the seller. Hansel asked me for the car keys, and, still having them in my hand, I tossed them to him, saying that I would wait for them near the front entrance. They both walked into the lift and were gone before I started to walk out into the banking hall.

I went to the front door, and seeing Fred sitting on a bench in the garden, reading a newspaper and having a smoke, I went back inside and sat down in the customer service area, looking around at the customers to see if I could see anyone who looked like a wealthy Arab. No one seemed to fit the bill, and I was starting to get suspicious that Fahad might be wasting my time again.

After sitting for another ten minutes or so, I got up and walked back to the front door. Fred, noticing me standing there, ambled over to see what was happening. We talked for a minute or two, after which he walked back out into the garden, and I headed back into the banking hall. As I did so, I was approached by a man in a suit who introduced himself as a police officer and asked if he could see my passport. Normally, I wouldn't have been carrying it, but because I had to identify myself to the bank manager that day, I had it with me. He looked through it for a short time, then, appearing to be satisfied, he handed it back and disappeared.

It must have been about the same time, or shortly after, that another plain-clothes police officer approached Fred in the garden and asked to see his passport. After inspecting it, he escorted Fred into the bank. Just before they entered, though, I was approached again, this time by three officers: two men in plain clothes and one, a woman, in uniform. One of the men, speaking reasonably good English, asked to see my passport once again, and though a little discomfited at being surrounded by police like this, I quite willingly handed it to him. Very shortly after that, Fred was brought over to join me.

Of course, everything is simple to analyse and explain in hindsight, easy as hell. But how many times have I asked myself over the years since that day, why, in the name of Christ, did I carry on with this deal? Why didn't I see right from the beginning that it was an agglomeration of confusion, half-truths and lies – in short, a con job?

The very first thing Hansel had said to me with regard to the letter of credit was that he had told the Arab that I was a Swiss banker. Then there were the numerous instances of what I had mistaken as Fahad's incompetence but which were nothing less than planned deception, pure and simple: wealthy Arabs who like to sleep late, free holidays, unscheduled lunches. And what about the suitcase? Why had a smooth operator such as Fahad entrusted his belongings to a dropout like Hansel? Why did Hansel ask me if he could put it in the boot of my car? If it contained Fahad's essentials for a trip to Phuket, why didn't Hansel take it with him to the ground floor of the bank when we arrived? After all, he knew that time was going to be short and that Fahad was going to be leaving directly from the bank to the airport after I had talked to the seller and done what was needed there. Why had the mysterious seller not shown up anywhere at any time? Why this and why that . . . I mean, what more did I need to alert me?

But I *wasn't* alerted, and now it was too late. After the police officers had inspected our passports, the older one, who appeared to be the superior, pointed to the lifts on the opposite side of the bank to the one that Fahad and Hansel had taken. Then his subordinate said in English, 'Please accompany us for a moment while I have these documents checked.' With a flick of his head, he indicated that we should precede them.

There were several other people in the lift with us initially, but by the time we reached the fifth-floor car park, just Fred, the police officers and I remained. Fred was looking worried, and I was starting to feel more than a little uncomfortable myself. However, we both nearly shit our pants as we stepped out of the lift and the cops grabbed us brutally around our necks from behind and bent our right arms up between our shoulder blades.

'Hey! What's going on?' I shouted out, as a knife of pain shot through my shoulder. Fred was a little more forthright and, struggling, screamed, 'What the bloody hell? Get the fuck off me!' but then choked as the cop's arm tightened around his neck. We were then handcuffed.

As this was happening, several other uniformed officers came running over from a group already standing near my car. We were then taken, shocked and confused, over to where Hansel stood, wearing what can only be described as a livid expression. There was no sign of Fahad.

'Can someone please tell us what this is all about?' I asked no one in particular, but there was no response. I looked over at Hansel. 'Hansel! What the hell is going on? Where's Fahad?'

Before he could reply, one of the uniforms punched me in the kidneys and said 'No speak!'

It wasn't until we were all dragged around behind the car that Fred and I saw the white suitcase that Hansel had brought with him to my apartment. It was still in the boot, but now its lid was open, and what I saw there made me feel sick to the bottom of my stomach. There were a number of packages in the case, wrapped in brown paper. One of them had been slit open and white powder was spilling out.

'What the hell is that, Hansel?' I shouted, though I knew instinctively what it was. He looked away, saying nothing. I tried to be calm as all kinds of possibilities began to flash through my mind, but I wasn't being very successful, and I knew my voice was shaking as I turned to Fred and said, 'Holy shit, mate. What's happening here?'

It was when the flash bulbs began to explode as one of the uniforms took photographs of the three of us beside the car that we both realised that something very serious was going down. A feeling of foreboding crept into my already knotted stomach. Fred, with trembling hands, reached into his pocket for a smoke.

Just a few minutes later, Fred and I were bundled into the back seat of a car and taken to the police station. We were handcuffed together by this time, with Fred's right wrist attached to my right wrist. He sat behind the driver while I sat behind the front passenger seat. We tried to talk to the two police officers in the front of the car, but were told to shut up. At one point, the officer in the passenger seat drew his revolver, pointed it at Fred's head and pulled the trigger. He then laughed himself to the verge of tears at the astonished and terrified look on Fred's face when there was a loud 'click' from the hammer hitting on an empty chamber.

'Try that again, you asshole, and I'll ram that fucking thing down your bloody throat, handcuffs or no handcuffs.' But Fred's displeasure only added to the cops' entertainment, and, delighted with the response, they both roared with laughter and continued to chuckle like hyenas almost all the way to the station.

'Listen, mate, we've done nothing wrong, so we've nothing to worry about,' I said to Fred. I was trying to be rational, though I knew my voice was still shaking. 'The suitcase belongs to Hansel . . . well, to Fahad, but Hansel had it, so that's his problem. They've probably already got Fahad. We weren't even anywhere near them when it was opened, were we? So what have we got to worry about? I think we'll be OK.'

But we both knew that what was in the boot of my car was a major problem that had to be overcome before we could start breathing easy again. However, believing that we would not be considered responsible for it being there gave me a little comfort – a false sense of security, as it turned out. Fred, not entirely convinced, managed a weak smile, but he was also still trembling. I think being shot at with an empty gun had unsettled him more than the contents of the suitcase and the flash bulbs. I didn't feel too good myself.

Hansel, for reasons unknown to us, was left behind, still standing by the car, with his hands cuffed behind his back, talking to the police officer who appeared to be in charge. Fahad was nowhere to be seen.

# CHAPTER 2

# Day One of Six Thousand Three Hundred and Thirty-three Before Liberation

WE ARRIVED AT THE NARCOTICS SUPPRESSION DIVISION (NSD) POLICE station at least 30 minutes before Hansel made an appearance. One of the duty officers removed our handcuffs once we were inside and took us over to a small alcove to be fingerprinted. By the time Hansel was bundled into the same room, this task had been completed and we were being briefly interrogated for the record. The officer doing the interrogating was the same one who had pretended to shoot Fred in the head.

'Officer, will you please tell me what this is all about? We have done nothing at all to warrant this.' I was trying my best to be polite, but it had no effect on this fellow.

He looked up from the paper on which he was recording our personal data and, with no attempt to conceal his arrogance, replied, 'You are being charged with buying and possessing the six kilos of heroin that was found in the suitcase in the trunk of your car. That's what this is all about.'

'That's absurd. I – we' – I swept my hand towards Fred – 'had nothing to do with that suitcase. Ask that fellow over there.' I pointed to Hansel, who by this time had been pushed into a seat at a desk on the far side of the room and was being questioned by one of the officers who had brought him in, now sitting opposite him, a writing pad under his folded hands. '*He* was carrying that case. It's not ours. It belongs to an Arab named Fahad.'

Hansel showed no sign of having heard what I was saying, so I raised my voice. 'Hansel, look at me! Where is Fahad? Please tell this officer that we had absolutely nothing to do with that suitcase.'

Hansel continued to stare vacantly at the wall in front of him, occasionally replying in Thai to the officer's questions. I was ready to rip his head off with my bare hands, such was my fury at being put in this embarrassing and humiliating position by him. This time, with no attempt to disguise how I felt, I yelled, 'Where the hell is Fahad?'

When he ignored me again, I stood up, my chair screeching across the floor as I did so, and headed towards him. I wanted answers and I wanted this German shit for brains to clear this mess up right there and then. It had got way out of hand, but he could clear it all up with just a few words and then Fred and I could be out of this place.

The cop jumped to his feet and another one who was standing beside Fred moved in quickly to block my way and restrain me. The trigger-happy fellow grabbed me by the shoulder and, swivelling me around roughly, told me to sit or I would be handcuffed again, and this time to his desk.

'OK, OK. But this is ridiculous.' I sat again, and he returned to his seat, pointing his finger in my face as a further warning as he did so. Still fuming, I continued, 'My friend here and I had nothing to do with any heroin. If you don't already have Fahad in custody, then that's who you should be chasing right now. That case is his.'

This information had no effect on the cop, and he continued with his questioning, more interested in our personal details than the events of the afternoon. With this completed, he stood and told us to follow him. I got up, but Fred stayed seated, saying that he wanted to speak to someone from his embassy before he went anywhere.

The cop just chuckled. 'The people from your embassy will find out soon enough. Now, you come with me or I will have you taught some manners.'

Fred, not needing any further lessons at that particular moment, decided to do as he was instructed and stood up beside me. We were then escorted, together with Hansel, along a corridor and through a heavy iron gate that led to the station holding cells. There were probably half a dozen of them altogether, some occupied, some not; in my state of mind, I barely noticed. 'Holy shit, not again' was a thought that tormented me all the way to the empty one at the end that we were shoved into, and as the clang of the door slamming behind us echoed through the building, a feeling of desolation and desperation, accompanied by chilly goosebumps, assaulted my very essence.

It was around 4 p.m. by that time, but it seemed more like late evening. I was physically and emotionally drained. Looking round the filthy cage where we were destined to spend the night, I felt as disgusted and sickened as I had on quite a few previous occasions, but this time I did not deserve to be there, which made it very much harder to swallow. Shortly after that, the fireworks started, and I swear that if Fred hadn't been there to intervene . . . well, I don't think I could have been held responsible for a little temporary insanity, rendering Hansel eternally speechless.

Hansel had thrown himself down into a corner, avoiding my eyes as I stood over him like an enraged bull. 'You stupid fucking moron! Just look at what you've got us into!' I shouted. 'You'd better start giving me some answers, and fast, or I'll knock your bloody brains out, if you've got any.'

I was breathing like I'd run a mile; my face was burning. 'What the hell were you doing with a bag full of heroin in the first place? And why did you bring it into *my* apartment and travel with it in *my* car? Lie to me, you bastard, and, so help me, you won't see the morning, and that's a promise.' I'd never felt so infuriated in all my life and was barely able to control the urge to thump him.

Though he hesitated for quite a few seconds, Hansel eventually spoke. 'Look, Sly, I didn't know there was heroin in it. I'd never have taken it if I did, I swear. Fahad gave me that bag at the Prince Hotel and told me to go to your apartment and tell you to meet him at the bank. He said it was his clothes for the trip and that he didn't want to take it to the airline office on his motorbike because it was not easy to carry. He asked me to take it with me so that we could leave directly from the bank to the airport. I was just helping him out. Honestly, that's exactly what happened. I had no idea what it had in it. I almost died myself when I saw what was inside after he opened it in the car park.' His German accent was quite broad at the best of times, but now, with his voice trembling, it became more pronounced, and he wasn't easy to understand.

'I don't believe you, Hansel. What happened to Fahad? He went with you to the car park. Where is he?'

'I don't know where he is. When we reached the car, he asked me for the keys, and I gave them to him. He opened the boot himself. After that, he spent at least a minute or two fumbling around opening the suitcase. *He* had the keys to that, not me. I was standing by the back door waiting for him. He stood back after he had lifted the lid of the case and took a penknife from his pocket, then he bent down into the boot again, and that's when I walked around to see what he was doing. It was *then* that I saw that there weren't any clothes in the case and that he was using the knife to cut into one of those brown packages.

'Truly, Sly, I didn't know that he had that stuff in there. After he cut the packet, he licked the blade of the knife, and I realised then that it must have been drugs. I got frightened and began to hurry away to the lift. That's when the police came out from everywhere. A couple of them grabbed me and took me back to the car, then they cuffed my hands behind my back.'

'So, what happened to Fahad? If the cops grabbed you, they must have grabbed Fahad as well. Surely he wasn't able to just run away?' I was trying to get it all into some semblance of logical sequence, but it wasn't making sense.

'No, he didn't run away. The police didn't touch him at all. He was talking to them like they were old friends, then he and another Thai guy got into a car that was parked almost beside your car and drove off. After they were gone, a couple of the police started to punch me, and when I fell down, one kicked me in the ribs and stomach.' He stopped speaking and rubbed his chest, as if expecting some sympathy, then carried on when he realised none was forthcoming. 'When I tried to talk to them, they told me to shut up or they'd shut me up. That was just before you two arrived.'

'This is not adding up, Hansel. Why would Fahad open the bag in front of you if he knew it had heroin in it? How come the place was already crawling with cops? How come Fred and I were brought up from the ground floor just at that moment? What game were you playing with Fahad, you bastard? Tell me. Tell me or I'll . . .' I was getting closer to Hansel, my face almost pressed against his.

'OK, Sly! Sly! Take it easy, mate.' Fred, who had been keeping out of things until now, finally entered the fray, possibly saving me from the further charge of assault, or worse, and no doubt wondering what the hell had happened to his anticipated afternoon of unhurried flat hunting.

He took my arm and eased me back a little, then fixed his gaze on Hansel. 'Hansel, I don't know you at all, and you don't know me. I've never laid eyes on you before today. Believe me, I would remember. But you can be sure that already I don't like you very much. I am also extremely pissed off, as is Sly, at being brought into this silly little game, so you had better start coming clean, mate, and tell us exactly what happened today and why.'

'Look, Fred, I don't know any more than I have just told Sly. That was Fahad's bag. *He* had the keys to it. *He* was the one with the combination number. *He* was the one who opened it. I thought I was going to be on my way to Phuket by now. I had no involvement at all in what was in that case.'

'Hansel, the cops must have known the bag had heroin in it. They must have known you had it in the boot of Sly's car, otherwise they wouldn't have been there waiting for you, would they?'

'I know, Fred. But I have no idea how they knew – truly.'

I burst in again, my heart pounding like a tom-tom. 'OK, then. What about the letter of credit? You were the one who introduced me to Fahad. So where is it? Where is the Arab who was supposed to be selling it? Have you actually met him? You told me you had met him and that you had seen the letter. Have you?'

'Um, no, I, um, I haven't met him, nor have I seen the document. I was just going on what Fahad told me. He told me to tell you that so you would get more interested in doing the deal.'

'WHAT! Why the hell didn't you tell me that at the beginning? I spent weeks running around trying to arrange a buyer for that letter. It cost me money and a lot of valuable time. Are you telling me now that there wasn't one to sell after all? Where did the copy you gave me come from?'

'Fahad gave it to me . . . Look, I need my share of the commission on that deal as well, you know. I just did what Fahad told me to do. I'm not sure if there really is a letter of credit or not. Fahad told me there was – why would he go to the trouble of trying to sell it if there wasn't one to be sold? I can't work it out either, Sly.'

I still wasn't convinced. Perhaps it was the way Hansel was refusing to look me straight in the eye when he spoke. 'Maybe you should start by telling us what you know about Fahad. How long have you known him? What does he do for a living? How long has he been in Thailand? Where does he live? What's the nature of your relationship with him?'

'Look, Sly, I'm really not up to this right now. My head is bursting; my stomach is in knots. Just leave me alone, will you? I've told you all I know.' He was on the verge of tears, but pity was the last thing he was going to get from me.

'Now, let me tell you something, you snivelling scumbag . . .' I was again so close to him I could feel his breath on my face. 'I don't care if you are up to it or up to your balls in brier. Tell us exactly what has been going on. We are in here on drug charges because *you* had heroin in *your* fucking suitcase, and you put that suitcase in *my* car. So don't give me any of this "I'm not feeling up to it" bullshit. Start talking . . . NOW!'

Fred put his hand lightly on my shoulder. 'Sly, simmer down, mate. Getting yourself in a state won't help us much. We'll talk to the people from the embassies tomorrow and see what they have to say about this. Anyhow, let's take five. I'm really knocked out myself. Let's think this thing through. There are some rather odd shapes developing here that don't seem to fit the puzzle.

'Hansel, why don't you just relax for a while and try to think of anything that may be of help to us all, OK? What we have to do is convince the police that the suitcase had nothing to do with any of us.'

Hansel nodded, grateful for Fred's intervention. I moved away from him, realising that my tantrum wasn't helping matters. 'OK, Fred. Yes, you're right. I am a trifle agitated. Let's sit over there by the door.' A trifle agitated indeed! I was frantic. All I could think about was the bars and the steel doors and the locks and the warders and the terrible food and the numbing boredom and all the rest of it that I thought I had long ago put behind me. I was on the brink of finalising arrangements for a decent little legitimate project, one with a big-bucks future, and this stupid bloody German, without my knowledge or consent, had me doing business with a drug dealer! I sat down on the floor with my back against the bars. Tilting my head back and closing my eyes, I took several deep, slow breaths.

'Something is not adding up here, Sly,' Fred said. 'I mean, I don't know what has been going on with this letter of credit deal, but if this Fahad guy was trying to sell one and you had someone to buy it, why would he be carrying heroin, or at least giving it to Hansel to carry, and then call the cops to arrest the very guy who was going to complete the sale? The cops said there was around six kilos in that case. Now, that's a lot of powder, right? I've no idea what it would be worth, but it wouldn't be peanuts, that's for certain. So why would Fahad have it in his case and then have the cops confiscate it?

'According to Hansel, Fahad was talking to the cops. It doesn't make sense that he was able to just escape. There were at least half a dozen cops up there when we arrived, not to mention that it's a long way down to the street. That makes what Hansel said about him jumping in a car and driving off feasible. That means, as I see it, that Fahad was probably in league with the cops for some reason. But why? What is there to gain?

'It might make sense if the letter of credit deal had been completed or if you actually had the cash in your pocket to buy it, but as it wasn't and you didn't, there doesn't seem to be a logical reason for all this drama at all. What I mean is, as far as a sting is concerned, it stinks. No one has got any cash, or anything else, out of you. Where's the benefit to the crooks?'

I agreed with Fred. It did look awfully suss on the surface. I spent the next hour going over it all with him, starting with my very first meeting with Hansel almost a year before. Fred sat and listened, mostly in silence, but the events of the past few hours had torn my nerves to shreds, and it was difficult to concentrate. I wasn't even sure that I was making sense half the time.

Today, after many years spent making it my business to find things out, the pieces of the puzzle fit together snugly, and I know exactly what happened and why. But that day, I had few pieces to work with and more questions were thrown up than answers.

I gave a long sigh as I capped it off with, 'Well, mate, you know the rest. Hansel arrived at my apartment alone, carrying a suitcase, and now we are here.'

We discussed lots of possibilities: maybe Hansel was taking the drug to Phuket to sell; maybe Fahad was; maybe Hansel was carrying it to Phuket for Fahad; maybe Hansel was selling the drug to Fahad. But we came up with as many questions: how come Fahad wasn't arrested along with Hansel in the car park? If Hansel did manage to get the dope from somewhere, unbeknownst to Fahad, how did the cops know he was going to be at the bank with it and at what time he would be there? How did they know it would be in my car in the car park? How this and why that? But we had no answers.

'The only thing that I can suggest at this point is that Fahad is in some way connected to the cops and is working with them. But why the set-up? It doesn't compute . . .'

'Beats me, Sly. Let's give the fat boy a chance to get his thoughts together and then ask him some more questions. I'm not real sure that I believe he knew nothing about this.'

'Yes, I think you're right, Fred. Maybe Fahad stabbed him in the back. But Fahad talking to the cops like that indicates that they knew him and allowed him to leave. Maybe there is a share of the rewards going to Fahad.'

'There are too many maybes, mate. But what do you mean rewards? What rewards?'

I explained what I knew of the rewards-for-drug-convictions system in Thailand. 'Every time there's a drug bust and eventual conviction that involves a foreigner, Fred, there's a cash reward for the cops involved in the arrest from the NSD and the DEA [Drug Enforcement Agency]. I'm not sure how much it is, but, whatever the case, it is becoming obvious that there was never a letter of credit. Where the dope came from is another question, isn't it? Hansel said that Fahad dug a knife into one of the bundles in the suitcase and then licked the blade, remember? If he knew it was heroin, why would he do that? Does it make sense to you that Fahad packed the heroin into his own suitcase and then in the car park dug a knife into just one pack and tasted it to see if it was heroin? It sure as hell doesn't make sense to me, unless he was actually marking the only packet that did contain the genuine drug so that when the cops did their field test they would get the positive result they needed to arrest us.'

I was a little calmer by now and beginning to think a bit more clearly. Hansel was sitting with his head resting between his knees, his hands cupped over the back of his neck.

'Possible,' Fred replied, 'but it could be that, like I said before, Hansel was selling the drugs to Fahad and Fahad had to test the packet to see if it was what he was paying for.'

'Yes, that's another possibility, I guess, but if that's the case, then the cops were certainly in on it, because they let Fahad leave, didn't they? Realistically, though, I doubt that Hansel has ever seen the kind of money needed to buy six kilograms of heroin, even at Bangkok prices. Since I have known him, he has always been on the bones of his arse and hounding me for small amounts of cash to feed himself.

'It's possible, though, that we became involved for no other reason than the dope was in my car or because Hansel was with us. There's no disputing that the cops knew he was coming and what he had with him. But I still can't see how the letter of credit fits in. Also, if Hansel was supposed to be carrying the case, why were the cops waiting in the car park for him to return there with Fahad? Why weren't they in the banking hall where I was waiting? Why weren't we arrested as soon as we arrived? I mean, he was carrying the case then, wasn't he?

'Anyhow, I've had enough of this for now. I'm going to see if I can make a call to my wife. She will get worried when I don't pick her up as promised. I can get her to bring us some decent food, too. Can't imagine we will be getting much of a catering service here.'

I stood up and looked through the corridor sidebars out towards the front gate. Several figures were milling around on the far side, so I yelled loudly enough for them to hear. 'Guard! Guard! Hey, officer! Come here a minute, please. I need to make a phone call.'

No one paid any attention, but I noticed a few guys dressed in plain clothes who appeared to be reporters. 'Shit, we're going to get our names in lights . . . Just what we need.'

God, what a friggin' mess.

We sat almost in silence, occasionally trying out a new thought on one another. We also had another go at questioning Hansel, but he was sticking to his story. Darkness fell, and at about 7 p.m. the sound of the gate to the corridor being opened made me sit upright. I nudged Fred, who had decided to ease some of his tensions with a little deep meditation.

One of the police officers we had seen earlier unlocked the door of the cell and indicated that we were all to stand while he cuffed our hands behind our backs. That done, he escorted us through the station and into a brightly lit room where there were a dozen or so people in civilian clothes, a mixture of Asians and Europeans. Some of them were the reporters I'd seen earlier. Between them, they sported an array of expensive-looking still and video cameras, which they focused on us as we were led to a table at one end of the room and told to sit down on chairs laid out behind it. The white suitcase was sitting open on the table, the brown packages exposed for all to see. The babble of voices immediately stopped as the police major who was responsible for the arrest raised his hands and began a speech, the meaning of which was clear even to Fred and me with our limited Thai. It was a self-congratulatory exercise on having apprehended all three suspects, red-handed, with at least six kilograms of heroin in their collective possession. The reporters shouted questions as the camera bulbs flashed in our faces. My heart sank into my boots, and, feeling sick and disgusted, I once again found myself thinking about the bars and locks of my past that I had so carefully concealed from all those I had become associated with since I'd left the UK.

Ten minutes later, we were back in the cell, feeling quite a lot less confident that things would get better in the immediate future.

# CHAPTER 3

# Pay the Price of Deliverance
# or Rot in Hell

I WASN'T ABLE TO SLEEP MUCH THAT NIGHT. IN FACT, I BARELY SLEPT at all, just dozing a little from time to time. It didn't help that the cell floor was cold, bare concrete and I had nothing comfortable to rest my head against, or that a foul smell was wafting over from the toilet cubicle. There was a ceiling fan, but one of the police officers had said it was out of order, so we were left to suffer the sticky heat and humidity as well as the stink.

To make matters worse, there were several Thai detainees in the adjacent cell who were making a terrible din, talking and giggling and emptying their bladders every ten minutes with the careless aim of the inebriated. They were also evidently reluctant to use the water scoop from the abutting reservoir to flush the toilet, and the whole place reeked of whisky-induced piss. The partition between the cells was made entirely of bars, and, as such, there was no respite from their fascination with the three foreigners locked up just like them. 'Hey, you. You like Thai lady?' and 'Thai lady good fuck?' were the standard of their questions, repeated time and again. Fred and I simply ignored them, though Hansel seemed to have some affinity with them and spoke to them in Thai on several occasions.

Time seemed to be standing still. Minutes seemed like hours. Hansel sat alone in one corner of the cell, his elbows propped up on his knees and his face cradled in his hands, staring blankly at nothing in particular. Fred and I sat on the opposite side, our backs to the corridor, by the cell door. At about 8 p.m., a police officer brought in some bags of boiled white rice, but they remained untouched on the floor. Fred asked for some fresh water and had to pay the guard twenty baht for a bottle that normally cost two baht. It was a matter of pay up or help ourselves to water from the tap next to the stinking toilet; not really a desirable alternative. This was the beginning of the routine extortion – albeit on a relatively small scale here – that was to become the norm for many years to come.

Every couple of hours through the night, a police officer would come into the corridor, noisily clanging open the barred gate that separated the cell area from the main police station. He'd shine his flashlight into each of the cell occupant's eyes long enough to make each of us cringe and put an arm over our faces to block the light. If he didn't get the desired reaction, he'd kick the cell bars or hit them with his baton until he did, then leave, generally with some wisecrack at our expense, causing the Thai party to start up their giggling again. An exaggerated slamming of the steel gate and the sliding of the metal bolt and lock added to the ruckus that kept the three of us awake.

No doubt this was standard strategy to make sure that those who were to be interrogated or coerced the next morning were not rested and as such would be unable to think clearly. In that respect, it certainly served its purpose with Fred and me because by the time morning arrived we were both exhausted. We had both smoked quite heavily during the night and had had nothing to eat since my wife's sandwiches the previous day, just before Hansel had arrived at my apartment. The pressure at my temples was causing my eardrums to thump, and I felt tremulous and light-headed. My mouth felt like I had eaten a kapok pillow, and the vertebrae between my shoulder blades and skull, which were prone to minor maladjustment, left my neck stiff and aching after the night of unnatural posture.

Fred was faring slightly better, being fitter than me and having employed the powers of deep meditation several times throughout the night.

As for Hansel, I don't think he had slept a wink. Though a non-smoker himself, the cigarette smoke generated by me and Fred, as well as the Thais in the adjacent cell, had left his eyes red and gritty. But, unlike us, he had surrendered to his hunger pangs and at some time in the night had unashamedly scoffed all three of the bags of rice we had been served earlier.

Breakfast was brought in at 7 a.m. by an officer dressed in government-issue dark-brown trousers, a white T-shirt with a red neckband and purple flip-flops. Once again, the victuals were not very appetising: another small plastic bag of boiled white rice, this time with a greasy overfried egg sitting on top. Both Fred and I passed on it in favour of another bottle of water and some coffee, for which the officer told us we would have to pay forty baht per cup, even though the Thais in the adjacent cell had paid just five baht per cup for theirs. We ordered two cups each.

Hansel ate his rice and, after establishing that we had no desire for it, ate ours as well. He was too miserable to pay the 40 baht for the coffee or the 20 baht for the bottled water, electing instead to drink from the tap by the loo.

Fred and I had interrogated him once again the night before, after the press conference, but had gained little further insight or anything more about his relationship with Fahad. He had spoken very little to either of us for the rest of the night, barely moving from his spot on the other side of the cell.

At about 9 a.m., I was handcuffed, taken from the cell and escorted into a large room on the second floor that was apparently used as the 'light interrogation' office. The door was closed behind me, and I was made to sit at a small desk opposite a uniformed police officer who introduced himself as Colonel Wirat. After I was seated, he told me, in excellent English, that he had not been directly involved in our case at the arrest stage and that he would like to talk to each of us individually.

We had talked for no more than five minutes before a fellow from the British Embassy, whom I'm going to refer to from here on only as Rodger, entered the room and introduced himself to me. After speaking directly to me for a few minutes, both he and Wirat interrogated me for almost an hour about the events of the previous day. I answered all of their questions truthfully, explaining my association with Fahad and Hansel and telling them all about the letter of credit and why I had been at the bank, believing that once all this was clear I would be released.

Shortly after that, Fred and Hansel, in the company of two other foreigners, both wearing dark suits, were escorted into the room and over to Wirat's desk. One of the suits was the drug liaison officer from the Australian Embassy and the other was the consul from the German Embassy. After introductions, Wirat told Rodger that he could use another office to continue his discussion with me, leading us both to an adjacent room. Once there, Rodger suggested that I write a statement of events in my own handwriting, providing me with several sheets of foolscap paper with the official Thai police header for the purpose.

During my absence, Fred and Hansel had been questioned separately by both Wirat and their respective embassy officials. They were then advised to write their own statements down, as I had done. When they had done so, Wirat took Fred and me aside and asked us both several times where the money had come from to buy the heroin, and we repeated time and again that we had no knowledge of the heroin prior to seeing the open suitcase in the boot of the car and that we had no knowledge of any money – or who might have provided it, if there was any.

The colonel had the three statements in his hand as he spoke. Finally seeming to get the message, he nodded reflectively and, hitting them lightly on the edge of his desk, ordered that we be taken back to the cell. It was after midday when once again we sat on the filthy concrete floor. Hansel, who had arrived back before us, was already in his usual spot against the far wall. Fred and I were to concur later that evening that Wirat seemed to be a little uneasy when discussing Fahad, and we agreed that he was probably not in the 'Fahad loop'. In fact, he had treated us all very courteously and professionally throughout the interrogation process, never once threatening or coercing us in any way.

A little later that afternoon, an officer entered the corridor, opened the cell gate and beckoned Fred and me to follow him. He then escorted us to an open visit area. There on the other side of the bars stood a smiling Fahad.

I immediately flared up, grabbing the bars with both hands and yelling, 'What the hell are you playing at, Fahad? Why have you done this to us?'

He was suavely dressed, as was his usual practice, in a tailored suit with sharp creases in all the right places. He wore a pair of what looked like crocodile-skin shoes and a matching belt. His shirt was navy-blue silk, with a row of matching blue buttons, and his silk tie depicted a golden vine wrapped around a silver sword. He was dripping in gold, from the Rolex on his wrist to the buckles on his shoes; even the diamonds studding his belt buckle appeared to be genuine. Mind you, they all could have been as artificial as he was himself.

He was not alone in the visit room. Several Thais had also arrived to meet other detainees, and they were huddled in their respective groups, intent on their own concerns and taking no notice of my little tirade. One other person stood there on her own, a few feet behind Fahad, though he seemed to be unaware of her presence.

'Now, now, Sly, calm down . . . we must not quarrel. I came to help you . . . I *can* help you . . . but only if you cooperate with me. You will get nowhere by making me leave in an unhappy mood. I can promise you that you will be out of here in no time at all if you do exactly what I tell you to do. It is as simple as that. No problems, no criminal charges, just walk away and go home. I can arrange it for you in five minutes. Now, do you want to listen to me or not?'

Fahad was speaking quietly and deliberately, the way he always did, and with the air of a man confident of his ability to make things happen. He looked directly at me when he spoke, his hooded grey eyes betraying his heartless disposition.

'OK, what's the rub?' I replied. 'I know you have set this whole charade up. That's clear enough now, but what for? What's the reason? What the hell do you want?' I was fuming and shot the question at him like a report from a .38.

As I spoke, I glanced inconspicuously over his left shoulder at the rather attractive girl standing behind him. Taking advantage of a momentary lapse in his concentration, I signalled to her with a creased brow and pursed lips, accompanied by a subtle shake of my head, to say and do nothing. She was close enough to be able to hear what Fahad was saying but not close enough to make it obvious that she was listening to our conversation.

Fred said nothing and exhibited no emotion. He had never had the misfortune to come into contact with Fahad previously, but, being more perceptive than most to the subconscious vibes and body language of your average Homo sapiens, he was quick to recognise Fahad for what he was. He stood quietly several feet away from me, smoking a cigarette and appearing to have little interest in the proceedings. However, he spent the entire ten minutes of our conversation scrutinising the Arab and listening to every word he said.

Though I had not seen it on my previous meetings, it was now becoming clear to me too that Fahad was a snake in the grass, a chameleon who changed his colour to suit his surroundings, a soulless and heartless eater of his fellow man.

'Really quite simple, Sly. You and your friend there are in a perilous situation. You have been arrested with six kilograms of heroin in your possession. That's the death penalty, mandatory in Thailand – did you know that? The chances of you proving your innocence – which, my friend, is what you will be required to do – are remote, because the dope was in your car, wasn't it? Your friend there is in the same boat, yes? As for Hansel, well, let's just say that he is up to his jowls in camel shit right now, and, as far as I care, he can stay there. He is nothing but a stupid mule, a sour-cabbage-scoffing ignoramus. He deserves nothing less.

'So, Sly my boy, you have two choices, as I see it. You can buy your way out – and I can help you with that – or you can rot in here for the rest of your miserable life, which probably won't be all that long if what I've heard about the gulags here is true.' Fahad's satisfied smirk indicated that he knew that he had cornered his prey and was confident that I would take the least painful option. 'Take the low road, Sly. After all, it's only money, isn't it? Smart fellow like you can replace what you pay to me in no time.'

'How much?' I spat at him.

'Let's say one million baht apiece. That's three million baht. Get that to me today and you are all out tonight. Case closed.'

'What the hell are you talking about, "case closed", you moron? We were presented to a press conference last night! That little twerp of a police major was telling the world that he had caught a bunch of international drug traffickers red-handed. Do you expect me to believe that he will now change his story and say he has made a mistake?' I was bellowing at Fahad again. 'Anyhow, I can't get that kind of money in five minutes. What do you think I am, a fucking millionaire? And what makes you think that I would pay you anything to get Hansel out? What the hell is he to me? He is the reason we are here, or at least part of it.'

'Well, my friend, I don't give a damn where you get it, but just remember that you shouldn't take too long to organise it because you will be staying right where you are until you do. But allow me to suggest that you do it well within the next six days. That's all you have left before you will be officially charged and taken to court. After that, it will cost you a whole lot more because there will be more people to satisfy and more paperwork to get rid of, if you understand what I mean. Choice is yours.'

Fahad smiled coldly as he spoke. Taking a step forward, he whispered, 'The German is the perfect scapegoat for you. You had better take advantage of that so the police have a head to put on the chopping block. He's served his usefulness, as far as I'm concerned.' He chuckled as he continued, 'Stupid man! Thought he was going to be in Phuket chasing little girls this weekend with his pockets full of money.'

When I asked him how I would be able to make contact with him if I decided to play the game his way, he took a small notebook from his hand pouch and wrote a phone number and 'Johnny' on one of the pages. 'Just ask to talk to Johnny. If I'm not there, leave a message. But don't waste too much time thinking about it.' He tore the page out and handed it to me before swivelling around, slightly alarmed as he did so to see a woman standing so close behind him. As he was leaving the room, he called back over his right shoulder, 'I will make sure that you will be permitted to make those calls.' Then he was gone.

As soon as he had left the room, the woman spoke. 'Sly, what's this all about? I saw your picture in this morning's newspaper, and the article said that you were caught dealing with drugs? Is that true? Who was that man? Why is he asking you for money?' She moved in close to the bars, concern etched into her face.

Om was not actually a woman, but the cosmetic modifications and surgery that she had undergone when she was younger made it almost impossible for the average Joe to recognise that. She was a relative of my wife's, though not an immediate one, and had become a close friend – a lot closer than my wife realised – shortly after we had been introduced not too long after my arrival in Thailand.

I went on to explain what had happened and that I was in the midst of a big con job, with a three-million-baht price tag, and that the slimy little Arab who had just left was the one doing the conning. 'Did you hear what he was saying?'

'Yes, I did, but why you? I mean, how come you are involved with people like him? Where does he get the idea that you can pay him so much money?'

Om had good reason to be concerned. That morning, the newspaper she usually read had carried a front-page story of our arrest, along with the pictures of Hansel, Fred and me with the suitcase. She explained that she had just taken a mouthful of coffee at the beginning of a late lunch break and had almost choked when she saw my image right in front of her. She had read the story with rising alarm and, almost in shock, had abandoned the food she had ordered and rushed home to change out of her work clothes.

Being a Thai national, Om was familiar with the way the police often treated suspects. Although she had never actually experienced anything at first hand, several of her transvestite friends had been molested and abused by the police in the past and had related to her their stories of rapes and beatings. Some had even been tortured, electric probes being forced into various body cavities in attempts to extract a confession.

After a quick shower and a change of clothes, she had headed for the police station, arriving just after Fred and I had been brought into the room at Fahad's request. She had grasped in those initial few seconds that Fahad was the recipient of my outburst and was about to speak to me when she heard his response. This prompted her to step back a little to let him speak, and she had managed to listen unnoticed to the subsequent exchange, hearing it all with the exception of the few words Fahad had whispered when he had moved in closer to me.

I was expecting to be returned to the cell at any minute, so, interrupting her explanation, I asked her to try to get in touch with Jaidow, to fill her in on the situation and to ask her to bring me some clothes and other essentials as soon as possible. I didn't know how long it would take to get this mess sorted out, but in the meantime I would need at least a little sustenance, a change of clobber and a bit of money, not to mention a ton of smokes, to carry me through.

I must have looked pretty terrible, because she took a comb from her bag and handed it to the guard with a request for it to be given to me. Then she departed, saying that there were several vendors outside on the footpath and that she would send me in some food.

As I watched her leave, I started to feel a little more positive. I felt sure that I could get Jaidow to ask her uncle – who was in a pretty prominent political position in the Roi Et Province – to intervene and get me released from custody, then have Fahad fixed for good. I also had some good contacts who might be able to assist.

I turned to Fred. 'I guess that solves the mystery, doesn't it? It's not just the reward they are after. Did you hear Fahad? He said Hansel had served his usefulness. I'm going to strangle that stupid bugger when I get back there. I don't know if he actually knew what Fahad's plans were, but he certainly seems to have been the one used to carry them out. How much money can you get your hands on in a hurry?'

Fred nodded thoughtfully and, after a moment's consideration, replied that there was no way he would be able to get his hands on the kind of money that Fahad was after in the short term. 'That's one very fiendish little motherfucker, mate. His evil is almost tangible. You know, I had a similar feeling when I first set eyes on Hansel yesterday. But with regards to him, maybe it will be better not to let him know too much for now. We may do a whole lot better if we have the upper hand here. If he did know the scam was being planned and was in on it, then Fahad has sacrificed him. Let's just keep it cool for now and see what happens. I am now quite convinced that the cops are in on this as well, from what Fahad said about being able to fix it for us to get out of here with no charges. So we had better tread carefully. At least until we *are* out of here.'

We returned to the cell laden with the plastic bags of rice, chicken curry, noodles and spicy soup that Om had purchased. Hansel was sitting in his customary spot as far removed from us as the cell would permit and was curious to know who had come to visit. But we sat facing the passage with our backs to him and appeased our grumbling stomachs. He looked on expectantly for a while, but we had no intention of inviting him to join us.

Fred and I spoke quietly as we ate. 'If I find out for sure that that fool over there was in cahoots with Fahad and trying to work me over . . .' I hissed. 'Anyway, if that's the case, then Fahad has screwed him big style. Serves him right.'

'Listen, Sly, he might be as innocent as you and me. I mean, Fahad might have just used him as an instrument to set the wheels in motion. He never actually said that Hansel had been in it with him. He just said Hansel was of no further use to him. But you could be right. Let's see what happens from here on in. If they were working together, then he will be particularly annoyed that he has been double-crossed and might spill the beans. Anyway, let's give him the benefit of the doubt for now but keep plugging away at him to see what reaction we get.'

I agreed that this was a good idea. 'Look, Jaidow should be here soon. If the worst comes to the worst, I have a few million baht in the company account and a couple more in my own personal accounts that

I could probably use. But, to be sure, that will be the very last option.' This last bit, being a trifle on the generous side of exaggeration and mostly bollocks, didn't strengthen my own optimism one iota, but it did provoke a momentary glimmer of relief in Fred's expression.

When we finished eating, we both turned and rested our backs against the bars. 'Hey, Hansel! We just had a talk with Fahad. He said he needs you to give him three million baht if you want to get out of here. Can you get hold of that within the next five days?'

'Wha . . . What! That . . . what did he say? Why didn't he call me out, too? Why does he want *me* to pay three million baht? I can't get three million baht . . . Where the hell does he think I'm going to get three million baht?'

'Well, I don't know,' I replied, 'but he said we have to pay him one million baht each if we ever want to see daylight again, and being as how you got us in here, it is up to you to get us out, right? So, you get to pay it all. Fair enough?'

'But . . . but . . .' – he was almost in shock by now – 'I don't have any money. He . . . he knows I don't have any money. How can I get that kind of money? He knows I can't do that. *You* have to get the money. *You* have the money, not me . . . He knows that. *You* have to pay him. How can I pay him?'

'Hmm, well, that aside, old man, it seems to me that you've been screwed. Look, why not tell us the whole story? Maybe we can turn the tables on him. After all, he just called you a stupid mule. Said you were an ignoramus, a heap of camel dung, among other pleasantries. He said you had served your usefulness. Looks like he's used you and is now ready to dump you like a big bag of poop. Did you know what he was planning, Hansel? Did you think he was your bosom buddy? Come clean, Hansel. We are all in this leaky old boat together now. Y'know what I mean?

'Do you know what I'm thinking, Hansel? I'm thinking that you and Fahad planned this little game together. I'm looking back over the past couple of months, and I'm seeing very clearly how it all fits together and how *you* are the connection. What I am seeing is a phoney letter of credit, and you and Fahad and a bunch of bent cops, and a bag full of washing powder, and a plan to get me to cough up a heap of money. I've got plenty of money, right? You just said as much a moment ago. I'm the one who's got to pay, right? You just said that, too. "He knows that," you said. So how does *he know that*, Hansel? Was that the plan? I have buckets full of cash. Is that what you told Fahad, Hansel? Well, if that's the case, you have screwed up again, old boy. You see, I don't have any money. So, *now* where are all these millions going to come from to get us out of here? Got any suggestions?'

Hansel sat as still as stone, but his face was puffing up and getting redder by the second. He sat glaring daggers at something only he could see.

'Better let him absorb that for a moment, Sly. Looks like he's having a little difficulty grasping what's happening here.' Fred stood and cleared away the aftermath of our lunch and lit two cigarettes, handing one to me as we sat back feeling a little more comfortable than before, but not a lot more confident that things would be getting better soon. Hansel remained motionless for at least five minutes, then he stood up abruptly and rushed to the toilet, where he proceeded to chuck up into the squat bowl.

'Guess he held his breath too long.' Fred was not a bit sympathetic, and I had a sudden urge to go over and push his head right down into his own vomit and hold it there.

'Hope the idiot chokes,' I said instead and stretched out on the cold floor. The lack of sleep and the stress of it all were catching up with me.

Hansel recovered to some degree and washed his face at the tap, rinsing his mouth several times as he did. 'I don't know what Fahad is doing. I don't have any money, and he knows it. I didn't know what was in the suitcase any more than you did. I have already told you that, so stop accusing me. I didn't know! I didn't know!' He was almost shouting now, and Fred and I looked at each other with our eyebrows raised.

'Maybe he *is* just the dispensable patsy,' said Fred.

'Maybe,' I conceded.

Fred was once again the pacifier. 'OK, sit down, Hansel, and we'll talk about it.' Hansel dried his face on his shirt and shuffled back to his spot against the far wall. He wasn't that tall, being not more than five-foot-six, but he was heavily built, with the hint of having once been a very strong person. His legs were thick, his shoulders broad and his chest deep and muscular. He was in his mid-50s, but the years had not been terribly kind to him, and his large paunch did him no favours. He had left Germany more than ten years previously and had lived in Thailand since then, sustaining himself mostly by guiding German-speaking tourists around the country. Consequently, he had a very good knowledge of its geography, customs and language. He was not a particularly bright man, except where money was concerned, and begrudged parting with every penny, unless it was spent on himself. He hadn't been out of Thailand to renew his non-immigrant visa for many years. The reason being – by his own admission – that it cost money to do so.

Fred began to quiz him again about Fahad, but we learned nothing new. Shortly after we abandoned that approach, a uniformed officer appeared at the cell door and told me that I could make some phone calls if I wished, motioning me to follow him out to the front office.

'Well, Fred, it looks like the Fahad machine is in gear. Let's see what we can do now. With some luck, we will be sleeping on a mattress tonight. I'll get onto Jaidow first and then try to raise a couple of the people at the office. Hang tight.'

The officer made no attempt to handcuff me as I left the cell and was chummy and courteous as he led the way to one of the offices, where he showed me to a seat and handed me a phone, patting me on the shoulder as he told me to take my time. A little surprised, I thanked him. It seemed that we had reached the turning point already.

# CHAPTER 4

## The Fiendish Enforcers of Law and Order

'NO, NO! STOP IT! STOP IT! LEAVE ME ALONE!'

'You come! *Now!*'

'Stop it, please!'

Muffled, desperate cries penetrated my sleep. The nightmare that was tormenting me slowly gave way to reality. As I gradually surfaced, the cries became louder, and I realised where I was. The haze clouding my weary mind faded, and I could hear the pleading again.

My body was in same position it had formed when I had passed into the nether world hours before. The side I was lying on was numb, and I had no feeling at all in the hip, leg and arm that had been in contact with the cold cement floor. My head still lay on the pillow I had fashioned by rolling one of my shoes in my shirt. The air was thick with the smell coming from the toilets. The one in the adjacent cell seemed to be the worst offender.

As I tried to turn onto my back, I heard the cry again. It was the voice of a girl or woman trying to resist someone, her protestations filled with terror. I turned my head in the direction of the sound, my eyes adjusting slowly to the dim light. Fred was still comatose. Like me, he had been totally exhausted when he had passed out at around 9 p.m. and appeared not to have moved a muscle since. Hansel was sitting against the far wall of the cell with his arms crossed on his knees and his forehead resting on them, also asleep.

'Let me go! No, please! Please don't!'

'Come! You come, *now*!' A heavy-set officer, dressed in regulation trousers and white T-shirt, was struggling with what appeared to be a young Asian female, whom I am going to call Corrie. She was resisting so much he had to force her quite roughly out of the cell door. As he turned her from the cell into the corridor, I could see that she was indeed quite young, probably no more than 20 years old. She was speaking English with a slightly Asian accent, indicating that she was probably not Thai.

It was hard to tell for sure, with the only light coming from a single dim fluorescent bulb in the centre of the corridor, but she appeared to be Japanese or Korean, very pretty, with a small frame, dressed in jeans and T-shirt. Another sound attracted my attention, and looking deeper into the cell, I saw another female, whom I am going to call Jennie, huddled into the far corner. She was cowering against the bars, her arms wrapped around them, and whimpering with fear.

The first girl was dragged, struggling, along the corridor and out of sight, into the main office area. The door of the cell that she had been taken from stood open, but the remaining girl made no attempt to leave. She seemed to be too terrified to move. About three minutes later, the officer returned alone and shut the barred gate to the corridor but still made no attempt to close the cell door. Raising my head, I watched him disappear then looked at my watch. It was 1.35 a.m. I called to the girl who had been left behind. 'Are you OK?'

She didn't respond. I called again and she answered in English. 'No.' She stifled a sob and sniffed loudly. 'I . . . I'm frightened.' She sobbed again, and I waited for her to continue. 'Why are they doing this? We didn't do anything wrong. This is crazy.' She started sobbing louder.

'OK, take it easy, then. Take it easy, love. How did you end up here? What have they got you in here for?'

Her voice trembled, and she sobbed fitfully as she replied. 'They just stopped us as we were walking in the street and told us to get in the police car. They said we were suspected of dealing with drugs, then one of them grabbed my handbag and stuck his hand in it. He showed us some small packets and said it was heroin – and that we could get the death penalty for carrying it.' She broke down, and for quite some minutes her sobs echoed around the cells.

Calming a little after a while, she began again. 'We didn't have any drugs, honestly. We don't use any kind of drugs. I don't know how that heroin got in my bag. I don't know where it came from. I didn't put it there. I really didn't. Oh, what are my parents going to say?'

Her sobs became more pronounced, and I did my best to console her. 'OK, OK, I believe you. Just try to settle down.'

It wasn't difficult to guess what had happened: two pretty, defenceless young foreign girls travelling alone in Bangkok, arguably one of the most dangerous and decadent cities in the world, believing all the tourist-brochure propaganda, expecting to encounter 'the Land of Smiles' and warm and accommodating multitudes; little girls with no knowledge of the fangs that lurk behind many of those grins or the underlying agenda hidden beneath many of those accommodations; no inkling of the deeply entrenched corruption, selfishness and perversity that is the foundation of so much of the authentic version of Thai society; the perfect target for a certain faction of the servants of the people otherwise known as the Royal Thai Police Force.

'I know that's easy to say,' I added, 'but try to take it easy and wait to see what your friend has to say when she gets back.' I had a feeling, though, that I knew exactly what she'd have to say. Drugs were evidently a tool that could be used for more than cash rewards. 'Look, if what you have said is true and you really didn't have any drugs, then I believe I know why these guys have done this to you. Unfortunately, this kind of thing happens often here. But I have a feeling that if you do what they say, they will probably release you. Just try to concentrate on handling it without making them more aggressive. Fighting these guys won't work. It will just encourage them to abuse you for longer – maybe even a lot worse than that.'

'You mean . . . they're going to rape me?'

'I'm afraid that's what it looks like. Listen . . .' She was crying again, and it broke my heart that I could do nothing to help her. I waited for her to stop. 'Listen, love, as repugnant as it might sound, you will probably be far better off if you play their silly game and then get the hell out of this country and never come back. When you get safely home, you can then make your complaints. Tell all of your friends what happened and tell the authorities and the media and make a big fuss about it. Where do you come from?'

'I come from Taiwan originally, but Corrie and I are on holiday from England.'

'Look, I'm not trying to make you more frightened than you already are, believe me, but you might as well know what to expect. I doubt they will want to keep you around for long once they've had their fun. I wouldn't be surprised if they took you to the airport in the morning and told you to get lost. But please do *not* threaten them with anything. That could lead to something far more serious and permanent. I'm sure they'd have no hesitation in slitting your throat if they thought that they were in danger of exposure. Do you understand what I am saying?'

She moved over to the bars directly opposite me. I could see the panic in her pretty ebony eyes. 'I can't go through this. Please help me! I have never had . . . They will hurt me . . . Don't let them hurt me! Oh, what can I do?' she sobbed desperately.

But I was powerless to prevent what was evidently already in progress. After some years of living in Thailand, and having heard many stories from the locals, I knew that attempting to intervene could well have a disastrous result as far as the girls were concerned. It was not uncommon for tourists to be found dead or simply to disappear altogether in Thailand. I really did not know what else to do, but I reasoned that it would be far more dangerous for the girls not to cooperate than it would be for them to do so.

'OK, OK, listen to me, love . . . Listen to me now . . . What's your name?'

'J . . . Jennie. J . . . Jennie Lee,' she sobbed in reply.

'Jennie, look. There is absolutely nothing I can do to help you, understand? I am locked in here, and you are over there. What can I do? For me to become involved could make things even worse, and they wouldn't listen to anything I have to say anyhow. Just try to be brave and try to minimise the danger by not antagonising them. As I said, it's more than likely that they'll just let you go after they have done with you. There is a chance that they will steal any money or other valuables you have, but what's a little money if you're still alive. After that they will probably make sure you are on the next plane out of the country.'

Jennie began to regain her composure and actually straightened her back as if she was gaining strength and determination. 'What's your name? You sound English.' She smiled faintly, letting me see that she was preparing herself for what she now expected to follow.

I told her my name, and we talked for a while. She told me some of what she and Corrie had been doing on their holiday. I gave her brief details of my own predicament but encouraged her nonetheless to believe that there was every probability that she and her friend would be home safely before long, as would I. In fact, I genuinely believed that I would be having the holiday I had planned with my mum in a few months' time. After telling Jennie this, she suggested that I ring her when I arrive and provided her phone number, which I noted on the back of a business card from my wallet.

The sound of heavy footsteps advancing towards the entrance to the corridor silenced us, and I put my index finger to my lips and laid my head back on the shoe pillow with my eyes almost closed, considering it safer for the girls if the cops didn't know there was an additional witness to their decadent brutality. I watched carefully as the same man who had taken Corrie out brought her back. He wasn't being rough with her now, and she wasn't struggling. She walked by his side as he lightly cradled her arm, just above the elbow. He let her enter the cell where Jennie now sat with her back to the bars. He then closed and locked the door behind her. It was almost 3 a.m.

As the cop turned to leave, Jennie got up and went over to embrace her friend, who was standing motionless in front of the door. Corrie threw her arms around her friend and, with her head on Jennie's shoulder, began to cry; deep heart-wrenching sobs that slowly subsided to a soft whimpering. Jennie held her, patting, caressing and whispering to her until she finally became silent and they sat together on the concrete floor.

As soon as the cop had gone, I sat up again. After waiting for the girls to settle down a little I called softly across the passage, 'Is she all right, Jennie?'

'I think so, Sly,' she replied, turning her head a little towards me. After a while, Jennie stood up and faced me, clutching the bars in front of her. 'You were right. They made her sign some papers, and then some of them raped her. They told her she would be charged with drug trafficking if she resisted and that I would also be charged and possibly executed, or go to jail for life . . . They said the only way to get out of here was for her to do what they told her and not to make any fuss. They said if we both do what they say, then we will be released in the morning and no charges will be laid against either of us.'

'That figures. Did they hurt her?'

'Not physically. I mean they didn't beat her or anything. They took turns on her, though. What kind of police are these, Sly? What kind of place is this?'

'Can't find a word off the top of my head to answer that properly, Jennie. How many were there?'

Jennie turned her head towards her friend and said something that I didn't quite catch, then she turned back and said, 'She's not sure.'

About 40 minutes later, a different cop came for Jennie. This one was shorter, a little younger and swayed as he walked – a characteristic that psychologists might have attributed to inner feelings of inferiority and inadequacy. He unlocked the gate to the corridor quietly and entered the passage. I could make out a lecherous grin on his face as he approached the girls' cell.

He was clearly taken aback, however, when Jennie met him at the door, standing straight and glaring daggers of hatred at him through the bars. His bravado seemed to evaporate in an instant: no stomach at all without his buddies standing beside him. He didn't grab her as the previous fellow had with Corrie; instead, he motioned to her with a flick of his head to precede him to the outer door.

While she was gone, I managed to engage Corrie in conversation to take her mind off the plight of her friend. She told me that she had a Korean mother and British father. She had spent most of her early youth in Korea, with annual visits to her father's home town, but since leaving primary school had lived in Britain, mostly in boarding schools, and had been back to Korea only for holidays.

She and Jennie had met several years previously at one of those boarding schools, where they had shared the same room. Eventually they had rented a small apartment and had been living together for the past two years. Jennie was 17 years old, and Corrie had just turned 18. They had chosen Thailand for a two-week holiday partly because they wanted to see at first hand a little of the culture that they had read so much about. They then planned to spend two weeks with Jennie's parents in Taiwan before going on to Korea to spend the rest of their vacation with Corrie's family.

Their expectations of being able to relate to their friends and families wonderful experiences of friendly people, delicious food and Buddhist temples had now been shattered. Of course, neither could have possibly anticipated that they would be seeing very little of that and would instead be subjected to fabricated drug charges, threatened with the death penalty and gang raped by a bunch of morally bankrupt thugs calling themselves law-enforcement officers.

They had been out for dinner and were walking down Sukhumvit Road near the Night Bazaar, doing a little window shopping on their way back to their hotel, when a police car had pulled up beside them and two uniformed officers had jumped out of the back. One of them spoke reasonable English and had asked them to produce their passports. They'd complied with the request, thinking that it was a routine check, but when the officer had said that they had to go with him to have the passports verified, they had both been shocked. They'd been bundled into the back seat of the car and sandwiched between the officers. One of them had then grabbed Jennie's handbag and had fished around in it for a few seconds, while the other had told them that they were suspected of dealing in drugs. The girls had been stunned when they'd heard that, having read about people being hanged in some Asian countries for possessing drugs. They'd never used drugs of any kind and had never so much as seen heroin, other than in the movies.

'There must be some mistake,' Corrie had said. 'We have no drugs.'

'Well, what's that? Looks like drugs to me,' the cop had replied, pointing to the several small plastic bags in the open hand of the officer who'd been rummaging around in the bag. Corrie had looked quickly at Jennie for some kind of explanation, but Jennie had shrugged her shoulders and responded with a wide-eyed look of shock.

'I have no idea,' they'd both said in unison. They were becoming very frightened.

'The penalty for drug-trafficking in Thailand is death. Did you know that?' The cop had then spoken a few words of Thai to the driver and the car had pulled out from the kerb.

When the cops had first taken her to the front office, the one who spoke English had told her to sign a paper, which she could not read because it was typed in Thai. He'd said that if she did not sign it, she and her friend would be charged with drug trafficking. If she did as he told her, they would not be charged and would be free to leave in the morning.

After she had signed, he'd explained that the paper was a confession and that if she made any accusations against the police, or made any complaints to anyone, he would have her arrested again immediately and she would not be released. He'd explained that he had sufficient evidence to have her and her friend convicted of trafficking in drugs and had numerous police officers to stand witness. He'd pointed out that she would have no possibility of winning a contested court case and then detailed the penalties they would face once convicted. He had also warned her that, in the event of a court case, all of those officers present in the station that night would testify that she and Jennie had been treated in accordance with the law, that they had been taken from the cell and questioned individually in relation to the drug offence in the presence of those officers and that nothing other than the interrogation had occurred. In short, there were no witnesses to the rape other than the offenders themselves, and any complaint from either of the girls would be considered to be nothing but an attempt to escape punishment. 'Just lie back and enjoy it. Then you can go home,' he had cautioned.

I was relieved for both girls when Corrie told me that the police had all used condoms, though they had hardly been thinking of the girls' well-being when taking this precaution. A little semen, after all, can be used as irrefutable evidence, and traces of it can be still present for several days after the act.

I was surprised at Jennie's composure and apparent fortitude after she returned. She had somehow been transformed from the whimpering terrified child I had spoken to earlier, clinging desperately to the cell bars, to a determined and courageous young woman. She turned and spat in the direction of the cop as he left.

Fred stirred. 'What's up?' he asked with a grimace, raising himself with difficulty onto one elbow and looking towards the girls.

'Tell you in a minute, mate,' I replied and turned my attention back to Corrie and Jennie.

Jennie had been given the same spiel in the front office and had been forced to sign the same confession that Corrie had. Then she'd been raped by several of the officers. She told me that she had seen two leaving the station through the front door as she had been taken into the small room, which contained a couch. Perhaps they had already had their fun for the night with Corrie.

Oddly enough, considering their ordeal, the girls dozed off in each other's arms, and, after a brief discussion with Fred, I decided to try to get a little more shut-eye as well. When I awoke, the girls were gone. I could do nothing but hope that they would get back to their families safely.

The story of Jennie and Corrie doesn't end there. Over the ensuing years, we became good pen friends, and they eventually helped to set up a website that detailed a lot of what was happening to me. Although they decided not to relate their own terrifying experiences to anyone, they vowed never to return to Thailand and to discourage any of their friends or associates from venturing into the Land of Smiles.

I learned later from their letters what happened after they'd left the police station that morning at a little before 6 a.m. Two of the police officers had driven them back to their hotel in Sukhumvit Road. In their hotel room, both cops had sat drinking tins of beer from the mini-bar while warning them to leave Thailand as soon as possible. One of them had tried to become intimate again with Corrie, but when she'd begun to scream, he'd been frightened off and told to stop by his colleague. After drinking all of the beer that was in the fridge and stuffing the mini bottles of spirits into their pockets, they'd left with a warning – make any waves and you will be arrested again.

As soon as they'd gone, the girls had rushed to pack their bags and had checked out, taking a taxi to a small hotel near the river on the other side of the city, not too far from Bangkwang prison, where I was destined to become a resident for about six years. They'd hid in their room for three days, not daring to go out, not even to visit the hotel restaurant; instead, they had all of their meals sent up. Their airline tickets were open, and they decided that instead of taking a flight from Don Muang International Airport, they would take a train to Butterworth in Malaysia and then go on to Taiwan from Kuala Lumpur. They booked first-class tickets and spent almost the entire 20 hours that it took to reach the border locked in their cabin.

# CHAPTER 5

## Your Money or Your Life

IT WAS BECOMING INCREASINGLY HARD TO BELIEVE THAT JUST 48 hours earlier I was living the comfortable life I had enjoyed for several years. I had a good, reasonably profitable business, a small office in a respectable part of town, a devoted wife (at least I thought she was), a comfortable apartment and a little cash in the bank. I travelled periodically, had some good friends, both in Thailand and abroad, and was generally content with my lot.

Of course, it hadn't taken too many years as a resident in Thailand to know that there was a high level of corruption within the Thai police force, as well as other government departments, and I was accustomed to being required to pay bribes of varying degrees for every conceivable official transaction. I was also accustomed to being subjected to the 'double standard' pricing, which meant that, for no other reason than that I was a foreigner, I was charged a considerably higher price than the locals for almost everything. I accepted that as part and parcel of living and doing business in Thailand, and although the blatant discrimination always riled me, I realised I was not able to do a whole lot about it. I generally budgeted for it, as do most other business people in the country I would imagine, but I had not previously been a victim of its most ruthless form.

Nevertheless, as I awoke that Saturday morning, I was reasonably confident that things would be sorted out and that Fred and I would be released in a short time. I believed, too, that my wife's family would rally behind me and that my connections would come through. I had also been encouraged by the conduct and attitude of Colonel Wirat and did not believe that a professional like him would deliberately victimise innocent people for personal gain. I felt certain, too, that he would not be a party to anything that involved a lowlife such as Fahad.

Hansel, I thought, would probably be detained for further questioning and possibly charged with drug possession. But Fred and I were nowhere near him when the suitcase was opened – even though it was in my car – and the police would, therefore, not need to detain us for long. They just needed time to check my reasons for being at the bank and what I had told them about Fahad and the letter of credit. Then they would probably go to see my wife and my business associates to verify that I was, in fact, who I said I was. Then they'd do the same for Fred, and we would be released. They were just doing their job, after all.

Jaidow arrived at the police station with Om that morning not long after 9 a.m. I was taken from the cell and led, unshackled, to a room at the back of the station where they had been told to wait. Although it was not too comfortable, we could at least talk privately, with only one set of bars separating us. Om had phoned Jaidow from the public phone booth outside the police station as soon as she had left me the previous afternoon and had arranged to meet her there as soon as she could make it. She didn't show up until well after 6 p.m. because she had been delayed in the afternoon traffic. Evidently, this was the reason that I was unable to get in touch with her when I had been given permission to use the phone. She was told by the duty officer that visiting time was over and that she would have to return the next day.

When she returned home, she called her uncle in Roi Et – let's call him Whitaya – only to be told that she was not to mention his name to the police under any circumstances. He also told her that I must shelter the entire family from any fallout; none of them could visit me or even let it be known that they were acquainted with me, such was their fear that their names would be linked to a drug scandal or, more importantly, to the officers of the NSD. That I had not been dealing drugs or that the whole affair was a set-up was of no concern to them at all; in fact, it had only reinforced the family's resolve to be distanced from me as far as possible. To be involved in any way was far too dangerous and the consequences could be costly. I was on my own, as far as they were concerned.

Fortunately, Jaidow and Om were not so easily intimidated and were there for me, even if they could offer little more than moral support. I was grateful for their loyalty.

Jaidow was on the verge of tears when I entered the room. She was very concerned that I had been beaten, tortured or otherwise maltreated, but once she had established that I was still in one piece and faring pretty well under the circumstances, she related her troubling news to me. As I absorbed what she told me, with more than a little disappointment, she explained to me what my business partner had done as soon as he had been informed of my arrest. In a word, vanished.

'Well, news moves quickly in this place, doesn't it?' I finally responded, but there was little else to say about it. I hadn't at all considered that there would be such a far-reaching and terrified reaction to what had happened to me, but as she spoke I realised that my arrest would have caused a major tremor.

'Anyway,' I continued, 'there's not a lot we can do about any of that at this stage. Look, Jai, this Arab is asking for one million baht to get each of us out of jail. He is quite obviously a professional extortionist, and it is apparent that some of the cops here are involved in his little game.'

We discussed what might be the best way to play things, until we were interrupted by the return of the officer, who beckoned to me that it was time to return to the cell. We said our goodbyes then I followed him out.

Jaidow had brought me a small carryall with some clean clothes and some toiletries. She had also included a carton of cigarettes, some confectionery, a couple of containers of fried rice with prawns and other seafood, and several sweet-bread rolls, along with 2,000 baht in small denomination notes. I was going to feel a little more comfortable, if nothing else.

Having given him the benefit of the doubt for the present, I invited Hansel to join Fred and me for lunch, but after eating he retreated to the other side of the cell and lay on his side with his face turned towards the grey concrete wall. Perhaps he was trying to make some sense of the various scribblings left there by previous occupants. Fred and I talked quietly for the next few hours before nodding off to sleep.

After the initial shock of being arrested and beaten in the Bangkok Bank car park had subsided, Hansel was more than eager to curry favour with Fred and me. He had no money, apart from the few hundred baht in his wallet, and told me quite frankly that he would need to rely on me for some support, at least as far as food was concerned, until he could make other arrangements with his girlfriend.

His visitor from the German Embassy drug-liaison office had told him that, as he had confessed to carrying the suitcase – even though he claimed it belonged to someone else – it was very unlikely that he would be released in the short term. He had conceded while talking to us that it was partly his fault that we were in this situation with him, though he kept to his story that he had been unaware of the contents of the suitcase when he had carried it to my apartment. He did tell us, however, that he had mistakenly believed that he was a close friend of Fahad's, having known him for quite a few years, and that he felt much betrayed by him. He assured us that, once he was out of his present predicament, if he ever met Fahad again face to face he would surely throttle him. 'For that satisfaction,' he snarled, 'I will not mind going to prison.'

I agreed to include him when ordering food and drink, and actually began to believe that he might be as innocent as he professed to be. It was certainly possible that Fahad had simply used him as a mule to accommodate his own agenda and then discarded him – a dispensable and convenient card for the cops to play in their game. After all, they would need to produce a drug dealer or courier to justify their claim on the rewards they would be expecting. As far as Fahad was concerned, as long as I coughed up the one million baht each for me and Fred, Hansel could burn in hell. That way he would get his share of the rewards, plus a percentage of the two million as well.

Jaidow and Om visited the police station each day during the initial seven days of our confinement, making sure that all three of us received decent food and essentials. On the Tuesday, they went to the Park-Inn Hotel, where Fred had been staying, to get him some clean clothes, toiletries and some cash from his luggage. On arrival, they were told by the management that there was nothing at all belonging to Fred being kept there, and their questions as to where his possessions were and who had taken them were met with indifference and blank faces.

Fred was astonished and more than a little pissed off when Jaidow gave him the news. The only explanation that he could conceive was that the manager of the 'Fark-Inn Hotel' (as he henceforth called it) must have heard that he had been arrested on drug charges and decided that he wouldn't be returning, meaning that anything left in his room was fair game and could be pilfered. Either that or the police had removed them and the manager was afraid to become involved. Regardless of how or why or who, everything was gone. He'd had at least 50,000 baht in cash and quite a number of important documents relating to his business locked in his briefcase in the room, along with several thousand dollars' worth of clothes and valuables. To add to the insult, he had paid one month's rent in advance just two weeks earlier. He promised himself that he would be having a word or two with that Fark-Inn manager.

It was fortunate that he had his passport, bank passbook and credit cards with him at the time of his arrest, though these were clearly of limited use at that moment. He had only 3,000 baht in cash in his wallet and had given 1,000 of that to me to give to Jaidow to help cover the cost of the food and sundries that she was providing. On learning of the plunder of his room, he gave her a further 1,000 baht to buy him some changes of clothes, and she brought these with her on her next visit.

The following Tuesday, at around 9 a.m., I was taken from the cell and escorted to the visit area, where I met, for the first time, the embassy welfare officer whom I am going to call Pat. Pat was a very pleasant lady of about 35, tall and rather attractive, who spoke in the unmistakable tones of a native of Yorkshire. She told me that she had learned of my arrest only that morning and had come to see me immediately. Rodger, it seemed, had forgotten to mention my plight.

I had a long discussion with her, during which I asked if she would make contact with my mother, now in her 80s, to let her know what had happened. But I asked her to stress that I was well and in no danger and that she should not worry because the whole affair was a mistake and would be sorted out quickly. Pat promised that she would arrange this as soon as she returned to the embassy and also that she would visit me the following week, after I had been transferred to the remand prison.

Fahad was another visitor that day. I was called out to see him at around 2 p.m. Fred stayed behind in the cell with Hansel.

'Hello, Sly. I'm pleased to see that you are still in good shape. Have they been treating you well? I instructed my friends here to take special care of you, you know, so I hope they have been doing that. Now, my friend, have you done what I told you to do?'

Merely the sight of this little twerp raised my blood pressure again. I spat, 'Listen real close, Fahad, because I am going to say this only once. I have no intention of paying you or your buddies here one single baht. Is that clear? Got the message?'

'Oh . . . Plead to Allah, and may he have mercy on you, Sly! This is not a very nice way to do business, is it? You're being a silly boy, now. Silly, silly.' He was talking calmly in a childish fashion, waving his forefinger at me and trying hard to convey the impression that he wasn't terribly concerned. 'Why are you tormenting me like this, my friend? It's not smart, you know. Not smart.'

'You're the one who should be getting a bruise on his fucking forehead pleading to Allah for mercy, old chap. You're going to be needing it soon. But, tell you what, why don't you just take your conniving arse and your big nose out of here and don't bother me again. I'll be out of this hole very soon, and when I am, you had better be watching your back real close because I am going to be looking for you. When . . .'

He interrupted me with half-pretend laughter. 'Oh, Sly, Sly, you are a funny man! I just love it when you get angry like that. But, please, be serious for a moment, Sly, because I don't have much time today. Now, do you have the money I told you to get or don't you? If you don't, then I'm terribly sorry to say that you will most definitely *not* be out of here next week. Actually, that's not quite correct. You will be out of *here* next week, but you will be in a much more hostile environment, and of that much, my friend, I can very confidently assure you.

'Now, why not make it easy on yourself? You have the money to end this tiresome nonsense. Why not just pay it over and go home to your lovely wife? I have warned you already that if you don't do so before Thursday, it will be too late to keep the lid on this little can of worms, and you and your friends will be taken to court. Then you will have to pay a whole lot more if you want to go free. Then, my friend, you will have to pay the judges and the prosecutors as well, and they don't come cheap, Sly. Don't be foolish, now. Get the money arranged. I can have you out of here in a flash, all the paperwork in order. Only Hansel will be left holding the bag.'

I turned and left without saying another word, leaving Fahad standing at the bars staring after me. Though he might have been a little less sure that he would be enjoying the benefits of my hard-earned cash, he was no doubt confident that he would still be getting his share of the reward money, which he knew would be half of the $6,000 per kilo paid by the DEA plus half of the 20 baht per gram paid by the NSD. Not a bad return on time invested. Not bad at all.

# CHAPTER 6

‖‖‖‖‖‖‖‖‖‖‖‖‖‖‖‖‖‖‖‖‖‖‖‖‖‖‖‖‖‖‖‖‖‖‖‖‖‖‖‖‖‖‖‖‖‖‖‖‖‖‖‖‖‖‖‖‖‖‖‖‖‖‖‖‖‖‖‖‖‖‖‖‖‖‖‖‖

# Hell Was Opening Its Doors

SEVEN DAYS AFTER THE ARREST, WE WERE TAKEN FROM THE CELL
that had been our home and put into an enclosed wagon with no
windows, apart from a small glass observation porthole between the
cabin and the back tray and one small opening covered with heavy
steel mesh at the top of each of the back doors. Benches had been
built over the wheel arches on either side, and we were handcuffed
to bars welded along the back of these, Hansel on one side and Fred
and me on the other. There was very little conversation during the
20-minute trip to the court building, mainly because the backdraft
created by the movement of the van caused the exhaust fumes to be
sucked into the canopy, causing us all to feel extremely nauseous.

It was about 9 a.m. when we were processed through the transfer
system at the court and handed over to the Corrections Department
officials. Our handcuffs were removed, and we were ushered into a
large holding cell in which several Asian men in civilian clothes sat
silently on the filthy concrete floor – like us, waiting for their initial
appearance before the magistrate.

Five identical cells stood in a row, each one separated from the
next by a shared row of bars – I was destined to become very familiar

with every one of them. The other cells were positively bursting with prisoners, every one of them, as far as I could determine, dressed in brown shorts and shirts and all shackled at the ankles with heavy chains.

'Where do we go from here, I wonder?' Fred was thinking out loud as we sat down, our backs against the dividing bar partition.

A foreigner in the adjacent cell answered with a question of his own. 'What have they got you for?' He was a tall Scandinavian fellow, possibly a Swede or a Finn, with very blue eyes and wavy sandy hair. He and his two companions, foreigners like himself, were dressed exactly like the others in the adjoining cells.

'Heroin possession, a bloody big bag full of the stuff,' answered Fred, with a what-the-hell-have-I-done-to-deserve-this expression.

'Well, in that case you will in all likelihood be headed for Bombat prison. Not a nice place. I was there for six months before they transferred me to The Prem [Klong Prem prison]. You had better keep your wits about you there, boys. It is a very dangerous place to be. Not so much from the other inmates, but from the scum they have running it and the trusties.'

'Trusties? What's a trusty?' Fred enquired.

'Convicted prisoners, just like the rest, but ones who have been given some level of protection and authority – and some privileges that other prisoners don't get. They're the lackeys of the warders – generally ass-licking swine who will be more than happy to set you up or squeal on you for anything that they think will get them a pat on the back or some favourable treatment.'

For the next ninety minutes or so, Fred and I sat and listened as these three fellows explained the workings of a system that I was to come to know as 'Justice Incorporated'. It all seemed to point to one stark fact: that we had virtually no chance of freedom until at least the first court had heard our case and handed down a verdict, and that could take months, even years.

Suspected drug offenders, particularly foreigners, were usually not granted bail, so the only thing that could facilitate our release before the court hearings began was if the police decided not to proceed with the charge or if the prosecutor considered that there was insufficient evidence to have the case presented to the courts – but neither scenario was likely to be forthcoming unless we parted with a pot of gold or two, and because no one would want to miss the gravy train, those pots had better be heavy. In such a case, the Scandinavians explained, the police would have to have an incentive for not presenting certain incriminating evidence, the prosecutor would have to have some incentive for not asking questions that would be detrimental to the defendant's cause and the judge would have to have some incentive for overlooking certain things and ensuring that the court transcripts were favourable to the defendant.

We became more and more despondent as one of them explained that he had been detained for 15 months so far and that the Criminal Court still hadn't completed the trial. He had been approached several times during the proceedings with thinly veiled suggestions that he could walk free if he had the resources to make all of the relevant parties happy, but although he had been trying hard to do so, he hadn't as yet succeeded. He said that he had come to Bangkok to purchase a quantity of heroin for his own use, because it was so much cheaper than in his home country, but he had been caught on his way through the check-in at Don Muang on his return journey. He had found out later that the Thai guy he had bought the drugs from was a police informant and that an Englishman he had met at Nana Plaza on Sukhumvit Road, and who had introduced him to the pusher, was also apparently working in league with the cops. He told us that he had initially pleaded innocent because he had been persuaded to do so by his lawyer – an exercise to allow time for an arrangement to be made. But having been unable to come up with the cash, he was preparing to change his plea to guilty so he could get the case settled that day and avoid the trauma of being dragged to court each month. He said he had been told by his embassy that he would be able to apply for a transfer to his home country once he had served four years, and would probably then be home in his own warm bed no more than a year or two after that.

Much later on, and after hearing many similar stories, I realised that the way this fellow was caught in the first place revealed quite a cosy arrangement between the pusher and the police. This was how I saw it: the police gave the pusher the drugs from their ample store of confiscated narcotics. The Englishman – being from the West made him more likely to be trusted by other foreigners – then introduced the buyer to the pusher. The pusher then informed the cops, and they apprehended the buyer with the drugs in his/her possession, preferably on their way out of the country. The Englishman shared with the pusher their percentage of whatever the buyer had paid for the dope – which could be anything from $8,000 to $12,000 per kilogram. Once the case was tried and the buyer convicted, he also took a share of the rewards on offer from the DEA and the NSD. If the cops could get the suspect to part with some exorbitant amount of money to have the case dropped, then the Englishman and the pusher got some of that, in lieu of the share of the rewards. The cops got the drugs back, plus, of course, the lion's share of the profits and rewards – or, in the case of a pay-off, the purchase price plus the payola – and could use the dope again for the next sting. In other words, they had a great time making lots of money out of nothing while getting paid by the government for being on duty at the same time. The cops also got all kinds of pats on the back and promotions for doing a great job, and the NSD office received additional subsidies and financial support from the USA and other countries to continue the so-called 'drug offensive'. And very damned offensive it is, too. Now that might *not* be exactly how it all works, but that's how I have pieced it together over the years, and it seems to fit pretty well when all's considered.

Our informants were telling us about the life that awaited us at Bombat prison when a uniformed official called them to the gate and, after cuffing their wrists together, escorted them out of sight along the corridor. Shortly after that, the three of us were similarly ushered from the cell to a courtroom on the second floor.

Our appearance before the magistrate was brief. We were told to stand side by side facing the bench while one of the police officers who had brought us addressed the court. Only Hansel understood anything of what was said, and he told us later that the cop had made a request that the three of us be detained for a further period of twelve days so that the investigation could continue. We were given no opportunity to speak, and the magistrate rubber-stamped the request. That was it. We were then returned to the cell, where we sat, mostly in silence, each submerged in our own private thoughts.

'Sly! Sly! Over here, honey. Sly!' The shouting must have been going on for some time before it registered above the din that someone was calling me. Recognising Jaidow's voice, I went to the bars on my side of a wide corridor, opposite a window that looked out onto the courtyard. The window was covered with thick wire mesh, and it took me a while to make her out among all of the other people struggling to communicate across the corridor. But there she was, standing with Om, the pair of them waving madly.

I gave her a rundown on events since I had last talked to her, but the effort required was almost as draining on the nerves and energy reserves as had been everything else, and it left us both exhausted and hoarse. There were just so many people shouting back and forth across the distance that divided them that we had to cup our hands around our mouths and yell every word at top volume, and then to try to catch what was said from the other side by similarly cupping our ears. In spite of it all, I managed to convey that we would in all likelihood be heading for Bombat prison on the afternoon bus and that in the meantime it would be lovely if she could buy us some food and drink. She promised to come to visit me the following day after she had checked that Bombat was where we would indeed be confined.

'It looks as if you're going to need a lawyer from now on, Sly,' she said. 'This has gone too far to try to tackle it on your own. You had better start thinking about who I should talk to.' She was desperately trying to sound positive, but her expression betrayed her fear and apprehension. I realised then just how deeply this whole affair was affecting her as well.

About ten minutes after she departed, an officer called my name and handed me through the bars a plastic bag filled with smaller plastic bags. Some were filled with curried chicken and rice, others with iced coffee and cold water. Lunch had been served, but had Jaidow not been there to purchase it, we would have gone hungry. No food at all is provided at the courts by the Justice Department.

It was late afternoon when we were taken out of the cell, handcuffed and led to a dilapidated old blue bus, with heavy steel mesh covering the windows, that was parked at the rear of the building. We were accompanied by at least 50 other prisoners who had been taken from the other holding cells. Most of them, having made this trip before, scrambled to secure a place on the benches along either side of the cabin. Those who were too slow or who preferred to stand were crushed together along the aisle, clutching bars fixed to the ceiling. After a barred door between the rear guard compartment and the passenger section was closed and padlocked, the bus moved out and headed towards our new abode.

Ninety minutes later, stiff and dazed from our initial introduction to a system we were to become all too familiar with, and with our heads aching from the thick blanket of exhaust fumes that is as much a part of Bangkok as the traffic that produces it, we arrived at Ladyao.

The bus swerved abruptly from the main road and after entering the front drive of what we later discovered was the Klong Prem men's prison, turned left down a narrow street that paralleled the prison walls. At the end, the bus then turned right and headed down a side lane. On the right was a high concrete wall, with guard towers situated at about 20-metre intervals, the occupants of which sat casually or stood cradling a rifle or in some cases manning a fixed machine gun, their expressions revealing the brain-numbing boredom they had to suffer, day in and day out, in their small boxes doing absolutely nothing.

Though these guards probably considered themselves to be rather important cogs in the state machinery, I realised later that they were in reality little more than prisoners themselves. In fact, most of those they were guarding had far more freedom than they did. At least the prisoners had human company and could talk and laugh and play games and walk or jog around the prison yards. True, the inmates were locked up in very crowded cells at night and had to endure other harsh conditions, but the tower guards were, in reality, in solitary confinement for their entire working day. They would never have admitted that, of course, but, when it's all boiled down, they were virtual prisoners for at least ten hours each day.

The bus turned right again, and I could see the prison wall extending for at least another 500 metres. On the left was a wide canal and on the far side of that a narrow stretch of greenery skirting another road blocked with traffic.

After being herded through the main entrance, we were moved into a long wide corridor and went through the induction procedure. All of our possessions were inspected and our valuables impounded, logged into the property book and put into plastic bags, to which the original copy of the property form, signed by the owner, was attached. No prisoner is allowed to have money or valuables in his possession, so any cash that he is carrying on arrival is impounded and is supposed to be put into his prison account so that each day he can draw a small amount in the form of a coupon, which he is able to use to purchase items from the prison store.

After the initial registration was complete, we all had to submit to cavity searches by one of the officers, who seemed to relish his job of poking his finger up everyone's backside. Initially, the three of us, being the only foreigners in the group, thought that we might be spared this humiliation, but we found to our horror that we too had to strip naked and bend over in front of the officer. He was wearing a glove but made no attempt to clean or sterilise his finger after each insertion, other than to rinse it quickly in a small bowl of water he had beside him.

Having had some first-aid training in the past – during one of my previous periods of incarceration, in fact, proving beyond doubt that some good can come from every adversity – I was terrified that I would become infected by some terrible disease that any one of the other 50 prisoners could have been afflicted with. But though I tried to resist the inspection, I was immediately manhandled into complying. For several weeks afterwards, I worried if HIV could be transmitted in this manner. I knew for sure that certain other STDs and bacterial and parasitic infestations could be. Due to the rapid escalation of HIV infection in Thailand at that time, I figured that there could conceivably be at least some level of infection of one kind or another among those who had preceded me.

This admission process was carried out in the front sector of Section 3. Because all other sections were closed off and isolated after 3 p.m. each day, it was necessary for those returning from the courts to stay in one of the Section 3 cells until the next morning. The only exception was on the rare occasion that a bus arrived from the court earlier in the day; only then would the inmates go directly to their own section after being checked in.

Each cell at Bombat is about eight or nine metres long by about four and a half metres wide, and there are ten such cells on the second level of each of the main confinement buildings. Each cell was initially built to accommodate a maximum of around 15 people in a semblance of comfort – that is with each prisoner having room to lie down and stretch out to sleep and to move around to use the toilet without encroaching on the space of others. However, during my period of residence, and according to other long-term inmates, none of these cells ever had fewer than 30 men quartered at any one time. On the days when the bus returned from the court late, several of the cells in Section 3 would be crammed with 50 or more prisoners, many with their legs shackled in heavy chains, only allowing them room to sit with knees up under the chin or, at the very best, to lie in a foetal position. Prisoners had learned that in order to get a little sleep some cooperation was required, and they would therefore sit back to back with their legs pulled up in front of themselves and support each other.

In a cell this crowded, a simple trip to the toilet became an agonising trek, an excursion through the mass of humanity that occupied every square inch of floor space. The encumbrance of having one's legs tethered together with anything from five to fifteen kilograms of chain made it a particularly awkward ordeal, especially if one happened to be located at the wrong end of the room and in urgent need of its temporary sanctuary.

To add to the absurdity and torment, a guard would call at each cell at hourly intervals during the night and rap on the bars of the door with his baton. One of the inmates would then have to stand and declare, in a clear voice, that all inmates were 'present and accounted for'. The responsibility for tendering this vital information – unverified, unrecorded and irrelevant as it was – fell only on the permanent occupants of each cell, who had worked out a system of taking turns to deliver it, giving each at least one night per month with very little sleep.

Fred, Hansel and I, and about 20 others, were taken up to the second level and put into a cell. The three of us were the only temporary occupants of the cell who didn't have leg chains fitted. As we entered, last in line, I looked around in astonishment. The room was almost solid with humans, and as those who accompanied us squeezed their way into the crowded depths to find a spot to squat, I could see no place left at all that was large enough for me to even put my bag, let alone sit.

There was a raised section made of wooden planks about six feet deep and nine inches above the floor on either side of the doorway and another along the length of the back wall. The space between them was bare concrete and was similarly crammed with standing, squatting or sitting men, most wearing leg chains and looks of misery and despair. At the top of the back wall were four small openings, each fitted with vertical iron bars about four inches apart. Two filthy ceiling fans that looked as if they had been installed around the time Methuselah was a lad rattled and whirred as they endeavoured to circulate the heavy, foul air. The only other ventilation was via the barred cell door and two openings, identical to those on the back wall, at the top of the corridor wall.

The once-whitewashed walls were a sooty grey after decades of cigarette smoke and other pollution, and the floorboards on the raised sections were raw sawn timber planks worn to a shine by the countless bodies that had lain upon them. At one time, they might have been tightly cramped together, but now there were wide cracks between them, which allowed numerous species of vermin to take up residence below. Huge, aggressive cockroaches, spiders, fleas, bedbugs and a myriad of other blood-sucking and scavenging parasites made a home of the sweat-soaked and mouldy accumulation of debris disseminated by the thousands of men who had lain there over the years.

On the wall beside the door at about head height was a small red-and-gold-painted Buddhist-offerings platform on which were set three tiny ceramic bowls and an incense-stick holder, among other essential merit-making and devotion-offering paraphernalia. Thailand is predominantly Buddhist, and even many of the worst criminal elements make daily offerings to the Lord Buddha, as is the custom, but mostly in Bombat with the view of getting him to intervene and set the devotee free. The small bowls were filled with items such as pieces of fruit, biscuits, red rice, green tea, cigarettes and, of course, a cigarette lighter. The brass holder held several smouldering joss sticks as well as the remains of at least 20 or 30 others that had seen better days, and the tray beneath it was thick with the ash and dregs of countless others that had burned away there.

Nobody seemed to consider, though, that the Lord Buddha might find consuming these heartfelt offerings from such a squalid dining table to be rather distasteful. Nor did it seem to cross anyone's mind that the fine dust from the spent incense was being wafted around the cell by the ceiling fan, rendering the air thicker and breathing even more difficult.

In one corner of the cell, I could make out what appeared to be an attractive woman, with a large breast exposed for all to see. This fleshy appendage was being lustily fondled by a Thai man, evidently of Chinese extraction. I didn't need a closer inspection to know that the owner of that manufactured mammary was more male than female – a lady-boy, as they are called in Thailand, and one who was being very accommodating, it seemed.

There was one other lady-boy in the cell, and although he sported a very large set of beautifully shaped breasts, of which he seemed to be particularly proud, he was otherwise quite an ugly and repulsive-looking creature. The following morning, this person approached me and, in a deep and abrasive voice, asked me in reasonably good English if we needed any help in familiarising ourselves with our new surroundings. Looks can certainly be deceiving.

Fortunately, as it turned out, Fred and I were the last to enter the cell. As the heavy iron door slammed behind us, and as we were trying to absorb and adjust to these mind-boggling surroundings, I heard a call from the other side of the corridor. Although my eyes were already stinging from the grime from the incense, I saw two Caucasian men at the door of the cell directly opposite.

'Hi, guys. Havin' fun? Do you smoke?' The speaker was clearly American.

'Well, mate, a definite *no* to the first and a *yes* to the second. Two of us do, but the bastards took all of our smokes when they searched us and wouldn't give them back.'

'Yeah, I know. It's a bitch, ain't it?' He tossed a couple of packs across the passage, and I retrieved them through the bars. After we introduced ourselves and had a short chat – during which we were advised that we would, in all likelihood, be transferred to Section 4 in the morning and should therefore stay as close to the door as possible so as to at least get a little fresh air – Fred and I sat down right where we were standing. Hansel tried to worm his way a little further into the cell and eventually managed to secure a spot on the floor in the centre.

The cell had one small toilet at the far end of the centre passageway, but it was nothing more than a raised concrete block with a squat toilet pedestal and a trough of water. There was no curtain at all, the only provision to afford a little privacy being a low dividing wall about two feet high.

Even with the constant shower of incense dust, which made us both dry in the nostrils and thick in the sinuses, the stench of the 60-odd cell occupants and the toilet – not to mention the hourly visits by the guard – Fred and I eventually managed to get a little sleep. We sat facing each other on either side of the aisle right up against the bars of the door and talked for several hours until the torment of the day at last caught up with us and we nodded off.

The following morning, we met the American who had been so considerate the previous night, as well as several other foreigners. One, an Australian whom I'll call John McPherson, helped us sort out something to eat and showed us where we could go and get ourselves cleaned up a little. He also advised us on what we could expect in Section 4 and warned us about a trusty there named Lek Pathan.

At around 10 a.m., we were taken to an area on the ground level of the confinement building to be fitted with shackles and chains. A large block of timber, possibly a discarded railway sleeper, sat on the ground. Filthy, rusty shackles, which were actually coiled bars of reinforcing steel rod with about ten kilograms of iron chain attached, were placed around each leg just above the ankle. The leg then had to be put up on the block of wood and a trusty with a heavy mason's sledgehammer slammed the shackles tightly into place with repeated strikes to the top of the coil.

I sat perfectly motionless, not daring to breathe, terrified that the slightest movement would cause the trusty to miss the shackle and hit my shin. I was later to witness such incidents and see the resulting injuries and agony that the recipient of these – often obviously deliberately inflicted – blows had to endure for weeks, even months, afterwards.

By 11 a.m., we were all transferred to Section 4 and shown to a cell. Though identical in size and layout to the one we had occupied the previous night, we were pleased to discover that it had just 38 people in residence. The downside was that Lek Pathan, the trusty we had been warned about, was the room captain. Over the following four months, I was to learn exactly what an evil little son of a bitch he was.

As terrifying and mind-bending as the events up to this point had been, both Fred and I were to discover that the nightmare had only just begun.

# PART 2

||||||||||||||||||||||||||||||||||||||||||||||||||||||||||||||||||||||||||||||||||||||||||||||||||||||||||||

# The Nature of the Beasts

Never underestimate these negative forces, these
evil forces. In many ways, we still live in the
Dark Ages here in Thailand.

*Anand Panyarachun,*
*Thai caretaker prime minister, 1991–2*

# CHAPTER 7

||||||||||||||||||||||||||||||||||||||||||||||||||||||||||||||||||||||||||||||||||||||||||||||||||||||||||||||||||||||||||||||

## Sadists in Uniform

'WHAT THE FUCK! SLY, LOOK! OVER THERE BY THE WALL! WHAT THE hell are they doing to that poor bastard?'

I turned my head and followed Fred's wide-eyed gape of horror. It was then I realised that a muffled thumping sound I had heard as we entered the prison yard was in fact the result of the repeated blows being administered to a prisoner by one of the uniformed guards.

The prisoner, a short, thin Asian man with a large blue tattoo depicting some kind of Buddhist symbol in the centre of his back, was tied to a tree with his hands pulled above his head and fastened as tightly as possible around the trunk. Though the inmate was limp and appeared to be unconscious, the guard continued to swing his baton haphazardly across his back and arms as if possessed by some enraged demon that had rendered him totally out of control of his senses, not seeming to care or even to be aware that there was no longer any response from his victim. He continued until he himself was exhausted and had to stop to rest, handing the blood-stained stick – which appeared to be similar in length to, but not as thick as, a baseball bat – to a trusty with orders for him to clean it.

The recipient of this barbarism was left hanging from the tree, both arms bleeding profusely, one of his elbows quite evidently shattered, his back lacerated and turning from crimson to black as Fred, the several hundred other inmates in the yard and I stood and watched. The guard ordered one of the trusties to bring him a glass of water – beating people to death is parching work – and, still breathing heavily, he slowly drank it, at the same time keeping his eyes anchored to the streams of blood running down the man's arms and back and saturating the waistband of his scruffy shorts. When it began dripping from the hems of both legs and splashing onto the dirt, the executioner ordered the man cut down and put in a box. Two trusties cut the ropes around his wrists, grabbed him under the shoulders and dragged him face down – dead or unconscious, we didn't know – towards the Section 4 confinement building.

Both Fred and I had stood speechless throughout the performance. Open-mouthed and wide-eyed, we barely dared to breathe until the guard had left the area and the man had been taken away, leaving a bloody trail across the exercise yard. Never before had either of us seen such a display of seemingly uncontrollable rage and brutality. It was simply beyond our imagination that such extreme cruelty was still practised in prisons, let alone that we would be witnessing it right before our eyes. Even more frightening still was the realisation that we might be the recipients of some of the same at any time.

'Fucking hell! What the fucking hell?' Fred was the first to utter a sound, but it was some time before either of us could muster sufficient control of our emotions to ask a foreign prisoner standing nearby what the victim had done to deserve such severe punishment.

'Nothing much. He'd just returned from the court. Sometimes a bus comes in around lunchtime. Doesn't happen often – must have been a full house over there today. Anyhow, the guard at the checking-in section found 200 baht tucked under his balls. He's from this section, so he was brought over here to be punished.'

'A couple of hundred baht? You mean that guy got beaten like that because he had 200 fucking baht? That's, what, less than $8. Is this for real?' Fred's astonishment was etched into his tone as well as his expression as he looked first at the informer then towards me. I was speechless.

'That's all. Doesn't need more than that to set that cretin off. He's a maniac, a complete nutcase. He does that kind of thing all the time. Bastard kills at least one a month in this section alone and hurts plenty of others. They'll put that guy in a box now, but it doesn't look like he'll come out of it alive.'

'What's a box?' we asked in unison and were told that they were small metal-sheeted punishment cells, measuring no more than about four feet square and the same high. Each section had several of them, and in Section 4 at least one of them was usually occupied by a victim of this sadist warder.

'I have personally seen one guy dragged out of them, stiff as my dick in the morning. This asshole was responsible for that, and I'll be surprised if we don't see another one tomorrow. His name is Mongkhon. If I were you, I would stay as far away from him as possible. He's totally unpredictable and completely off his fucking rocker. He clearly gets off on this kind of cruelty. If he ever tries it on me, though, believe me I'll ram his fucking stick right up his arse and pull it out of his nose.'

'Oh shit, man! What have we landed in here?' Fred's voice was shaking. 'How can this kind of treatment be concealed from the outside? Someone must get to hear of it. What about the relatives? Don't they ever complain? Don't the newspapers ever expose this shit? What about the bodies? The families, or someone, must see the injuries. That guy's arms are broken. The fucking bones are poking out of his elbow. He looks like he's been hit by a truck. He's probably got a bunch of broken ribs as well. How can that be explained away, for Christ's sake? And he must still be on remand. His trial must still be in progress, otherwise he wouldn't have been to court today.'

Fred was becoming very frightened, and he wasn't the only one. Having seen the shambles in court the previous morning, we knew that we were stuck between a rock and a hard place for the foreseeable future. Knowing now that we had this maniac for company certainly wasn't helping us to cope.

We shook hands with our new acquaintance, whom I am going to call Geoff Higgins, and introduced ourselves. Geoff, a Canadian, was a jovial sort of fellow, over six feet tall and carrying at least thirty kilos of excess fat, most of which hung obscenely over the waistband of his shorts. He had been arrested along with two other Canadians several months earlier for possession of heroin.

Geoff, however, shared his status with Fred and me, being another innocent victim of circumstance. He was unfortunate to have been accompanying his co-accused – who I'll call Kevin and Danielle – at the time of their arrest. He was ignorant of the fact that they had heroin in their possession, but soon discovered – a little too late for comfort – that they had bought a small quantity of the drug for their own use while they holidayed in Thailand. Unfortunately for them, they had bought it from a police informant.

'This kind of barbarism is pretty hard to swallow from where we stand, that's for sure, but it's not only these Thai assholes who kill people here,' Geoff continued. 'My case partner died less than a week after we arrived in this hole, and as far as I'm concerned his death was a direct result of insensitivity and inaction by a certain faction wasting space at the embassy here – the Canadian Embassy, that is.'

'How's that, Geoff?' I was curious to know how the man's own embassy could possibly be responsible for his death. I foolishly – as it turned out – believed our embassies were there to help us – they were the good guys we could turn to when we found ourselves in trouble in a foreign country. That they could be otherwise had never entered my mind.

Geoff went on to explain how he had met Kevin, who was about 30 years of age, and his girlfriend Danielle, who was perhaps in her mid-20s, on the plane on the way over from Vancouver. They arranged to have some dinner together and then to take a look at some of the entertainment in town the following night. He had arrived at their hotel room at about 7 p.m., and they invited him in for a drink before they left. Not more than ten minutes after he had settled on the couch with a cold tin of beer for company, there was a knock on the door.

Kevin answered it and about seven cops burst into the room, a couple of them with guns drawn.

'I nearly pissed in my pants, I can tell you. I didn't know what the hell was happening. Neither did Kevin. Danielle was still in the bathroom with the door shut, putting on some make-up or something, but when she heard the ruckus, she opened the door and one of the cops grabbed her and pulled her roughly into the room. She screamed and ran over to Kevin. Then another one spoke in English directly to Kevin and told him that they were going to search the room. I was still sitting – close to shitting myself by now, I might add – on the sofa with one of the uniforms pointing his piece right at my head.'

He then detailed the inevitable result of the cops going through the couple's luggage. They had searched Geoff as well but had found nothing of an illegal nature. He assured us that he didn't use dope and had not been aware that the other two did. But even though Kevin told the cops that the bags of powder they had found in his suitcase were his and that Geoff had nothing to do with them, they ignored him and took Geoff to the police station, eventually charging him along with the other two with possession of heroin.

Something he didn't know until a little later, though, was that Kevin was diabetic and regularly had to have insulin shots. During the search, the cops also discovered his kit, containing several syringes and insulin vials, but took no notice of them. Evidently, they knew exactly what they were looking for and had found it. Kevin was even permitted to take that kit with him when they were taken to the police station, and while they were all locked up there, he was allowed to use it after someone from the embassy explained to the boss cop that it was prescription medication. That same embassy fellow also went to the Bangkok Police Hospital with Kevin's prescriptions and returned with enough additional insulin to last him another month.

'Actually, the cops there were OK. They treated us OK. One even offered us a hit of dope each for free! Can you believe that?' He chuckled at the memory.

Things got a lot worse when they were transferred to Bombat, however. As they were being registered at the front office of Section 3, the guard who was going through their possessions – more than a little worse for wear after a liquid lunch – decided to demonstrate to his Thai brethren (both official and captive) that he was a force to be reckoned with when it came to handling farang detainees. Apart from his loud pidgin-English abuse and deliberate carelessness with how he pulled things out of their suitcases, throwing them on the floor in front of them, he confiscated Kevin's insulin. Despite their collective attempts to explain the need for Kevin to be permitted to retain it, the guard refused to give it to him and screamed at them both – Danielle had already disembarked at the Ladyao women's prison on the way through – to pick up their belongings and move to the next bay for the rectal examination.

'Kevin was real worried by the time we had been taken upstairs and put into a cell for the night,' Geoff went on. 'He knew, of course, what would happen if he didn't have his insulin, and because I had no real understanding of the condition myself, he filled me in. The next day, after we had been moved here, I was pretty concerned, so I arranged with one of the foreigners who gets visitors a few times a week to ask one of them to call the Canadian Embassy and explain the situation. That same day, a friend came to see Kevin, and after the visit he called the embassy and talked to staff in the consular section, explaining what had happened and the danger of real problems developing if Kevin didn't have that insulin when he needed it.

'Well, nothing happened. Not a damn thing. The embassy was called again two days later and told that Kevin was already beginning to get ill. It was explained that a phone call by the consul to the prison director was all that was needed and that it should be made urgently, requesting that Kevin be given access to his insulin when he required it. But still nothing happened.

'Within four days, Kevin was very sick. The embassy was called yet again, and the visitors returned that same afternoon to let us know what was going on. This time, they called me out as well. They told us that they had spoken to the consul personally this time, but that he had been quite rude and offhand, giving the impression that he was not interested in Kevin's problems. The visitors were upset and said that they didn't know what else they could do. The next day, Kevin collapsed in a coma.

'Believe me, this was really pissing me off. For four days, I had tried to talk to the commander [the prison director]. I had even tried to talk to that cretin Mongkhon, and I'd tried to get the trusties to ask the commander if Kevin could be taken to the hospital. No one would listen. No one did anything at all. When he collapsed, they finally did take him to the hospital here – if you can, by any stretch of the imagination, call it that. And do you know what the idiots there did? A moron trusty, who evidently knew zilch about diabetics but who worked in the hospital as an orderly, put him on a glucose drip, even though the insulin that had been confiscated from him was right there. It was put with his possessions that went to the embassy later. Fat lot of good it was to him then, of course. Can you believe it? Well, the next thing we heard, a couple of hours later, he was dead.'

Geoff was sweating quite heavily and was clearly upset. He sat down and wiped his face on his shirt. We sat down beside him and waited for him to go on.

'Kevin was on daily insulin shots. That means he had too much glucose in his blood during an attack – or what's called hyperglycaemia – and needed insulin, but they gave him more glucose, which only made matters worse. Six days, man. Six fucking days, and the embassy did absolutely nothing. Nothing . . . All they needed to do was make one phone call to the commander here. All they had to do was arrange for Kevin to have his insulin available to him and to make sure he got new supplies every month. Not much to ask. If they had taken the ten minutes to do that, Kevin would still be alive.

'I mean, what was the man's crime? The guards here sell dope all the time. Why was Kevin's little bit of smack so fucking important to everyone? What the hell were the bastards trying to do? Protect him from the terrible effects of using dope? That's all that he had it for. To sniff it up his own nose and get a bit of a buzz.'

After being shocked into silence for the second time that day, Fred was again the first to speak. 'My God, Sly. Remind me never to go apartment hunting with you again, will you?'

Of course, we didn't know for sure that the embassy hadn't tried to make contact, that they had taken the matter seriously but had been prevented from getting involved for some reason. This was what both Fredrico and I considered to be the reasonable explanation, believing that we could surely rely on our own embassies for help. That they could be otherwise had never crossed my mind.

A few hours later, we returned to the tiny space we had each been allocated in Cell 5 on the top floor of Section 4 to be locked up for the night. As we made our way in, a track of blood mapped the route of the man who had been beaten. After being dragged inside, he had been hauled up two flights of stairs to the second floor – his knees and shins would have been scraping over every concrete riser as he went. The track of blood ended in a pool near the end of the corridor, where a row of five small steel cubes stood in line with a row of lockers between the cells – the boxes we had been told about. Each cube had a small opening, about six inches square, cut into the top. The front panel housed a small door about 18 inches wide by 30 inches high.

The following morning, when the door was opened, his body was pulled out, as stiff as a plank, in the same twisted posture in which it had apparently been forced inside: head first, his back to the top and his legs bent up under him. Lifeless though he had appeared to be out in the yard, there was evidence to suggest that he had not died until some time later. Blood had spread across the bottom of the box and congealed there, and the man's bowels and bladder had drained at some time, leaving a large stain in his shorts and a track of almost-dry excreta down the back of each thigh. Apart from the overwhelming stench that wafted from the box as he was removed, our already fragile senses were assaulted by the sight of the body, and the blood, which was covered in a blanket of flies and small black ants.

It was to be no more than three weeks before we were to see a repeat performance by the maniac Mongkhon, and another shattered corpse. In the meantime, we were to witness numerous savage beatings by him and several of the other pitiless swine who made up the guard contingent of the prison.

I remained curious as to how the prison could explain away these deaths and mutilated bodies and why there seemed to be no official repercussions. Fred and I agreed that some kind of report must have been necessary, possibly even an autopsy. That it was possible to murder people in such a brutal and unconcealed manner and not have those murders exposed by someone was, in those early days, beyond my sense of reason.

After some time, though, I realised that almost all of those who were flogged to death or severely maimed – not only in Bombat, but also at the other two prisons I was to occupy – had few, if any, visitors. Even if they were not actually alone in the world, there were many possible reasons for their isolation: their family or friends could have been in a low-income bracket and located far from the city, making it impossible for them to be in contact; they could have simply been too terrified of the authorities to dare to put themselves in a position where they would have to become directly linked to someone who was in prison on drug-related charges, as was the case with my wife's family, none of whom ever made an appearance for the entire duration of my imprisonment; the inmate could be an illegal immigrant worker from one of the neighbouring countries; and so on. That being the case, there would be no one to whom the authorities would have to account for their deaths. The injuries, if ever questioned, could also be passed off as the result of an accident or brawling, but never sadism by maniac officials. How the bodies were disposed of, though, remained a mystery for longer.

Throughout the years of my imprisonment, I counted at least 50 deaths at the hands of prison staff – deaths I either personally witnessed or that were witnessed by those around me. Never once did I hear of any appropriate disciplinary response.

# CHAPTER 8

████████████████████████████████████████████████████████████████

# A Touch of German Brilliance
# It Certainly Wasn't

TRUE TO HER WORD, JAIDOW ARRIVED AT THE PRISON AT 2 P.M. THAT
same afternoon to visit me. Om and a young girl named Nok, who
Hansel referred to as his girlfriend, were with her. Nok had visited
Hansel once whilst he was being held at the police station after Om
had made contact with her at his request. During that visit, she'd
told him that she had very little money and could not give him more
than 1,000 baht. That hadn't pleased him much, and he'd sarcastically
reminded her that she knew how to make money, instructing her to
get out and start earning some.

Nok was almost nineteen years old, no more than five feet tall,
and had a plump, moonish face. A rather plain-looking girl, she had
been used and abused by many men since childhood and had had
the misfortune to end up with Hansel. She had been crying when
she'd left him that day, and Jaidow had comforted her, having heard
what Hansel had said to her. Taking pity on the girl, she'd invited
her to have some lunch after they'd left the police station.

Nok had told Jaidow that Hansel was a close associate of Fahad's
and that she had been with him many times when they'd met. She'd

told Jaidow that she had lived with Hansel for almost a year, and how, during that time, he had taken all of her savings, about 30,000 baht in all, and had pawned her gold jewellery, worth about 12,000 baht, promising to repay her but never attempting to do so. She'd explained to Jaidow that she had no money to give to him and that she would have to prostitute herself again simply to survive and pay the rent.

Jaidow had given her a little money and had told her to go home, pack some clothes and then come to stay with her at our apartment. She'd figured that she could use some help with a small business she ran and would be doing herself a favour while at the same time giving the girl clean, respectable work and accommodation if she wanted to take advantage of it. Nok had been very grateful for her understanding and generosity – most other Thais would have shunned her like a roach – and had accepted the offer, arriving at the apartment that same evening.

That Friday afternoon, when the three women visited Bombat prison for the first time, Hansel took Nok to the far end of the steel-mesh wall that separated prisoners from visitors, leaving Jaidow, Om and me out of earshot. He then demanded once again that she get him some money. He also told her to pack his clothes and some of his other possessions into a suitcase and to bring it to him the next time she came to visit.

Nok, who had spent her life surrendering to the demands of others, was intimidated – even though Hansel was in no position to do her physical harm. She promised to comply with his orders, deciding at the same time that she would let Jaidow know exactly what he had said and that she would not visit him more than once each week from then on. She continued to accompany Jaidow to the prison at least three times each week, but only called Hansel out on Wednesdays when she would speak to him but tell him, truthfully, that she had no money. Anyhow, as I was providing him with food and other essentials, there was really no need for him to be asking Nok for money that she didn't have to give him.

On the fourth Wednesday, Hansel once again beckoned Nok to the far end of the visit room. He told her that she was to tell Jaidow that he would testify that it was she, Jaidow, who had provided the heroin that was found in the suitcase and that he would ensure that she was arrested unless she paid him 50,000 baht. Nok sat aghast while he dictated these terms, terrified that Jaidow would be put in jail if she didn't agree. When the visiting period was over, she told Jaidow everything and declared through her tears that she had determined to wipe him from her slate and never to see him again.

Jaidow was equally astonished but told Nok not to worry. They would visit the prison together the following day, she said, and explain the situation to me. Needless to say, I was surprised and extremely irritated to think that Hansel could behave like this after everything I had been doing for him, but I convinced them that there was nothing to be concerned about. If Hansel were to change his story and his own written statement, he would implicate himself in something he had professed to know nothing about. I assured them that it was nothing but an empty threat. I also assured them that Hansel would now find himself in a far less favourable position as far as my support inside the prison was concerned.

I discovered some time later that he had actually begun to receive a monthly prisoner-assistance payment of 3,000 baht from his embassy the week before he made this threat. Apparently, he had considered this to be none of my business and had neglected to mention it, preferring to continue to sponge off me instead.

That night as I lay on my back trying not to listen to the oohs and aahs coming from two of my fellow inmates over in the corner of the cell, I silently fumed as I considered what I would do with Hansel. His influence on my life had already been staggering enough – to have the fool now trying to blackmail me was the limit.

All but ten of the cell occupants managed to fit on the raised wooden platforms, and the two disturbing the still of the night with the sounds of their coupling were among the fortunate ones who had wood instead of concrete to sleep on. They were husband and wife, in Bombat speak: a pretty lady-boy of about 20 and a Thai man, roughly 50 years old, who, like the 'husband' on our first night at Bombat, was evidently of Chinese origin or extraction. He had purchased the 'wife' from the commander for 10,000 baht, and he was making sure that he got what he had paid for – at least a couple of times a day.

The lady-boy was not much more than five feet tall, had wavy, shoulder-length ebony hair and was well proportioned, with apparently genuine, though small, breasts. She had been arrested in Pattaya – a bustling seaside resort on the northern shores of the Gulf of Thailand, which has, in part, a rather long-standing reputation for being a sleazy, sex-for-sale, criminal-and-thug-infested holiday location for international and local tourists – for possession of marijuana and had been sentenced to three years in Bombat (which, incidentally, means 'to rehabilitate and make well' in Thai). As was the practice with most of the lady-boys who found themselves locked up for one reason or another with a bunch of sex-starved, horny males, she was earning her keep and, more importantly, protection by willingly agreeing to be sold, enjoying decent food and no prison work as a result.

The couple had located themselves in the bottom right-hand corner of the cell, adjacent to the corridor, and had fashioned a curtain between them and the rest of the room with a bed sheet hanging from a cord that they had strung from nails driven into the walls.

The only other sound that could be heard, apart from the occasional snore and the constant buzz of mosquitoes, was the incessant chanting from the nearby Buddhist temple. It went on for an hour each night and again early each morning. When the air was still and the prison hushed and inactive, the nightly session was disturbingly audible, even though the temple was about a kilometre away.

Fred and I had managed to get ourselves a place beside each other on the platform on the right of the cell near to the door. Hansel, thankfully, had been delegated a space well away from us in the middle of the room, between two rather odd specimens of humanity who, although harmless enough, exhibited certain idiosyncrasies that made them rather undesirable bedmates. At least that's the way I looked at it.

One was a tall, pencil-thin African, his black skin sporting a deep-purple shine. His curls were as tight as a knot of steel wool, his nose broad and flat with wide gaping nostrils, seemingly forcing apart the coal-black eyes that were tucked in under protruding brows. When he laughed, which he was prone to do most of the time when he wasn't asleep, he displayed a perfect set of sparkling white ivories and a vaginal-pink tongue and gums. He had the deepest voice I'd ever heard. He ate, talked – or rather bellowed – and laughed all at the same time, following this up by noisily picking his teeth with a chewed chopstick or twig he'd carried up from the yard. As for the python that had a habit of poking its head out from the leg of his shorts and at times looking him right in the eye . . . Well, let's just say I was glad not to be any closer.

The other man was even less desirable. He had ventured to Thailand from Hong Kong several months before with grand visions of becoming a trillionaire by simply taking a big bundle of heroin back to his homeland. His dreams had been shattered, however, when he was caught at the airport with a suitcase full of the stuff and a few more kilos strapped to his body. Slightly built and no more than five-foot-six, he was almost always spaced out on dope. He pissed in his pants, spilled his food and forgot to wash. When he was conscious, he smoked continuously, and when he wasn't, he farted non-stop. To cap it all off, he grated his teeth at 100 decibels in either state.

He also had a particularly irritating tendency to fix a penetrating though vacant stare right into a person's eyes without blinking, as if he could see the very soul that dwelled within. Just imagine, for a moment, waking in the early hours and being confronted by a pair of bloodshot eyes no more than a foot away from your face.

These strange bedfellows certainly gave Hansel cause to exercise his venomous tongue, though the resulting dissension was more damaging to his own well-being and contentment than it was a disturbance to the others: the Chinese junkie was never in any mental condition to acknowledge or be concerned about threats, insults or abuse, and the African was simply amused and laughed longer and louder, spitting his food in Hansel's direction and snoring in his face. Nothing could rouse him to anger – he was just a happy soul caught in an imprisoned body. Life was good – well, it had been better – and God was with him all the time. His Bible told him that, and he read it every day. As he saw it, he was where he was for a reason – apart from being caught with dope, that is. Perhaps it was a sign from the heavens, a cross that he had to bear for the sins of man.

Many of his black brethren who were sharing his present penance, besides being the noisiest of all groups represented, were also the most genuinely religious, jovial, friendly, helpful and loyal to each other when needed. They banded together like one big happy family – conflict with one and you conflicted with them all. In stature and number, they were a force to be reckoned with – at least 90 per cent were the giant sons of Nigeria.

Most of them had been used as mules for organised criminal gangs and had been promised a couple of thousand dollars, plus expenses, to courier a few kilos of heroin. The majority had little or no understanding of what they were getting themselves into and no real concept of the dangers or risks involved. Certainly not many were aware that a lengthy prison term in extremely harsh conditions would be the only reward for their efforts if they were caught. Most had agreed to courier the consignments so that they could provide a little comfort for their struggling families back home. Very few had any other agenda at all, and none actually used dope themselves.

I had made a small sleeping mat about one inch thick and eighteen inches wide by folding a towelling blanket that Jaidow had sent in for me and sewing it together, similarly fashioning a small cushion for my head at the same time. The prison authorities provided absolutely nothing apart from the food they expected us to eat, which consisted of two basic meals of boiled red rice and fish soup per day. Anyone who wished to take advantage of that had to first get down on his knees and thank the King for his support. Those who had no one on the outside to provide for them simply had no options other than to eat what was provided or die. They slept on the bare floor and, regardless of whether they were convicted or remand prisoners, were made to work in the prison workshops as virtual slaves, payment for their labour being just one can of tinned tuna fish – valued at six baht (at the time, the equivalent of about ten pence) – per month.

Sleeping on bare floorboards or concrete, however, is not necessarily of major discomfort or distress to your average Thai. Many Thais, even wealthy ones, prefer to sleep on the floor, though they will usually have a thatch mat to lie on. It is we softies raised in the West who suffer this hardship the most, and I was one of them. My back ached under my weight, and the points that made contact with the mat soon became numb, necessitating frequent repositioning, which, in turn, disturbed my sleep.

To add to the discomfort, and as if by design, there was no mosquito net over any of the openings in the outside walls, and the room was always alive with plagues of them as a result. And they had company: moths, bugs and on occasion, after heavy rain, clouds of flying ants, attracted by the small lights that were left burning all night. The ants didn't actually bite, but they did irritate and annoy by crawling into hair, ears, noses and anywhere else they could find to invade. Those positioned directly below the lights were the worst affected, but really no one was spared.

The only bug repellent permitted was the little white, almost translucent, sticky-footed gecko lizard, or *ching-chock* in Thai. These creatures congregated around the lights and walls and filled their bellies with all manner of creepy-crawlies. But as quaint and amusing as they were to watch, the problem was that what goes into a ching-chock's mouth as a squirming bug must eventually come back out of the opposite end as ching-chock shit. It was a veritable ching-chock circus up there every night, with hundreds of the little buggers scampering around, eating tons of bugs and having a great time hanging upside down while they manufactured lots and lots of ching-chock offerings, which rained down like leaves in autumn. Sleeping on one's back did have its disadvantages as a result . . .

But that night I couldn't sleep. I was thinking of the blackmail demands Hansel had made to Nok. The more I thought about it, the angrier I became and, of course, the less likely I was to nod off.

'Hey, Fred,' I whispered. 'You awake, mate?'

'Yeah. Too bloody hot to sleep. And these mosquitoes! What's up?'

'I had another visit from Jaidow this afternoon. You aren't going to believe what she told me.' I was trying my best not to let the fury that had been building inside me since the meeting affect the volume of my voice. I wasn't entirely successful, and Fred rolled to face me as he raised himself expectantly on one elbow.

'I didn't get a chance to talk to you privately this afternoon, and I was too bloody cranky to talk anyhow. Believe me, mate, if that bastard Hansel had been in sight when I came out of the visit room, I would have floored the sod.'

I related what Nok and Jaidow had told me. By the time I'd finished, Fred was wide-eyed with astonishment. He had pulled himself up to a sitting position and was looking over to where Hansel was sleeping. His expression of loathing was not masked by the dim light, and the muscles in his jaw were flexing as his teeth grated together in anger. I recognised at that moment that Fred's calm and cool exterior concealed a far more tempestuous core, one which would not be pleasant to have to confront head on if it was ever allowed to surface. He actually made a move as if he was about to get to his feet, but I reached out and held his arm.

'Hold on a minute, mate. I've been thinking about doing something like that myself, but let's think before we do anything silly here. If we thump the fucker, it will only make things difficult for us. He'll get sympathy because he's half-crippled, and we'll look like bullies and probably end up in the shit with no evidence to show that he deserved what he got. Now he can't, and won't, do what he has said he will do. That doesn't make any sense at all. He's just trying to bluff that little girl into doing something to get him some money. He doesn't know that she is actually living with Jaidow or that Jaidow has been fostering her, so we have an advantage there. Let's do it another way and see what he does next.'

I was no less incensed but had calmed down sufficiently to realise that no purpose would be served by smacking Hansel around, other than giving me a little rather expensive satisfaction. Ending up on the business end of Mongkhon's baton was certainly not beyond the realms of possibility.

'OK, OK. Yes, you're right, of course. So, what do you want to do?'

We talked quietly for some time and then both tried to get some sleep. The following morning, Hansel came staggering around the corner of the building and over to where we were standing just as we finished cleaning up after breakfast. We had deviated from our routine of eating with Hansel at around 8 a.m. That morning we had prepared and eaten breakfast before 7.30 a.m.

'Did you get a visit from your wife yesterday, Sly? Did Nok come? I expected to be called out. She told me on Wednesday that she would come again yesterday.'

It seemed that Hansel had actually expected Nok to arrive with the 50,000 baht! I glanced at him briefly, but we both ignored him and carried on with our conversation. I then turned my back on Hansel and, picking up my bag in which I kept my breakfast-making paraphernalia, took Fred by the elbow and walked slowly away, talking to him as I went.

Hansel was left standing there staring. 'What about breakfast?' he finally managed to croak, but we ignored him.

He would, of course, have fully expected Jaidow to report to me the ultimatum that Nok had passed on for him, but he also evidently believed that I would be too terrified not to bend to his demands so as to save my wife from the traumas that I myself had been experiencing. That was how this brilliant scheme of his would work: through my fear. He actually believed that I really had no choice but to play the game his way.

At lunchtime, he appeared again and came over to where Fred and I were sitting, expecting to join us as he usually did. He probably even figured that he would be given a higher level of courtesy, now that it was understood he was in control. However, as he was about to sit down, Fred looked up at him with eyes of blue ice and said quietly, in perfect German, 'Fuck off out of here, you cretin. Sit down there and you won't be getting up again.'

'What!' Hansel dropped his jaw and looked in astonishment from me to Fred and back again, expecting that I would jump to his defence, expecting me to be terrified that my wife would be put in jail. You could almost hear his tiny mind working: 'Hey, guys, haven't you read the script? This isn't the way it's supposed to go. I'm in charge now. Don't you understand that?' I glanced up at him like he was a dung slug and continued to eat.

'I . . . ah . . . I have no food . . . The Thai food is finished,' he stammered, confusion etched into his expression.

'Your ears broken as well as your arse? I said fuck off.' The hair on the back of Fred's neck was beginning to bristle, and Hansel evidently wasn't so dense that he couldn't recognise the menace in his tone because he took two or three uneasy steps backwards and then turned abruptly and stormed away, fuming and muttering obscenities. As the prison authorities provided no food after lunch, he would have to rely on his ample supply of blubber to see him through until the next morning. Having already missed breakfast after I hadn't catered for him – the prison fare was usually finished before 7.30 a.m. – he had a long wait.

Just a few days after arriving at Bombat, Pat from the embassy visited me again, as she'd promised she would. She told me that on returning to the mission the week before, she had spoken to the consul and passed on my request for someone to call my mother. With apologies, she then confessed that, though she had been assured that this would be done, the matter had yet to be dealt with.

Mum's 87th birthday was just a few weeks away, and she would certainly be expecting me to give her a call. When that didn't happen, she would get worried, and, though her health had been excellent, I was a little concerned. Mind you, I was a lot more concerned about how the news of my being arrested – yet again – would affect her, but she had to be told.

Pat left with a promise that she would make certain that this was taken care of and in an appropriately sensitive manner. Four days later, she returned with terrible news. As delicately as she could, she explained that my mother had died. She had no details as yet but promised to return as soon as she knew more.

I was simply too stunned to respond for quite some minutes. Gaining control of my emotions, I eventually managed to provide the names of several friends in the UK who would be able to take care of funeral arrangements on my behalf. For the remainder of the day, I was consumed with grief. I spoke little and ate nothing, retiring to the filthy cell, crammed with gibbering and shackled men, that afternoon at around 4.30 p.m. Lying on my stomach, my face buried into a folded towel, I quietly wept. I silently asked my mum to forgive me for all the torment and anguish I had caused her over the years, with my seemingly endless stupidity and selfishness. I also asked her to forgive me for not being at her side when she needed me this time – once again on the unfriendly side of bars and electric fenced walls and out of reach. Was she aware of my absence? I will never know.

I am not a religious man by any means, but I silently projected an impassioned epitaph to the heavens during the early hours of the following morning, for I had no other way to say goodbye. Then, thoroughly drained, I slept.

# CHAPTER 9

iiiiiiiiiiiiiiiiiiiiiiiiiiiiiiiiiiiiiiiiiiiiiiiiiiiiiiiiiiiiiiiiiiiiiiiiiiiiiiiiiiiiiii

# Hansel Biffed Gretel

SEVERAL OTHER INCIDENTS DURING THE FIRST WEEKS OF OUR RESIDENCE in Bombat had given both Fred and me an inkling as to the true nature of Hansel, but we continued to give him the benefit of the doubt in respect to the drugs in the suitcase. His extortion attempt, however, was not to be ignored, and we henceforth ostracised him.

Hansel was a very easy person to dislike. His deep-seated vindictiveness, selfishness and jealousy invariably repelled others like skunk farts, and now that Fred and I were offside, he spent most of his time sitting alone as the hate for everyone and everything grew like a cancer in his gut.

The first of these enlightening occasions occurred just one week after we arrived at Bombat. I was sitting in the shade of the main building writing a letter, and Fred was standing nearby talking to one of the other foreign prisoners, when a Thai fellow, who seemed to be a little peeved about something, approached and in a rather belligerent tone said, 'Hey, you! What are you giving that little guy a hard time for? What's he done to you?'

I didn't have a clue what he was on about and told him as much, just before telling him to fuck off or he'd be the one getting a hard time. Fred interrupted his conversation and approached us. 'Got a problem, Sly?' he asked.

'Well, I'm not sure, mate. This goon seems to have a thorn in his arse about something, but I have no idea what he's bitching about,' I responded, with an accompanying shrug.

'So, what's up, then?' Fred asked, turning towards the Thai with a slightly raised voice and his head tilted backwards, his blue eyes spitting daggers.

The Thai shrunk away fractionally as he replied, a little less confidently, 'That Thai guy over there, the lady-boy, he keeps hiding away from you new guys. He's scared stiff of you. So what are you doing to him?'

I stood up, and both Fred and I looked to where the man was pointing. We saw a smallish Thai male, cringing behind several other Thai inmates. Judging by his stance and shape, and the fact that his small but well-shaped breasts were revealing themselves through his white T-shirt, it was quite evident that he was a very effeminate boy of no more than 19 or 20 years.

'That little guy there with the white shirt and tits?' I asked.

'Yes.'

'Never seen him before in my life, so how can I be bothering him?'

'Don't know, that's why I'm asking you. He's been nearly shitting his pants every time he sees you two and that fat friend of yours in the yard.' His tone was a little more civil now.

'Well, why don't you ask him yourself?' Fred remained confrontational and just a touch louder than normal.

'Did already, several times, but he won't tell us what the problem is. He just keeps hiding every time he sees any of you.'

I suggested that he be brought over so I could ask him what he was afraid of, glancing at Fred as I spoke. Fred just shrugged his shoulders. He didn't know the boy either.

After an assurance from Fred and me that we meant him no harm and simply wanted to find out what was bugging him, the boy explained that he had robbed Hansel of 6,000 baht quite a few months before and had recognised him as soon as he had seen him enter the section. He was afraid that Hansel would exact some form of revenge, and because Fred and I were Hansel's friends, he had been trying to hide from all three of us.

He explained that he had been a lady-boy prostitute while outside and had worked mainly from a coffee shop in Soi Nana. He had solicited Hansel in front of a bank near there, promising him a good blow job for 100 baht. Hansel confessed to Fred during one of his hate rages several years later that only minutes before the encounter with the lady-boy he had gone to an ATM machine to withdraw the money from Nok's savings account. When Hansel accepted the offer, the boy had taken him into a lane nearby and provided the promised service at the back of a car that was parked there. While doing so, however, he had lifted Hansel's wallet from his trousers and run off with it.

'A small world, it surely is,' I said, smiling at Fred. I then continued, saying to the boy, 'Well, you can relax, sonny. First, we're not his friends. And second, he's too fat and gutless to do anything to you anyhow. Just ignore him. If he gives you any grief, just tell him that you'll report him to Mongkhon. That'll stop his rot.'

I chuckled as I remembered the occasion when Hansel approached me on Sukhumvit Road near Soi Nana and asked to borrow 5,000 baht. His tale of being robbed had apparently been quite true, though at the time I hadn't believed him.

Ironically, this little lady-boy and that two-quid head job were, in fact, the spark that ignited the inferno that would be the source of my tribulation for the next 17 years. As nonsensical as it might have sounded to me at the time, I would reflect later that if this boy hadn't given Hansel that few moments of bliss and then pinched his wallet, I most certainly would not have become involved with him, would not have been introduced to Fahad and would not have ended up in this mess.

It was just two days after this incident, however, that another Thai man came across Hansel out in the exercise area. This person had just been transferred to Section 4 from another in the same prison. When he saw Hansel, he immediately began to abuse him loudly, attracting the attention of everyone in the yard at the time. He then became violent and began to punch him. Hansel went down trying to fend off the kicks that followed as two guards ran over. Restraining the man, they took him, struggling and yelling obscenities at Hansel, to the section chief's office.

It was at least 40 minutes before he reappeared. However, to the surprise of everyone who had witnessed the incident, he wasn't beaten as we all expected he would be. Instead, he was transferred from Section 4 to Section 5 so that there would be no further trouble between him and Hansel. He had been pardoned for his aggression, and as this was a very rare occurrence, everyone in Section 4 was curious to know why he had been let off so lightly – standard procedure for fighting among inmates was that everybody involved was flogged mercilessly by the guards.

Later, one of the trusties who had accompanied the guards to the chief's office related the story to a couple of his buddies, and it wasn't long before the whole section knew what had happened.

Apparently, several years before, Hansel had lived in the central district of Nakhon Sawan with a local woman – let's call her Gretel – in her small home on a few acres on the outskirts of the town. He had purchased 50,000 baht worth of weaned piglets and told Gretel to raise them, which she had willingly done. A few months later, being large enough for the barbeque spit that awaited them, she sold them at the local market. She then took 50,000 baht from the proceeds and gave it to Hansel as reimbursement for his initial investment. Naturally, she was keeping the profit for herself – after all, she had done all the work, and he was living at her home rent free, not to mention the carnal benefits.

Hansel, who was far from pleased by this, demanded 50 per cent of the profits as well. His reasoning was that he had provided the funding for the enterprise and as such was entitled to his share. A reasonable enough assumption from your average Westerner's point of view. However, that's not the way most Thais think when it comes to foreigners and their money. In fact, Hansel should have been very thankful that his 50,000 baht was returned at all.

The woman, of course, flatly refused to give him any part of the profit, which infuriated him even more. In his rage, he punched her, bruising her eye and splitting her lower lip.

Now, one doesn't need to be Einstein to work out that foreign men – if they have any intelligence at all – simply do not beat up Thai women, at least not in their own home town. Gretel contacted her three brothers, who lived not too far away in Phichit Province. They responded post-haste and arrived at the house to have a word or two with Hansel.

Hansel, being Hansel, however, could not control his spiteful tongue and began to mouth off to the three already rather hostile siblings. The predictable result of this folly was that they gave him the father of a beating, which landed him in hospital for three days. By the time he had recovered sufficiently to leave, he had hatched another of his brilliant plans and subsequently filed charges against the three men at the local police station, alleging that they had beaten him up and stolen 500,000 baht from him. The case went to court, and Hansel perjured himself by sticking to his story that the assailants had stolen his money, as well as beating him senseless and causing him injury. This little falsehood had the effect of making the offence robbery with violence as opposed to assault, and the consequence was that Gretel's three loved ones were convicted and each sentenced to eight years in prison. They actually spent three years incarcerated after good-behaviour credits and royal amnesties reduced the detention period.

After the trial, the locals in Nakhon Sawan gave Hansel a piece of advice that they recommended he take heed of real quick: 'Hit the road, Jack, and don't you come back no more, no more, no more, no more . . .' Well, even Hansel wasn't stupid enough to refuse such sound counsel and, realising that he was indeed in a hazardous situation, quickly evacuated the town and moved to Bangkok.

It turned out that the chap who had given Hansel the beating in the exercise yard that day was none other than Gretel's youngest brother. He had not been directly involved in the case but knew Hansel well and had recognised him as soon as he had entered Section 4 . . . It is a very small world indeed! The commander had for some reason decided not to punish the boy for his attack. Perhaps he harboured a certain antipathy towards Westerners – many of the locals do – or maybe he just sympathised with him and figured he deserved a little revenge.

Hansel was later to brag arrogantly to Fred and others that there really was no 500,000 baht. He had included the robbery in his allegations for no other reason than to get revenge on Gretel and the three men. Having them imprisoned for aggravated assault and robbery with violence was one of the outstanding achievements of his life and one of which he was evidently particularly proud.

# CHAPTER 10

# Lek Pathan v. Karma

LEK PATHAN WAS A DEVILISH LITTLE HEROIN JUNKIE, THAI OF INDIAN extraction, with the Indian side dominant. He was Mongkhon's inside drug dealer and informer for Section 4 and as such was protected. Being a pathological lying parasite, with a passion for informing on other inmates for the slightest breach of rules, he was the perfect collaborator for Mongkhon, who virtually lived for each time he had an excuse to beat up on or murder another prisoner.

He had paid for his trusty status through Mongkhon, a standard procedure for those who wanted to take advantage of the privileges such an appointment would ensure. The going rate at the time was 60,000 baht, most of which went to the director, but, naturally, Mongkhon reaped a percentage as the go-between.

The set-up was simple. If Mongkhon supplied first-grade heroin to Lek, then Lek could supply it to his own distributors and anyone else who wanted it at a highly inflated price. As Lek was a heavy user himself, he would cream off a portion of each consignment for his own use and cut the remainder with something suitable, such as powdered glucose tablets, to bring the volume to its original level. The portion he took for himself was his reward for being the dealer and informer.

Of the receipts from the sales, 95 per cent had to go back to the supplier, with Lek keeping the other 5 per cent for himself. Mongkhon's share was a predetermined figure; therefore, Lek had no way to short-change him, though he was streetwise enough to realise that he could increase his own return simply by diluting the drug with more glucose powder. He was fully aware that to cheat Mongkhon would be a very foolish thing to do, but he could, and did, cheat his fellow inmates at will and with impunity.

Lek and Mongkhon had other spies assisting them as well, mainly the other cell captains . Their main function was to inform on anyone they saw using drugs that didn't originate from the sanctioned source. Offenders were usually subjected to a touch of Mongkhon's sadism, and, unfortunately, this had a nasty habit of being the ultimate solution to their drug problem.

Lek also had another scam in place in Section 4, both sanctioned and participated in by Mongkhon. The guard had given Lek control of all of the lockers in the section and had purchased padlocks for them, which he sold to Lek at twice the price he'd paid for them. Lek then charged each new inmate who entered the section and wanted a locker double that as a rental fee. Unbeknownst to the renter, however, he always kept one of the three keys provided with the locks. This allowed him to replace the lock at any time and also gave him easy access for malicious or revengeful purposes. It was common practice for Lek to plant drugs or other restricted items, such as pornographic magazines, needles, syringes and so on, in a locker so as to cause problems for someone who crossed him. He often used this ploy to justify a transfer or, in particular with drug plants, to pave the way for a substantial bribe to Mongkhon for the case to be dropped or to avoid a severe flogging.

Frequently, he would use the spare key to thieve items from a locker when the renter was at court or receiving a visit and then sell the goods to prisoners in other sections. As soon as an inmate was transferred or released, Lek would replace the lock with a new one, giving him another one to rent, sometimes – if few were available – at a premium.

Lek also had a private scam in place, one that Mongkhon was not aware of because he was not able to speak or understand English. This involved two bent lawyers – not at all a rare commodity in Thailand, nor the rest of the world, for that matter. When a new foreign inmate arrived at Bombat, Lek would make it his business to talk to him privately at the earliest possible opportunity. He would introduce the services of his lawyer buddies and assure the foreigner that his case could be manipulated if these men were employed, advising that they could arrange to have all charges dropped and a release guaranteed for a certain price, or for a 'not guilty' verdict in the first court, with no appeal by the prosecutor, at a different price.

Of course, Lek always cautioned his victims that everything had to be done in strict secrecy – no one at all could be told, otherwise the lawyers would not proceed – and those gullible and frightened foreigners who had sufficient means at their disposal usually swallowed the bait and embraced the opportunity. Lek would then arrange a meeting, and the sucker would be told to have the necessary funds transferred before the next hearing date. Once that was done, the victim would not see the lawyer or his money again. Lek would then arrange for him to be transferred to Klong Prem prison by bribing Mongkhon with a couple of thousand baht.

It was about an hour or so after Fred had unceremoniously dismissed Hansel from our presence at lunchtime – about a month after our arrival at Bombat – that we saw this snake in the grass tackle one of the Thai prisoners, accusing him of possessing heroin. We were sitting together in the exercise yard, with our backs against the wall of the main building, taking advantage of the shade. I was reading a magazine, and Fred was meditating, as he often did.

Lek's victim was a heroin addict and usually made his purchases through the protected channels; however, on this occasion, he'd obtained his fix – generally referred to as a 'paper', consisting of about a half-teaspoon of diluted heroin wrapped in the silver paper from a cigarette packet – from another source.

True to form, Lek immediately informed Mongkhon 'the Terrible', who wasted no time in having the junky apprehended and brought to him. He spent the next ten minutes or so slapping the poor fellow around with his hands and fists, demanding to know who had sold him or given him the dope. The Thai wouldn't cooperate, triggering Mongkhon's uncontrollable temper. He took his baton from his belt and began to lay into the prisoner, knocking him to the ground with heavy blows to the head and face. He then continued to flog him on the back as the man knelt on the concrete ground, his ears bleeding and spewing a mixture of teeth and gum and blood into the dust beneath him.

The more Mongkhon flogged him, the more his rage or lust for blood – or whatever it was that drove him to such extremes – increased, and he was soon totally out of control, screaming abuse and obscenities. His face was crimson, and his eyes were ablaze with madness as he relentlessly smashed the stick into the man's body. The only things that existed for him on the planet at that moment were himself, his implement of destruction and the body he was pulverising.

On reflection, it must have been only moments before his victim collapsed to the concrete and lay flat on his stomach completely still – though we had no perception of time as we witnessed the third murder since our arrival. Mongkhon wasn't to be cheated, however, and screamed at the several trusties standing nearby to lift the man and hold him. Terrified themselves, they dragged the man by the arms so that he was upright with his head slumped, facing the executioner, but after landing several blows to the knees, thighs and pelvis area, Mongkhon decided that the position wasn't to his liking and ordered them to hold the man against the tree that had supported his previous two victims, and then proceeded to flog him every which way, even though the man was completely out of this world and could not have felt anything. It must have been at least five minutes before he eased up, exhausted from the effort and unable to swing the stick any longer. By that time, the object of his fury was mutilated. Several of his veins had burst, and blood was pouring out of his body like a fountain. His back was so severely damaged that broken bones protruded from the skin, and one of his shoulders was quite evidently dislocated. The trusties standing behind the tree, holding the body up by the arms, were also covered in the blood that had been splashed over them with every blow.

None of the more than 400 other inmates who witnessed this butchery that day could possibly have known for certain if the victim was still alive or not. It was doubtful that Mongkhon knew himself, but even so he yelled at the trusties to put him in the box and then stormed away, throwing his baton to another trusty as he left, with orders to have it cleaned and returned to him.

The two trusties who had been holding the victim moved around from behind the tree and, lifting him under the shoulders, began to drag the man face down towards the main building. However, before they had taken more than a few steps, he convulsed once, vomiting blood at their feet. They changed direction and headed towards the gate to the hospital section. No point in putting a dead man in a box, after all.

Not all of the prisoners were afraid of Mongkhon, however, despite his fearful reputation, particularly those who had large or influential families on the outside. A lot of these prisoners knew that Mongkhon was afraid of being too severe with them. He would also have instinctively known that whilst off duty his own life might well have been put in jeopardy if he was to injure or kill any of this class of inmate, so in the main he ignored them. Like most brutal bullies, he was gutless and impotent when not able to rely on his position and uniform to give him power and protection.

One such prisoner, however, failed to understand that Mongkhon's mental instability had a nasty habit of throwing him completely out of control of his senses and that at these times nothing short of Godzilla could stop him once he got started. This fellow wasn't actually doing anything apart from sitting in the shade against the prison wall that separated Section 4 from Section 5.

Seems his gods were busy someplace else that day because just as someone threw a small packet containing heroin over the wall from Section 5, Lek – who was standing about eight feet away from him, talking to another trusty – looked in his direction and saw it hit the ground. The prisoner didn't see it land and evidently wasn't even aware that it was there on the concrete near him until Lek ran over and picked it up.

With a practised lick to the tip of his finger and a dip in the powder, Lek determined that the substance was what he knew it would be and ran to inform Mongkhon, who ordered the chap who'd been sitting by the wall to come to where he was standing in the shadow of the main building. He asked him who had thrown the packet, and the man answered, in a rather belligerent tone, that he was sitting with his back against the one-foot-thick wall and didn't know who had thrown it from the other side. He denied that he had anything to do with it and said that he had simply been sitting there out of the sun.

Mongkhon struck him on the face with his stick, but even that failed to improve the man's eyesight, and, rising to the occasion, he yelled at Mongkhon to back off and repeated that he knew nothing about it. Mongkhon became instantly enraged and hit him heavily across the head again with his baton, screaming, 'Listen to me. I know you were waiting for that packet to come over the wall. Now tell me who threw it or you will be in very serious trouble.'

The inmate was by this time furious himself and confronted the threat face on. 'I can't tell you who it is! How the fuck can I tell you who it is if I don't know, you crazy bastard?'

Mongkhon grabbed him by the right arm and began to drag him, blood already trickling down his forehead, to the gate that separated the two sections. Just before they passed through to Section 5, though, the prisoner struggled and yelled again that he couldn't identify the culprit because he didn't know who it was and went to throw his left fist into Mongkhon's face. Mongkhon deflected the blow with the baton he still held in his right hand and, twisting the man around, began to pummel him across the ears and neck. The inmate pulled free and, spitting right in Mongkhon's face, screamed a warning that if he continued his bullying he would find himself being beaten to death himself on his way home from work one night. 'I've got six older brothers on the outside, and they will kill you, you bastard, so you better stop right now.'

Mongkhon simply went berserk and smashed his baton down onto the man's head, splitting it and knocking him to the ground, then, standing over him and using both hands to grip and direct his weapon, he landed blow after blow, mercilessly shattering the man's skull and arms. He then ordered two trusties to pick him up and handcuff his arms around his favourite execution tree in the yard, where he proceeded to kill him.

Not too many minutes later, the body hung from the tree, and Mongkhon was panting with exhaustion. He instructed the trusties to take the man and put him in a box and not to let him out for two days. Once again, this was unnecessary because as they pulled him from the tree, his brain partly exposed, it was obvious that he was already dead. Mongkhon, recovering some presence of mind, the demons in him temporarily appeased, just shrugged and told them to take him to the hospital and put him in a body bag.

It had been just three weeks since Fred and I and most of the other inmates in Section 4 had witnessed him murdering his previous victim.

'Bloody hell, Sly. I can't handle this, mate. I mean, how can this maniac keep killing people like this? I knew that guy. I was talking to him only last week. He could speak English quite well and was obviously reasonably well educated. He told me that he was still fighting his case and gets a visit at least twice a week from his wife and two kids. How can these murders be covered up? The family must get the body. I mean, those injuries can't be hidden. Someone must see them. You would have to be blind and stupid not to realise that he had been flogged to death. These people can't just disappear . . . Can they? With all the bullshit we have to go through every time we go to the court, there must be records of where everyone is. How come no one does anything? Surely the family can complain, can't they? He told me that he didn't commit the crime he was here for – said it was his neighbour's son but that the family was very wealthy and the father a politician. The cops just came and arrested him, then he ended up here. What the hell kind of place is this, man? Shit, I've been coming to Thailand for years, but I never knew it was anything like this. Nobody back home would believe it if you told them. I don't believe it myself, and I am seeing it with my own eyes.'

'I don't know, Fred. I really can't get a grasp on this myself, but we're stuck here for God knows how long, so try not to let it get to you, mate. I know it's hard to just stand by and watch it happen, but we can't do anything about it in here. Main thing is to keep out of the way ourselves until this is over and we're out – shouldn't be too long now. Once we are out, maybe we can expose this horror house and try to do something about it, but there's no point in trying to do anything now. Best to keep a very low profile and stay in the shadows, or we could end up in one of those body bags ourselves. Wouldn't help us, or anyone else, if we were to find out first-hand what happens to the bodies, would it?'

'I guess you're right. Let's take a walk. I feel like I'm going to puke.'

Lek's reign in Section 4 lasted for a total of five years. Eventually, however, there was a change of director at Bombat, and many of the inmates made complaints about his behaviour and thieving. He was henceforth transferred, powerless and penniless, to Klong Prem prison. Within one month, he was dead: poisoned with cultured salmonella bacteria by one of the fellows for whom he had previously caused heartache and who had been transferred to the same section many months before Lek's arrival. With no suspects and no inclination to find one, the cause of death was recorded as food poisoning, a common enough complaint and one that's often fatal. But as far as most of those who knew of him were concerned, Lek got precisely what he deserved and not a tear was shed.

It was just a few weeks before my transfer to Klong Prem prison that another rodent, who was also a cell captain trusty in Section 4, met his match and, as a result, his maker. His propensity to snitch on and take advantage of his fellow inmates' weaknesses was the catalyst in a plot to do away with him at his own hand.

Cell 1 was his domain to patrol and control, and it accommodated a higher proportion of heroin junkies than most of the other cells in the block, this cell captain among them. Not unlike a pyramid-marketing scheme, the dope that entered Bombat flowed down from the top via distributors, and cell captains were generally chosen for their position because they were on the down line and could help to keep the customer base loyal to their supplier: buy from the distributor and there was rarely a problem; buy from outside of that structure and invariably, sooner or later, there would be hell to pay for the privilege.

This captain – let's call him Slim – unlike Lek, was not a stoolie for Mongkhon. He was terrified to be even in close proximity to the 'Mad Dog', as Mongkhon was often referred to. Instead, he had forged an alliance with another of the more ruthless guards in the section, and when he saw anyone in his cell using dope that had not come via his distributorship, he would confiscate it and march the culprit off to have a chat with that guard. The end result would usually be a sound biffing – but generally not unto death – for the offender and a transfer to a less hospitable section. Slim would then be given the confiscated dope as a reward for his vigilance.

Monopolies have a tendency, however, to become the breeding ground for greed and exploitation, and the heroin trade in Section 4 was no exception to this rule. A couple of the regular users in Cell 1, as a result of the high prices and the dictatorial attitude that Slim was in the habit of employing to get his own rations for free, decided to do something about it – the Thai way.

I was destined some years later to see a very similar trick to the one they used to commit their own version of the perfect murder, only on this occasion the show was a whole lot more entertaining. There are plants that grow in some parts of the highlands in South East Asia that are so toxic that just a tiny drop of the sap or juice from them is sufficient to render a person unconscious. A little more will kill an adult within seconds. Apparently, some forms of it are often used by lady-boys and prostitutes in the tourist haunts in Thailand to put their foreign clients into a temporary coma so they can pinch whatever they can get their hands on from their wallets and luggage. A light smear on an inviting nipple is all that's needed to send the victim into orbit for up to 15 hours, sometimes for eternity. If administered in a deadly dose – as little as a couple of drops – one variety triggers a fatal heart attack, among other things, and is said to leave virtually no traces. The cause of death is, as such, usually diagnosed as heart failure.

Soon after the plan was made, one of the disgruntled fellows in Cell 1 received a bag of peanuts and some other vegetables, sent in from the outside by friends or relatives – a practice that was permitted in those days. Several of the peanut shells had been carefully cracked along the seam and the kernels removed and replaced with gelatine capsules, containing a quantity of lethal dried sap. The shells were then glued back together and put in with the others in the bag. Once recovered, a little of this sap – sufficient to have a rhino turning feet up – was powdered along with several glucose tablets and the blend wrapped in a piece of silver paper from a cigarette box to make it look like a regular heroin fix with which those who indulged were all too familiar.

A few minutes before the cell door was unlocked the following morning, the chap who had received the vegetables pretended to get ready to inject himself with the formula, making sure that Slim saw him do it. As had been anticipated, Slim rushed over and confiscated the paper and, as soon as the door had been unlocked, dragged the protesting man – soon to be a member of the perfect murderer club – off to see his favourite guard, handing over what he believed to be smack as he made his report. That done, the guard returned the paper to Slim, as usual, and started to discipline the offender. The victim vehemently denied having any connection to the paper or knowledge of its origin but, of course, that wasn't going to stop the guard from giving him a thumping.

Slim, however, didn't stick around for the show. He wanted to get the fix into his veins before anyone could take it away from him and slipped off back to the cell. Within minutes of his departure, and while the guard was still administering his discipline, a blood-curdling scream that must have lasted about a minute or more echoed through the section, followed by a deafening silence. Such was the spontaneity and the insinuation of extreme torment it provoked that everybody who heard it stopped in their tracks, looking this way and that with expressions varying from horror to excitement but not uttering a word. Finally, after what was probably only seconds but seemed like a minute or two, several trusties accompanied by a couple of guards, one being the murderer's disciplinarian, ran up the stairs to investigate. A few minutes later, Slim was carried down to the ground floor, his torso as stiff as a board, apparently frozen in shock, his eyes open like saucers, a look of total terror stencilled on his face.

Now, I don't know exactly how that stuff would react when injected directly into the blood, but Slim seemed to have found out the hard way, and it certainly didn't look like it had been a whole lot of fun. The corpse was taken to the hospital, and the substance that remained in the paper, which was found on the floor in the cell beside him, was tested to establish whether or not it was heroin. No positive identification was made, other than that the major portion was glucose powder. The guard who had given the paper to Slim evidently realised, however, that things had taken a rather sinister direction and that Slim had obviously been the victim of a pretty clever reprisal. When he suggested to the chap he had been biffing that the paper contained some kind of poison, the only response he got was that it proved the heroin wasn't his. 'I would hardly have been going to poison myself in such a terribly painful manner, now would I?' The guard took no further action. How could he? Slim had injected himself, and the guard had personally given him what had been injected. Within one hour, the murderer was transferred to Klong Prem and the cause of death recorded as heart failure. Another perfect murder and a little more justice, Thai style.

I often wondered after that why Mongkhon hadn't ended up the same way. He was always humping the lady-boys, and they all hated him with a passion. It would have been a simple matter for them to use the same trick by putting a little poison on a nipple and then dropping a bit more into his mouth after he had passed out. But this never happened, and he continued his sadism without reservation.

\* \* \*

It was only days before I left Bombat that I saw Mongkhon do something that left absolutely no doubt of his insanity. It was the fifth murder I had watched him commit since arriving there, and he did it in front of most of those being kept in Section 4. For whatever reason – and he didn't really need a good one – his victim was tied to the usual tree, and Mongkhon flogged him with his baton until he was bleeding all over but still conscious, which wasn't all that common after he had done his worst. Evidently, he wanted to play a different game this time, and ordering the trusties to untie the imminently deceased he had them drag him over to an old tree stump, in and around which was a large red-ant colony.

The locals have a tendency to name things according to the sounds they make or their colour, taste, feel and so on. For example, a brown and black scrub pheasant, because its call is something like 'pooot pooot', is called a *nok a-pooot* (meaning 'bird that goes pooot'). They call this species of red ant the fire ant because its bite is like being burned with a concentrated beam of fire, causing intense pain that takes an hour or more to wane.

After the inmate was secured to the stump, Mongkhon poured a little raw sugar-cane juice – a popular Thai beverage – over him and sat back in a white plastic chair, which he had a trusty fetch for him along with a glass of iced water, to watch. Within minutes, the ants had swarmed all over what they probably considered to be their next meal or perhaps an invader that had to be repelled. The man started screaming and twisting and pleading, until he went completely off his trolley. Finally, when he was unable to endure any more, he collapsed unconscious. With the show over, Mongkhon stood and ordered the trusties to put the man in one of the small metal punishment boxes in the corridor on the second floor of the confinement building. After throwing buckets of water over him to remove the ants, they did as instructed. When he was removed the next day, he was dead. His body was covered with thousands of red lumps. It was difficult to believe that the brutality and torture could go so far, but it did, and this instance wasn't the least of it.

# CHAPTER 11

‖‖‖‖‖‖‖‖‖‖‖‖‖‖‖‖‖‖‖‖‖‖‖‖‖‖‖‖‖‖‖‖‖‖‖‖‖‖‖‖‖‖‖‖‖‖‖‖‖‖‖‖‖‖‖‖‖‖‖‖‖‖‖‖‖‖‖‖

# The Pointing of the Bone

AS WELL AS WITNESSING BRUTAL BEATINGS ON AN ALMOST DAILY basis and the occasional barbarous murder, we had another regular trauma to endure. Every 12 days for a total of 84 days, we were herded together with 50 or more other men, shackled by a trusty swinging a stonemason's hammer – those already sporting chains receiving an additional set – and subjected to the agonies of being taken in the crammed blue bus through the traffic-clogged streets of Bangkok to the court buildings. There we would spend the entire day sweltering in the overflowing, filthy holding cells for no other reason than to stand for a few minutes, cuffed to at least another ten detainees, before a magistrate. A cop would then read from a sheet of paper, and the magistrate would wearily rubber-stamp another 12-day extension to our detention, theoretically allowing the police to continue with their investigation. Then, late in the afternoon, when the traffic was usually at its peak, we were returned, in the same excruciating fashion, to Bombat to suffer through the reinternment procedure and another night in the standing-room-only cells of Section 3 before being transferred back to Section 4 the following morning. It was a system so totally void of reason and logic as to be naught but an absurdity.

Life went on with monotonous regularity for the next few months until one afternoon early in May. About one week before my first actual court-hearing date, as Fred and I were sitting in the shade of the Section 4 confinement building, we heard a lot of commotion nearby in the exercise yard. That, of course, wasn't an unusual occurrence. By this time we had become so accustomed to the guards beating up Thai and other Asian inmates that we scarcely took any notice. However, this uproar was different because someone was yelling abuse in English, and that wasn't something that happened very often. We both jumped up and went to see what was going on.

'You are fucking dead! Understand, you motherfucker? DEAD! Got that?' The ruckus had attracted the attention of nearly all of the inmates within earshot, and all eyes were turned towards John McPherson, who was confronting one of the guards and pointing his forefinger directly into his face.

McPherson had initially been convicted and sentenced to one year in prison for possession of a small quantity of marijuana. Since being in Bombat, however, he had been given two additional one-year sentences for possession of small quantities of heroin. He wasn't a serious junkie; rather he was a user when he could get his hands on a little dope. The guard on the receiving end of his wrath this day was one of the more brutal sadists at Bombat prison: a man of average size by Asian standards but who appeared to be convinced that he grew to ten feet tall and sprouted muscles of steel every time he donned his uniform. Although not quite as bad, or as mad, as Mongkhon, he regularly beat prisoners with his baton and at times caused serious injuries to those he attacked.

Normally, the guards did not use violence on Western prisoners. The embassies could become involved if that happened, which was best avoided from the Thais' point of view. This fellow, however, had made the mistake of trying to impress the Thai prisoners and other guards by showing them that he really was the powerful man he perceived himself to be and had no fear of beating a white foreigner.

He had approached McPherson from behind, savagely whacking him across the back with his baton, knocking him to the ground.

McPherson had sprung to his feet and retaliated, shoving the guard and shouting at him in English that he was a 'dead man', then repeating the threats in Thai just to get the message across clearly. All of the other guards in the section at the time witnessed the event but none ventured to assist their colleague. Mongkhon was conspicuous by his absence – fortunately for McPherson, it was his day off.

The assaulting guard offered a little laugh, evidently triggered by his uncertainty as to how far McPherson might go, and then slowly backed off and left. He had lost some face, which meant he would now be a serious danger to McPherson.

A little more than an hour later, a group of guards came into the section. Two of them pointed at McPherson and the others looked at him closely, albeit from a safe distance. They talked quietly among themselves, timidly glancing at him from time to time but not attempting to go anywhere near him. Soon after they left, another group entered the section and then another, all repeating the performance. Fred and I were as puzzled as the three other inmates we were talking to when we saw this very unusual behaviour and like McPherson himself, as it turned out, feared that he was being sized up for some very heavy punishment.

After this had happened several times, one of the trusties – a long-term resident whom I actually got on quite well with – came running back from Section 3. After talking excitedly to several other trusties, he came over to where I was still speaking to Fred and the other three fellows. He told us that he had just returned from the main front office, where there was a major gathering of all of the guards and prison officials. They were discussing none other than John McPherson.

At first, we listened in horror, but as the story unfolded and drew to a close, I had to stifle an urge to join Dave – one of the foreigners with me – who wasn't able to control himself and had burst out laughing fit to choke. In fact, we were all chuckling by the time the trusty left.

McPherson had to be informed, and quick. Though we hadn't talked to him since the attack, we all knew that the procession of inquisitive guards must have made the poor fellow terrified that he wouldn't survive the day. His relief on hearing what the trusty had said to us, however, was unmistakable, the tension ebbing from his face like a receding tsunami as he started chuckling himself. 'I think perhaps there's a little potential advantage to be taken here, fellahs,' he responded after a few moments of deliberation.

The guard who had hit him had been so furious after he'd left the section for his lunch break that, jumping on his motorbike, he'd informed a colleague that he was going to have a few drinks. Less than an hour later, he was lying on the floor of the main office, badly mangled and as dead as salted mackerel. As dead as McPherson had told him he would be. McPherson had not touched him directly, of course, but all those gathered around the body were quite certain that it was McPherson who had not just killed him but mutilated his body almost beyond recognition.

The guards who had witnessed McPherson pointing his finger in this unfortunate's face and informing him of his imminent demise had repeated this to all who hadn't been there. Now they and all their colleagues believed that McPherson was able to summon the power of the Devil himself. They were unanimous in thinking that this could be the only explanation for what had befallen the man who had dared to cross him.

He had been plucked from his motorcycle and thrown into the path of a loaded ten-wheel truck out on the main road and killed instantly. Several guards walking by on their way to the prison for the afternoon shift had witnessed the accident, but on hearing the story were also convinced that McPherson was responsible. From this moment on, he became an untouchable, a man to be feared and treated with the utmost respect.

'Well, talk about poetic justice!' McPherson continued, his mirth still very much evident. 'Let's think of a few ways to reinforce this fear of the incredible power I possess. What a bunch of morons. They beat people to death every other day, and here they are terrified of the bogeyman!'

But he wasn't going to have the opportunity to exploit his newly discovered powers in Bombat. The guards immediately convened a meeting with the prison commander. They demanded that McPherson be moved to Klong Prem, or somewhere well away from them, and were all prepared to go on strike if their demands were not met. Two hours later, he was shipped out, accompanied by a couple of very nervous and extremely accommodating uniformed escorts.

His incredible and fearsome reputation preceded him to Klong Prem, however, and when he arrived, he was treated with exaggerated civility and courtesy. From then on, none of the officials there spoke to him, unless in very polite terms, and no one ever tried to make any complaint or trouble for him at any time right up to the day of his release. He was given favourable treatment wherever he went and was never so much as touched by any guard or trusty. He smoked marijuana in the foreigners' garden when he pleased and even handled cash right in the presence of the building chief.

He took full advantage of the situation, not only for his own benefit, but also for the benefit of certain other Western inmates. For the remainder of his term at Klong Prem, he had freedom to move where he wished and often smuggled letters out for inmates who wanted to bypass the censor – no guard ever refused to post a letter if asked by McPherson and none had the nerve to ask for payment for the service.

It was just a couple of years after he was transferred that he completed his sentence and was repatriated to Australia, much to the relief of the officials and many others at The Prem. It was later reported – though I was not able to confirm this absolutely – that approximately 12 months after his return, he was arrested in Australia on drug charges and sentenced to 15 years in prison. Maybe by then his powers had been depleted by all the pot he'd smoked while he reigned supreme. One thing is certain, though: he became a legendary figure in Thailand's prisons.

Ask any Australian Aborigine about the ramifications of 'pointing the bone', and they will all cringe in fear and unanimously confirm that being on the receiving end means certain death.

# PART 3

## And the Slug Advances on Its Path of Slime

Since Thailand's society is highly moral in character, with its shy, modest people who are easily offended by sexually related material, established in a country where sexual exploitation is virtually unknown, the use of the Internet to access indecency and improper information should be blocked.

*Someone who appears to be terribly ill-informed at* The Nation *newspaper, Bangkok*

# CHAPTER 12

‖‖‖‖‖‖‖‖‖‖‖‖‖‖‖‖‖‖‖‖‖‖‖‖‖‖‖‖‖‖‖‖‖‖‖‖‖‖‖‖‖‖‖‖‖‖‖‖‖‖‖‖‖‖‖‖‖‖‖‖‖‖‖‖‖‖‖‖‖‖‖‖‖

# My New Home Was
# Definitely Not My Castle

I SPENT JUST OVER FIVE MONTHS AT BOMBAT BEFORE BEING transferred to Klong Prem. My first real day in court had been about midway though the previous month and the second just 12 days later. Five days after the second hearing, along with my co-accused, I was given just ten minutes' notice to pack my belongings and was taken by covered van to The Prem, where I was installed in Section 2.

Located on Ngamwongwan Road in the Chatuchak district of Bangkok, The Prem is part of a large block of prisons that includes Bombat, the Ladyao women's prison and the main – though decrepit – prison hospital. A few years, later it would also accommodate the new Ladyao remand prison, which was destined to replace the 100-year-old Mahachai remand prison, where Brent – a fellow I will soon introduce – spent a terrifying 14 weeks at the beginning of his detention. A new seven-storey, reasonably well-equipped and staffed, general hospital was also destined to feature as a major improvement of the facility about a decade hence.

There were fewer incidents of brutality by guards at The Prem, and the building chief, although as corrupt as most of the officials I had encountered, was generally too lazy to exert himself, spending most of his day sitting in his little wooden air-conditioned office, which was built over a small lake between what we generously called the 'coffee shop' and the foreigners' garden.

The foreigners' garden was a small compound of about a sixth of an acre at the far-left back corner of the section, with the back wall abutting Bombat prison and the left-side wall shared by Section 1. It was actually like a small village, with five rows of huts constructed from bamboo poles and thatch walls. The roofs were made from some kind of wide-leafed grass or reed matted together and fixed to bamboo rods then attached to the framework with strips of the same material, which was surprisingly waterproof, even in heavy storms. There were reticulated power lines and outlets for electrical appliances, and the floor and paths were concrete. Many of the 'houses', as we called these huts, but which were actually just small segments of the main thatch buildings, had gas stoves, iceboxes and other appliances, such as electric fans and rice cookers.

The area was fenced off from the rest of the section and had only one entrance. Most of the Thai, Cambodian, Burmese and Laotian prisoners were not permitted entry unless they were working for a foreigner, in which case an identity tag had to be obtained to be used as an entry pass by the manservant. These men took care of the drudgery of washing clothes and blankets, cooking meals, washing dishes, tidying up the grass and bamboo shacks in the garden, and so on. If sharing a cell with his employer, he was generally responsible for cleaning its toilet and washing its floor each day, too.

Initially, there had been nothing on this land, and it had formed part of the open area where all of the inmates in the section spent their free time. That was until an Australian inmate got the idea of building a shelter. He approached the building chief, who together with the prison director, no doubt seeing an additional way to fleece their captives, agreed to allow anyone who had the necessary money to build a hut. For the privilege, the director had to be paid a monthly registration fee, the construction material had to be purchased through him and the labour cost of the Thai prisoner workers who built the huts, and who received just one small tin of tuna per day for their efforts, was charged out at the normal daily rate that applied on the outside.

To be permitted to have an electrical or gas appliance, it was necessary to pay an additional monthly fee, depending on the appliance. To get it into the prison required yet another fee, then the power had to be paid for and gas had to be purchased through the coffee shop at inflated prices.

Nevertheless, in spite of all these costs, over the years the garden grew, one building after another, and by the time I arrived, the entire area was covered with these native-material structures. There was a gym of sorts, with proper equipment, where inmates could do weightlifting and other exercises, and, believe it or not, a small restaurant, where a hot meal could be purchased. Although at the time of my initial residence it was owned by a Chinese heroin junkie who was not at all reliable, it did add a welcome convenience most of the time. There was also a community TV area, where every Saturday and Sunday afternoon inmates could sit and watch a movie, and during the week selected inmates could occasionally tune in for a short period to watch the news and a little sport.

A reasonably well-stocked library of novels and magazines was provided by one of the residents in an area built into the back of his house, a valuable facility that was very much appreciated by many of the foreigners in the section. Reading helped pass the time in a quiet and relaxed manner, and as there were numerous nationalities represented, the available material was quite diverse and grew continuously as new books and magazines were sent in by friends and relatives on the outside.

Several years before my arrival, some of the foreigners had pooled their money and paid to have a tiled toilet and shower area built. Although this was not under cover or in any way private, it was usually clean and was easily maintained, unlike the one on the Thai side, which was bare concrete and had grown black with mould and grime.

Those who owned houses generally rented or shared some of the space with one or more other inmates. Those who weren't so fortunate usually spent their time in the garden at the common area, where a number of fold-up easy chairs were available, in most cases to use for free. Many of the inmates spent their days wandering around the foreigners' garden visiting other inmates at their houses or using the large area outside the garden compound for exercise, jogging or just to sit talking while playing chess or some other board game.

Most convicted foreigners in Section 2 paid a monthly fee of 150 baht to the building chief so that they could be exempted from doing prison work. Those who hadn't yet been convicted and whose trials were still ongoing could, if they were represented by an embassy, avoid the prison work as well as the payment by simply refusing to do either. This stance generally resulted in a confrontation with the building chief, although as soon as he had been informed that an embassy had advised a remand prisoner that he didn't have to work or pay, he usually exempted that inmate from the requirement; but this kind of impertinence did have its drawbacks.

There were two small lakes in Section 2, and both were used to raise tilapia fish, a small African cichlid species that is a prolific breeder and a favourite food of the Thais. Every few months, the lakes would be dragged with nets and the catch made available for the inmates to purchase.

Once settled in, I spent most of my time during the day at the 'coffee shop'. This was a small store where inmates could purchase a variety of foodstuffs and other essential items, but not one where they could buy a cup of coffee and a bun and sit in comfort to enjoy it. I always tried to make myself at home there just the same, settling down in a corner to write or study and drinking coffee if I felt like it.

It was located at the back-right-hand corner of the section, almost against the wall that separated Bombat from Klong Prem, and was managed by selected long-term inmates, mostly Westerners, who took orders twice each week and kept records of the costs to be deducted from the buyers' prison accounts. One of the guards was store controller for the prison director and was responsible for arranging for goods to be sent in. Prisoners were permitted to spend as much of their account credit as they wished at the store. Although cash was outlawed, it was used by some inmates. Funds could be transferred from the outside to prisoners' accounts or even from the account of one inmate to that of another – but that service carried a 10 per cent surcharge. It was possible to order meat, vegetables, fruit, gas for preparing hot meals, toiletries and so on, and also to buy from stock many other items such as sugar, coffee, canned milk and tinned fish.

One drawback was that many of the items that could be obtained were either out of date or in damaged containers. For example, almost all products that came in a can were quite obviously rejects from supermarkets or wholesalers, the cans being dented or very close to or past their expiry date. Other items had stained labels as a result of breakages or spillages and as such were not suitable for sale through normal channels. Almost all bags of rice, flour, grains and cereals were contaminated with weevils or other vermin. Each bag of rice had a high percentage of the lowest-quality broken or rejected rice, together with a liberal portion of plain starch mixed along with a little better-quality rice to increase the weight at the lowest possible cost. Its plain, unlabelled packaging was proof enough that it had been prepared specifically for our consumption. The price, however, was still well above what one would pay for good-quality rice in a supermarket.

At one time during my residence, a consignment of canned tuna and canned condensed milk appeared, which had apparently been salvaged from a building fire – this was pretty obvious, because all of the labels showed signs of scorching. It was sold at the normal price, and no other stock was available until we'd consumed it all. If an inmate requested canned tuna or milk in his weekly order from the outside, he was told that the available stock had to be finished before any more could be brought in.

It was rare for any of the fruit and vegetables purchased through the coffee shop to arrive fresh. Most items appeared to be rejects from the markets and were already bruised or spotted or in some way unsuitable for sale to the general public. One kilogram of tomatoes, for example, would yield, at best, 800 grams of usable fruit, with the remainder being rotten or with bruised sections that had to be cut away and discarded. The potatoes, onions, cabbages and lettuce were usually similarly affected, and the cucumbers and carrots were often shrivelled and rubbery.

The cost to prisoners, however, was at least 50 per cent higher, and sometimes up to double, the price one would pay for fresh top-quality produce on the outside. The price of all other available items was similarly inflated. Very popular, though, were the long, thin loaves of fresh bread that were baked at the prison bakery and on sale almost daily. The almost daily ice delivery was just as well received.

Who reaped all of the rewards from this rather lucrative enterprise? Well, it's not difficult to guess. Needless to say, with more than 6,000 captive customers at Klong Prem being forced to buy their supplies through the coffee shops, there was a huge profit to be made each month.

Added to this, however, was the return from building materials and labour sold to inmates and registration fees, as well as from the sale of numerous goods that were manufactured in the workshops – most sections had at least one. In Section 2, several of them were housed in a long building that extended along the right-hand side in front of the coffee shop almost to the exit gate. Here inmates produced a variety of consumer products at little or no labour cost – most receiving the standard monthly payment of just one small tin of tuna – quite a bit of which was exported overseas to large multinational retail outlets. Mountains of artificial flowers and clothing made by inmates at The Prem certainly found their way to overseas markets; the barcodes and labels that were attached during the process proved that. The prisoners were given a quota each day and most were able to complete their assignments on time. Those who didn't were punished. The then prison director sanctioned such abuse to ensure that his shipments went out to the destination countries, which on the one hand – and for public consumption only – decry the use of slave labour, but on the other turn a blind eye to products produced by it being sold for huge profits by these manipulative and exploitative companies.

Although the coffee shop couldn't be compared to popping down to the supermarket, for those with credit in their accounts it was nevertheless convenient and made life a little more bearable. For the rest, things were less comfortable unless they had a service to offer.

One particularly unpleasant aspect of the garden area was an open sewerage trench that ran along the side and back wall of the section. All waste water from the wash troughs and all human waste from the toilet areas, on both the Thai and foreigners' sides, went directly into this trench and flowed along the full length of two sides of the garden perimeter to eventually exit through the wall and continue on to Section 1. At all times, it was black with mosquito larvae, flies and the slime and algae that usually grow in sewage. During the rainy season, it frequently overflowed and spread its contaminants across the major part of the yard and garden area.

Nevertheless, apart from the health hazards and extortion, when compared with the torturous conditions in Bombat and the dark cells at Mahachai, The Prem garden was heaven. At least I could go out in the fresh air – or as fresh as it gets in Bangkok – have a reasonably comfortable place to sit and eat, and enjoy very little restriction on my movement within the section.

It was just a few months before old George started chasing his former mate Saddam out of Kuwait, that Brent, an Australian, found himself struggling to maintain his sanity in another part of the city. Like me, he had been catapulted into a world that he could never have dreamed existed and could certainly never have envisaged becoming part of as another innocent victim of Justice Incorporated. His only error had been to allow a Thai family, whom he and his Thai wife had been fostering and assisting financially for many years, to gain the impression that he had a lot more money than he actually had.

I first met Brent at the coffee shop just a few days after he was transferred to Klong Prem. I was sitting inside enjoying a cold drink whilst writing in my notebook in Thai, which had attracted his attention. When he enquired, I explained that I was learning the language because all court proceedings were in Thai and that my lawyer wasn't translating what was going on. As a consequence, I was leaving court with no idea about what had been said or recorded during the session.

Even though Hansel was able to converse in Thai fairly well, the language he had learned over the years was that used by the lower caste – the slum dwellers, prostitutes and uneducated villagers – which was totally inappropriate as far as the courts were concerned. Accordingly, he couldn't understand more than 20 per cent of what was being said in court either. As such, I decided that I had no option other than to learn to read and write Thai.

I had been advised that it would take in the region of two years for the case to be completed in the first court – which turned out to be a pretty optimistic guess – and even then, regardless of the verdict, it would probably have to go to the Appeal Court, either at the demand of the prosecutor, if Fred and I were acquitted, or at our own demand if we were convicted. As it appeared unlikely that I would be able to get bail before the end of the Criminal Court proceedings, time was on my side, so I spent a lot of it learning the formal language.

Over the next few months, Brent and I became friends, talking for an hour or two every day. Our conversations usually ended up drifting back to the same subject – our respective cases – and it wasn't long before we had a complete understanding of each other's situation.

I remember well the first day Brent told me of the frustration he was experiencing and how it had all started for him. You could see his despair written all over his face. In fact, at first, I thought he was suffering from cancer or AIDS, or something just as destructive, because he was terribly emaciated and was having trouble with his breathing. It was when I asked him what he was suffering from that he started talking about his case and what he had been subjected to prior to being sent to The Prem.

His story was a long and complicated one. Suffice to say, he'd spent the usual seven days in the police station cells, all the time being encouraged to hand over a bundle of cash to secure his freedom, and a further three months or more at the infamous Mahachai remand prison in conditions that could not even be imagined by most people when he'd refused to comply. He then joined me in Section 2 at The Prem for about another year.

Several months before Brent's arrival, Hansel approached Fred and me in the foreigners' garden and handed down his second ultimatum.

We had not forgiven him for trying to coerce Nok into blackmailing Jaidow, and as a result we had stopped all support for him, even civil contact. However, since that attempt, and on the advice of officials from his embassy, he'd changed his plea to guilty as charged at the last but one hearing of the prosecution case. Embassy officials told him that there appeared to be no way he could win a contested case and that by changing his plea he would be convicted quickly and sentenced to no more than 25 years. The embassy would then arrange for him to be transferred back to Germany shortly afterwards, where his hip injury could be operated upon. He would soon be granted parole by the German authorities on medical and compassionate grounds and would be a free man in no more than four years. This, however, was little more than a lot of piss and wind. The fact that none of it ever eventuated was ample evidence of that.

Both Fred and I warned him that it was nothing but a trick to get him to plead guilty, but he wouldn't listen. He expected to be convicted and sentenced the same day that he changed his plea and was very annoyed when by four in the afternoon nothing had happened. He was even more annoyed when nothing had happened before the next hearing date and he was required to accompany us to the court as usual.

I guess that as a result of his realising that we had been right and that he had now sunk his chances of acquittal, he figured that he had nothing to lose by having another crack at us. With an arrogant smirk, he declared that he would testify to the court that both Fred and I were involved in the drug deal with him and that it was Fred who had given him the suitcase with the drugs to carry to the bank unless we met the following demands:

1. He was to be provided with decent food twice every day;

2. Fred was to agree to be his manservant for the duration of his stay; and

3. I was to agree to give him one million baht in cash immediately after I had won my case.

He then demanded that a contract be drawn up to that effect and signed by both of us. I laughed in his face at the stupidity of the demands and flatly refused to give him as much as recycled toilet paper. Fred, on the other hand, was a little more realistic. On reflection, he appreciated the implications and additional problems that we could conceivably face if Hansel did as he had threatened. Fred eventually convinced me that we could make it appear that we had agreed to the demands without committing ourselves to anything much at all. The main thing was to appease the fool until the trial in the first court was over. He reasoned that Hansel was so thick between the ears that he wouldn't know that such an agreement would be meaningless and that we could in fact word it in such a way that he would only end up facing additional charges if we ever brought it before the courts.

We decided to go ahead and draw up an agreement for his approval. Fred was willing to play the game as Hansel's manservant if that was what was required, but I made the negotiations appear tougher by refusing to provide him with food, reasoning that the German Embassy was providing sufficient money for him to feed himself. However, he could hardly contain himself when I told him that I would agree to the one-million-baht payment provided it was spelled out very clearly in the contract.

We had it drafted in duplicate by a Swiss inmate in Section 5 who was in for possession of a small quantity of ganja (marijuana) and who, unbeknownst to Hansel, had his own score to settle. This fellow had already confided to Fred and me whilst we were in Bombat that he knew Hansel, and he had told us a story that would later be confirmed by Hansel himself.

He had a friend, a fellow Swiss, who also liked to smoke ganja and who employed Hansel as a guide while he travelled upcountry. When they were getting ready to leave Ang Thong Province, Hansel went off alone for a short time, leaving his client to wait at a restaurant. When he returned, they headed towards the bus terminal ready to set off on the next leg of the journey. The Swiss bought the bus tickets, and they sat on a bench to await the boarding announcement.

They hadn't been there more than ten minutes before they were approached by a police officer who demanded that the Swiss submit to what he called a routine search. After a pat down and a quick check of his passport, the officer asked to search his luggage. There in his backpack the officer found what he knew would be there: a packet of ganja. Hansel was not searched or asked any questions.

The Swiss was arrested and taken to the police station, with Hansel accompanying him as his loyal guide and interpreter. This was his introduction to Justice Incorporated, and for the next few days he was given a tiny taste of the horrors that he could expect to encounter from then on if he didn't play the game by the rules.

Hansel strongly advised his client that he should try to make a deal with the police chief and volunteered to negotiate a settlement on his behalf, assuring him that he could speak Thai fluently and had a good chance of getting him out of his predicament.

As the fourth day of his confinement dawned, and more than a little worse for wear after being locked in the station cell with a number of Thai detainees, the Swiss paid the police all of the cash and traveller's cheques that he had with him, a total of 120,000 baht, and was then escorted to a bank to withdraw a further sum using his credit cards. He was then released and, with his trusty guide for company, returned to Bangkok because he had no money to continue with his holiday.

At that time, Hansel was shacking up with a Thai woman in the Huay Kwang district of Bangkok, and the first stop they made when they arrived in the city was at her apartment. The Swiss was very grateful to Hansel for getting him out of a potentially disastrous situation, even though it had cost him dearly. That same afternoon, he wired his family in Switzerland to have a little more money sent over so that he could return home, and he promised to give Hansel some of it as a reward for his assistance.

Four days later, he returned to the apartment to give him 3,000 baht, but Hansel wasn't there. However, his girlfriend was, and she invited him in for a cup of coffee. Inside, he immediately noticed a major change in the contents of the apartment: a new and larger fridge had replaced the old one; a new cabinet displayed a new TV set with video recorder and stereo equipment; the bed covers were new; there was an artificial teak laminated table with four upholstered chairs that had not been there before; and there was a new vinyl-covered sofa. On the floor was a large rug, which the Swiss reasoned must have cost at least a couple of thousand baht. In a nutshell, the apartment had been completely transformed since his previous visit.

The woman explained that Hansel had bought everything just two days earlier, telling her that he had been paid for a job he'd done. A little further discreet questioning revealed that Hansel knew the police chief from Ang Thong quite well.

Beginning to feel highly suspicious, the Swiss decided against leaving the 3,000 baht and asked instead for Hansel to come over to his guesthouse to see him. On his return there that day, he told several of his friends of his suspicions that Hansel was involved with the cop and that they had jointly stung him for what amounted to $10,000. This Swiss who was helping Fred and me with the contract was one of those friends.

Two or three days later, he and a couple of the others went to visit Hansel to ask him about the incident. They were told that their friend had got exactly what he deserved, because he was stingy and had tried to cut the price for his guide services after already agreeing on it. Apart from that, he complained that his client always picked the cheapest places to stay and eat. He didn't actually admit to a conspiracy with the police chief, but he didn't deny it and appeared to be quite pleased with himself. He then told the three friends to get out of his face and not to come back or they would suffer a similar fate. He assured them that he was well connected and could speak Thai fluently, and as such was able to do many things that normal tourists, like them, could not. Not wanting to risk becoming victims, they made a hasty exit.

The agreement to pay Hansel one million baht was drawn up and worded in such a way that it clearly showed the swindle for what it really was. He was delighted with it and handed one copy back to Fred, satisfaction written all over his face as he slowly folded the other and put it in his pocket. Although he wasn't going to be getting food from me, he was going to be waited on hand and foot and would have one million baht to take home with him. Not a bad day's work at all.

# CHAPTER 13

‖‖‖‖‖‖‖‖‖‖‖‖‖‖‖‖‖‖‖‖‖‖‖‖‖‖‖‖‖‖‖‖‖‖‖‖‖‖‖‖‖‖‖‖‖‖‖‖‖‖‖‖‖‖‖‖‖‖‖‖‖‖‖‖‖‖‖‖‖‖‖‖‖‖‖‖‖‖‖‖

# Prison Rats

ALL PRISONS HAVE THEIR 'PRISON RATS'. THAT'S THE TERM USED for inmates who wield influence or take advantage in one way or another of other prisoners for their own selfish benefit. Human rats, parasites, leeches, vermin, sharks, piranha, call them what you will, no prison is without at least a few, and Klong Prem was no exception. In Bombat Section 4, we suffered the little rodent Lek Pathan, who eventually stole some poisoned cheese and got his just deserts, but there were others.

In Section 2 at The Prem, we had a fiendish rogue – a German fellow whom I've named Mikhail Rhonald – who was a rather more sinister influence than even Lek had been, and he caused people serious problems, me included, after he had established himself as the kingpin.

Rhonald had been convicted, along with his case partner, let's call him Wolfgang, and sentenced to 33 years' imprisonment (just a couple of years short of a sentence that would have required the maximum-security confinement of Bangkwang) for blackmail and extortion. His vast experience as a con-man and swindler, together with an ample supply of ready cash, made it a relatively simple matter for him to start building himself a position of strength and influence almost as soon as he arrived at The Prem. He set himself up with one of the best houses in the garden by buying out the then owner and then had it furnished with all manner of luxury items that he was happy to hand over the inflated price to have installed: a cane table and chairs; a matching sofa with cushions; a few bookshelves; and cabinets with locks on the doors. He even had cane blinds placed over the openings and hung a couple of paintings on the thatch walls – a veritable home away from home. But he knew that the appearance of wealth impresses your average Thai more than anything else. To attract the interest of those he wanted to use, all he had to do was fabricate that image and he was halfway there.

Very early in the game, he made a point of getting very friendly with the building chief. This was simply achieved by having a confederate on the outside meet the chief and take him to dinner one night at one of the better restaurants in Bangkok, during which he was propositioned and given a wad of cash, as well the delicate hand of a beautiful young maiden with whom he could do as he pleased for the following few hours.

From that moment on, and as long as he kept the crocodiles adequately fed, Rhonald could do no wrong. He was often seen sitting with the chief at his desk drinking coffee and talking as if they had been friends for ages. He sounded out the section guards one by one and became very friendly with most of them, too. It was simply a matter of reward. Most of the lower-level prison staff had a monthly wage of less than what Rhonald spent on his periodical magazine subscriptions, meaning that it required only a small monthly supplement to their income to have them cleaning his boots.

He was, according to Wolfgang, the product of a reasonably wealthy family and received regular deposits to his bank account in Bangkok from his sister in Germany. The person doing his dirty work on the outside was able to access this account using withdrawal slips that Rhonald would send out from the prison duly signed and with instructions on what to do with the money withdrawn.

He soon arranged to be given access during the day to the main confinement building – it was out of bounds to most of the other inmates at that time – and this allowed him to sell the services of several lady-boys who were regularly brought in from Section 1 to accommodate his customers. He also found out which of the guards already brought drugs into the prison or were willing to do so under his direction and made a mutually beneficial deal with them.

Money was exchanged via his friend on the outside and paid directly into the officers' bank accounts. When they received their payments, they brought the dope in for him and arranged for the movement of the lady-boys between sections. For some of his wealthier inmate clients, the same principle was employed. They arranged for funds to be transferred to his bank account *before* the service or dope was provided, meaning that though Rhonald was paying the guards before receiving the goods, he was in fact using his clients' cash to do it.

He had the building chief appoint him foreigners' mail monitor and foreigners' cell monitor, the latter allowing him to reap a percentage of the sale price of the better-quality cells as they were vacated. He was also put in charge of cell renovations and foreigner inmate placement inside the main building. The result was that those foreign inmates who wanted to move from one cell to another, or those who wanted to reduce the number of occupants sharing their space or to make their cell a little more habitable, would have to pay Rhonald for the privilege and on a cost-plus basis. The building chief and director were happy to oblige, for the lion's share of the proceeds of course, but Rhonald did pretty well out of it, too.

He subscribed to numerous high-calibre magazines and periodicals, such as *Time*, *Forbes*, *Science* and certain medical journals, all of which arrived at the prison addressed to Herr Dokitor, or Herr Professor-Dokitor, M. Rhonald, Apartment 2, 33/2 Ngamwongwan Road, Bangkok. He did this specifically to impress the officials, and although he could barely write English, he passed himself off as a medical doctor and boasted of several other phantom degrees in science and chemistry as well.

Rhonald actually loathed Thais, considering them to be not much further up the evolutionary ladder than chimpanzees. He often said as much when he watched them squatting on their haunches around their bowls of rice and stinking fish soup at meal times, chattering simultaneously. But even though he despised them, he knew their psychological make-up – or thought he did – and was fully aware that a significant percentage of the population were in awe of doctors. Someone who was perceived to have a high level of education or wealth could also quite easily influence the lower classes – into which category fell the majority of Thai prison officials – and he took full advantage of this. He was also very familiar with their passion for money and young pussy and knew precisely how to use these infatuations to suit his own evil ends.

He managed to convince the doctor at the hospital that he had been a professor of English, even though his knowledge of the language was nothing more than rudimentary. Then, with the help of the building chief in Section 2, he was granted permission to teach English to the nurses there, a cunning manoeuvre that effectively allowed him to wander around the hospital at will. However, this seemingly unselfish and generous offer to donate his time was nothing more than a front that he used very successfully to gain access to some of the fresh young olive-toned, and often very accommodating, nurses and to the prisoner trusty who was in charge of the dispensary. Using his powers of persuasion and credits to the trusty's prison account, he managed to get his hands on a regular supply of Temgesic tablets – a synthetic morphine – which he then sold in Section 2 for 100 baht each. Just 20 tablets per day at that price would net him a worthwhile reward for the time he spent at the hospital.

After a short time in residence, he had become very influential, working with some of the guards to intimidate selected prisoners and to blackmail others into doing his bidding or conforming to his dictates. Junkies who bought their dope through his channels were rarely caught using it or with it in their possession. However, those who didn't were a target, and using information given to him by his protected spies, he made himself even more popular with the building chief by informing on them so that the chief could catch these transgressors in the act. In so doing, he earned himself some credits by having them charged or some additional income if the case was dropped in favour of a cash settlement. The latter option was often the most acceptable to those who could afford it, because even a small inside drug conviction would result in six months' solitary confinement with only leg chains for company and cost the offenders an additional two years in the can. It would also affect their eligibility for reduction of their sentence come amnesty time.

Rhonald often used his outside contact to dig into the private lives of the guards and trick them into revealing their financial situation. Once he knew a guard was in financial deep water, he would offer a life jacket, knowing full well that if he helped to relieve the burden, he had found himself another confederate.

It was about two and a half years after I had been transferred to The Prem that one of my cellmates – another German whom I'm naming Reinhard – and I began to have a lot of trouble with Rhonald. This started to get quite serious during May when we confronted a dilemma that could have caused us both a lot of grief if it had been left unchallenged.

Reinhard and I shared a cell in the main confinement building at night, and I usually shared space in his house in the garden during the day. The previous owner – a fellow countryman – had taken Reinhard in almost as soon as he arrived and, because he was stony broke, had supported him with essentials until he started to receive the monthly embassy allowance. Not too long after that the owner was released and transferred the house registration to Reinhard at no cost to him.

A couple of months later, Reinhard established what became known as the 'German Library'. Using strips of plywood that he'd managed to scavenge, he constructed several bookshelves along one wall of the shelter. He then arranged for all of the German-language books and magazines that were already in the section, as well as those that were subsequently received from the outside, to be kept in this library and made available to anyone who wanted to borrow them. He didn't keep anything in any other language, because the other library catered for those quite adequately already.

Not too long after the library was set up, we both noticed that books were being taken out and brought back the same day. I mean, inmates would come in and take a 300 or so page book and then bring it back a couple of hours later. Now, there were not a lot of speed readers in The Prem at that time, and this was just a little bit abnormal, but we became even more suspicious when Chinese, Pakistani, Australian and British men started filing in and taking out German books.

We decided to covertly observe for a couple of days and, noticing some quite strange behaviour, decided to investigate further. Early one morning, before we had our usual morning cup of coffee, we pulled all of the books off the shelves and inspected them thoroughly. To our mutual horror, we found at least ten ounces of heroin in small containers and dozens of papers, plus three hypodermic needles. The papers were slipped between the pages, and the containers and needles were inserted in the back binder or in small compartments that had been cut into the pages of a number of hard-cover books.

Needless to say, we both immediately began having palpitations that surely could have been heard in Pattaya. A conviction for possession of drugs of that quantity was not at all what either of us needed at that rather inopportune moment – is there ever an opportune moment? We were not merely perturbed, we were literally shaking with fear, terrified that a guard or a snitch would come in as we piled the lot onto the table. Neither of us had any doubts about who had set this up.

Rhonald was always out of the confinement building and in the garden very early in the morning, well before any of the others were let out of their cells, unless they were heading to court that day. We knew that for certain because on court days we had to get ready for the bus trip before 6 a.m., and Rhonald was always already in his mansion, sitting in his big cane easy chair with his feet up, like a Gestapo general, sucking on his pipe and drinking coffee whilst reading that morning's *Bangkok Post*. Putting his deliveries for the day in the German books would take just a few minutes and then all he had to do was give the customer the name of the book to collect. It was an extremely iniquitous manoeuvre, because although there was no risk to himself if the dope was discovered by an unfriendly party, it would be impossible for Reinhard or me to convince any inquisitor that we knew nothing about it.

Once we had made sure that we had it all, I bundled it together and walked quickly to the lake in front of the garden and tossed the lot in, rendering it instantly harmless to us and, of course, worthless to Rhonald. We then removed all of the books and put them in the common area and dismantled the bookshelves. The German library was closed.

Later that morning, at around 10 a.m., a positively livid Rhonald came rushing into Reinhard's house. Even his bald patch was scarlet. He wanted to know why the library had been dismantled and where all the books were. When he was told, he became quite hostile and yelled at Reinhard in German. 'You two bastards had better be real careful,' he said before storming off.

About 20 minutes after that, the building chief arrived at the house – the first time he had ever done so since Reinhard had taken it over – and he too was not a bit pleased. He asked Reinhard in Thai why we had done what we had done, and as Reinhard couldn't speak or understand Thai, I explained for him that it was not convenient to continue having the library located in the house because the people walking in and out all day disturbed my work. As I turned to pick up a Thai-language text book from the table to emphasise what I meant, he suddenly lashed out and smacked me across the head with his fist and yelled at me that nothing was ever to be changed in Section 2 without his permission – even though no permission had been sought or given to establish the library in the first place.

Naturally, I was taken completely off guard. It was the very last thing that I expected him to do, and, I might add, it was totally uncalled for. That I didn't retaliate just as suddenly still amazes me, but perhaps sensing that I might, he swivelled round and stormed off, denying me the opportunity, his face turning purple with rage.

The German library was never re-established anywhere, and the books and magazines remained in the common area for as long as I remained at The Prem.

Rhonald continued to be let out of the cells just before dawn and enjoyed having the morning newspapers delivered to his door, even though they were restricted items and none of the other inmates were permitted to have them. However, robbing him and the building chief of the returns on what went into the lake that morning, along with their convenient method of distribution, was not to be forgiven, and it wasn't too long before there was retaliation.

Rhonald seemed to have it in for me well before this library incident, for reasons that I could not even speculate on, other than that Hansel might have had something to do with it. As he was also German, and nothing short of satanic himself, he would have had no compunction in spreading misinformation and employing Rhonald to make waves if he considered it would serve his own spiteful ends. But I barely knew the man initially, and I kept well away from him, realising that he was an influential figure. For the first 15 months of my residence at The Prem, I had never so much as spoken one word to him.

Whatever the reason, he began to target me and became a major disruptive influence as far as my trial was concerned and caused me no end of additional torment that I could have done without.

He initially orchestrated his revenge via his position as the foreigners' mail monitor, which gave him the opportunity to have my mail intercepted. After the stamps had been removed from the outgoing post and the incoming post had been opened to remove anything of value, such as stamps or stationery, he simply destroyed the letters. This went on for quite some time before I discovered what was happening. In the meantime, his treachery reached new heights when, in collusion with one of his lackey guards, he set about trying to have me entrapped with a trafficable quantity of heroin. This heinous little stunt would have had a devastating effect on my fight for vindication in the courts if it had been successful.

The plan was made after he had been informed by one of his junkie customers that there was some disharmony between me and the other inmate who shared my evening accommodation, a Cambodian man named Seth. Reinhard and I shared the cost of his upkeep, providing decent food and other essentials, along with no prison work, in return for his domestic services – washing clothes, cleaning the cell, cooking meals, washing dishes and so on. There *was* some friction between us, due mainly to his becoming a little too complacent with his duties, and we had quarrelled several times. But it was nothing serious.

Rhonald, no doubt sensing that he could take advantage of this discord, approached Seth one morning and propositioned him with a plan whereby they could both get some satisfaction at my expense. He gave Seth 15 silver papers of heroin, along with 1,000 baht in cash, and told him to put the papers in my belongings in the cell that afternoon, promising him an additional 1,000 baht on completion of the task. Seth accepted the assignment and the money, agreeing to do exactly as he had been instructed.

Seth, however, was a whole lot smarter than Rhonald had given him credit for, and within one hour of taking possession of the dope, he had sold it all for 250 baht per paper to Thai junkies, effectively netting himself a cool 3,750 baht, plus the 1,000 baht he received in cash from Rhonald. That beat 2,000 baht any day – there were no flies on Seth.

He didn't mention anything to Reinhard or me, though, and went to the cell that afternoon as usual. The lock-up bell had been sounded earlier than normal that day, no doubt by Rhonald's design, and all inmates were locked up by 4.30 p.m. Roll call was completed quickly, and less than five minutes later a guard – let's call him Tinakorn – along with three others and three trusties, arrived outside my cell. They unlocked the door and ushered the three of us into the corridor. They then told me to go back in and to take everything that belonged to me and put it in the corridor.

After that had been done, Tinakorn watched as the other three guards searched through every item. They then told Reinhard to do the same and searched his belongings, too. Seth in turn got the same treatment. Every single item was checked, and by the time this had been completed, nothing remained in the cell except a small pile of magazines. When they found nothing incriminating in any of our belongings, the three of us were individually searched, but nothing at all of an illegal or restricted nature was found. The guards then went into the cell and searched it thoroughly, including the pile of magazines.

I noticed that Seth was looking uncharacteristically unperturbed by all of this; in fact, a slightly devious little smile caressed his lips on occasion during the proceedings.

Both Reinhard and I, not being privy to Seth's secret, were mystified as to why we would be singled out for such a shakedown. We did not have a reputation for taking or dealing drugs; the whole charade was, therefore, totally out of place. The other prisoners in the section, well aware of this, were watching with keen interest.

When nothing at all was found that could constitute a breach of the rules, Tinakorn, with a worried expression on his face, walked out of the cell and down the corridor to where Rhonald was standing. He spoke to Rhonald for no more than 30 seconds, after which Rhonald hurried off down the stairs, returning a minute or two later. Reinhard, the other three guards and I, along with half of the occupants of the cells nearby, witnessed Rhonald passing something to him. Tinakorn then hurried back to our cell and went inside again.

The magazines were stacked in the corner near the toilet. They had already been searched, but Tinakorn picked several up and began to leaf through them. Replacing them and moving out of the cell, he again instructed two of the trusties to search through them all carefully. Thirty seconds later, one of them found one silver wrapper containing white powder – a paper – slipped in between the pages of one of them, a *National Geographic*, that Tinakorn had opened just minutes before.

'So whose magazine is this?' Tinakorn demanded. Reinhard said truthfully that all of the English-language magazines belonged to him and all the French ones belonged to me. Tinakorn looked crestfallen. He had apparently assumed that I would be reading English; it never occurred to him that I might read French, too. Nevertheless, it had gone too far for him to turn back, and, though not at all pleased with this outcome, he ordered Reinhard to follow him to the office on the ground floor. I wasn't invited, but I tagged along anyway.

When the content of the paper was field tested and found to be heroin, I began to scream at the guards in Thai, 'Fit-up! Frame-up! This is a deliberate set-up! What the hell are you bastards on about?'

Though all other inmates had been locked up for the night, Rhonald was still standing there with the guards. He had a wicked smirk on his face. Knowing that none of the lackeys present could speak or understand English well, he said to me, 'These idiots can't do any fucking thing right, can they? Next time I'll do it myself.'

Things had obviously not gone quite as he had planned. Being in possession of one paper was an offence, to be sure, but a relatively minor one. Being in possession of 15 papers would constitute drug dealing, which was a serious crime with serious consequences.

'I know who put you up to this, Tinakorn. I saw you put that paper in that magazine, and I saw this asshole, Rhonald, give it you!' Pointing to Rhonald's face, I bellowed, 'I'm going to see to it that you pay for this, you mongrel.' I made a move towards him, fully intending to flatten him. Tinakorn intervened, threatening me with his baton, and ordered the trusties to return me to my cell. I went with them under protest, all the while yelling to the other inmates as I passed their cells that this was a set-up and that Rhonald was behind it. Several of them didn't need convincing; they had seen Rhonald palm the paper to Tinakorn with their own eyes and, in any case, were fully acquainted with his shenanigans.

Reinhard was taken back to our cell, ordered to pick up his small towelling mat and then escorted to a filthy cell on the Thai side of the building, almost directly opposite the one he had shared with Seth and me, where he was locked up in solitary confinement. After moving our belongings, as well as what remained of Reinhard's, back into our cell, Seth and I were locked in for the night. It was then, as we were putting everything back in order, that Seth confessed what he had done that day, explaining what Rhonald had tried to get him to do and how he had profited handsomely from his double-cross. He was a little concerned that Rhonald would take some form of revenge against him for his sleight-of-hand trick but figured that he would worry about that when, and if, that time came. It didn't. Rhonald must have realised that to start playing games with the natives could backfire disastrously, which in Seth's case it surely would have.

At around 10 p.m. that evening, two of the three guards who had accompanied Tinakorn during the search came to my cell and spoke to me at length. They told me that they had seen Rhonald give the paper to Tinakorn and knew that the whole episode had been staged and was grossly unfair. One gave me his name and position and also wrote down the names of the other two officers who were present, promising to make a report to the building chief the next day.

The following morning, soon after the rest of us had been let out for the day, Matti Anderson, one of Rhonald's collaborators, went to talk to Reinhard through the bars of his still locked cell door. 'Be smart, Reinhard. Change your story. Say that the magazines belong to Sly, and Rhonald will fix it with the building chief that Sly takes the rap and you get released.'

Reinhard's response was intense and laced with contempt. Barely able to control himself, he screamed at Anderson, 'Fuck off, you stinking fucking faggot! I'm going to get you and that cretin Rhonald when I get out of here, you can count on that. You have fucked with me once too often. I won't be making any false statements about Sly or anyone else. I'll be making real ones about you and that devil. Now get the hell out of my face.' Narrowly escaping the indignity of having to wipe from his face a dollop of spit, which had followed closely behind Reinhard's last words, Matti hurried away.

When the building chief arrived for work that morning, I went to see him and complained that this was a deliberate attempt by Rhonald and Tinakorn to have me charged with possession of a trafficable quantity of heroin. I repeated what Seth had told me, omitting the fact that he had sold the heroin, telling him instead that he had thrown it in the lake because he didn't want to be caught with it in his possession. Seth, of course, corroborated that slightly modified version of the truth very convincingly.

The building chief initially brushed off the accusations and tried to protect both Rhonald and Tinakorn, but after three weeks of constant complaints from all directions, including the German and British embassies – as a result of the details being provided to them by me and Reinhard – he was forced to listen. Written statements by the guards who had witnessed the whole thing, together with letters sent to the director by various inmates, also contributed to his change of heart.

Reinhard and I were brought to his office, where he proceeded to rationalise his decision to drop the matter. 'I have had tests done on the contents of the paper that was discovered in your cell,' he said. 'It has been ascertained that the substance was not heroin after all, but a powdered Tamchai tablet [Tamchai is a Thai pick-me-up, with a heavy dose of caffeine]. No charge will be laid, and you, Reinhard, are to be released from solitary confinement with immediate effect.'

Reinhard knew full well that what was in the paper had tested positive as a narcotic. After all, Rhonald would hardly have been wasting his time peddling Tamchai tablets. But rather than make a fuss and risk the chief changing his mind, he swallowed his disgust and mumbled a weary expression of humble gratitude followed by a request for permission to be transferred to the hospital for a few days.

Tinakorn was transferred from Section 2 that same morning and punished with a two-month stint of tower duty. He was later transferred to Bangkwang prison, where I was unfortunately destined to come into contact with him again.

The guards who had supported me and Reinhard told us later that Tinakorn had also earned himself a four-year suspension of promotion, which would surely mean that I had made an enemy who would hold his grudge for ever.

It was all just another charade, a hasty attempt at damage limitation, because the whole affair was ballooning out of control. If it had been allowed to go much further, it could have caused more senior officials to become involved – a devolopment best avoided. The principal outcome of all this manoeuvring was that the building chief could now be seen to have the matter in hand and to have taken the appropriate remedial action, but it didn't improve his opinion of me or Reinhard one bit, and it also made Rhonald even more determined to make things difficult for us both.

\*\*\*

During his three weeks in solitary, Reinhard became quite ill with severe diarrhoea and stomach pain, accompanied by fever. Whether or not this was a result of his food being deliberately contaminated is not known for sure, but it certainly was a possibility. He made requests to see the prison doctor, but they were ignored. It soon became evident that Rhonald, being a 'Dokitor' and all, and as such in charge of the requests for hospital visits, was not including his name on the hospital list that had to be submitted to the chief. When I discovered this, I challenged him in the presence of several other inmates and advised him to include Reinhard's name or be reported to the director. He added Reinhard to the list, but it made little difference, and Reinhard remained where he was for the duration of his solitary confinement. By the time he was released, he was in pretty bad shape, and it was only then that he was granted permission to see the doctor.

Rhonald, however, was not to be beaten. When it became evident that Reinhard wasn't going to cooperate with him, he began to attempt to discredit us and cause friction between us and the other inmates, particularly the junkies who relied on Rhonald for their fixes. I subsequently had a few minor skirmishes with some of them, but when I threatened exposure of their names and habits to the director, they backed off. They were more afraid of being randomly dragged up before the big boss without a minute's notice and made to piss in a little bottle than they were of Rhonald. With the spotlight already on him, and his valued lackey Tinakorn gone, his power had been eroded just a little, and I planned to continue chipping away at it at every opportunity. That was a very dangerous undertaking, no question about it, but certainly no more dangerous than doing nothing and allowing him to remain the section's little Hitler.

# CHAPTER 14

‖‖‖‖‖‖‖‖‖‖‖‖‖‖‖‖‖‖‖‖‖‖‖‖‖‖‖‖‖‖‖‖‖‖‖‖‖‖‖‖‖‖‖‖‖‖‖‖‖‖‖‖‖‖‖‖‖‖‖‖‖‖‖‖‖‖‖‖‖‖‖‖‖‖‖‖‖‖‖‖‖‖‖‖‖‖‖‖‖

# The Root of All Evil

VERY SHORTLY AFTER HIS EXPERIENCE WITH THE DRUG PLANT IN our cell and his subsequent three-week stint in solitary, Reinhard was again to witness the seemingly bottomless depths of perversity that he was rapidly learning were endemic in Thailand's penal and judicial system. On the day of his release from solitary, he had been transferred to the prison hospital suffering from a severe stomach disorder and was admitted to a ward along with a number of other patients, most of whom he discovered shortly thereafter were either dying from third-stage AIDS or suffering from TB or malaria, some with the lot. All of them with the exception of Reinhard, regardless of their condition, had heavy chains fitted to their legs – those that had adorned his ankles had been removed on the orders of the building chief after his release from isolation.

This extreme precaution, had been initiated some time before because an Australian man, after meticulous planning, had managed to escape over the outside prison wall, and remained at large long enough to take the first available plane out of the country as a free man. The appropriate course of action for this impertinence, as the Thais saw it, was to shackle every Australian in the entire prison with heavy chains and to leave them like that for an indefinite period, and of course, due to its close proximity to the perimeter prison wall, all patients at the hospital had to be similarly tethered.

Reinhard had been there for just a couple of days when he realised that the trusties in charge of the wards at night were, to a man, sadistic barbarians who treated all of the Thai and other Asian patients with extreme cruelty and brutality at every opportunity. As soon as the doctors and nurses went off duty each day, they would begin to torment and assault those not able or too weak to defend themselves. Reinhard, though disturbed when he saw what was going on, was unable to do a lot to prevent it. He was terribly ill himself and in no condition to take on a crusade to save anyone else.

It came to a head, though, on the first Saturday night of his stay. Two men in his ward, both suffering from full-blown AIDS and TB, were having a lot of difficulty breathing, and when they did manage a breath a very disturbing noise emanated from them. One of the trusties whose duty it was to stay in the room at night, kept yelling at these two patients to shut up and stop making such a terrible din; he wanted to sleep, and the noise was preventing him from doing so. Eventually becoming very irritated, he smacked both on the head several times with his stick. When that proved to be an inadequate remedy, he took a roll of wide sticking plaster and placed several strips across their mouths, all the time abusing them and telling them to die and be done with it.

Reinhard, feeling a little more like living himself by this time, got off his bed and, pushing the trusty away from the men, removed the gags. The trusty summoned the night guard and reported Reinhard for attacking him. Alhough Reinhard tried to tell the guard what had just happened, he was ignored and taken from the ward and isolated in another small cell. The following morning, he watched as the two patients were carried out of the ward, their eyes bulging from their sockets like ping-pong balls and as lifeless as bricks. Less than an hour later, before the doctors and nurses had arrived, he was transferred back to Section 2.

* * *

Reinhard had every reason to be very cranky with Mikhail Rhonald. His being sentenced to nine years in prison for fraudulently uttering traveller's cheques and travelling under a false passport was, in essence, the result of a premeditated Rhonald conspiracy.

Reinhard was not really a bad person; he was a desperate person, and it was this desperation that had caused him to do something that he would otherwise have never dreamed of doing. He had been living in Manila for many years with his Filipino wife and three children, and worked for a tourist hotel located near the Mount Pinatubo volcano. As fate would have it, the volcano erupted, and the hotel suspended operation, leaving him without an income.

Having ample savings to fall back on, he wasn't terribly concerned at first. However, shortly after his suspension he was involved in a serious car accident, suffering kidney damage as well as head injuries, and he lapsed into a coma for several months. He finally recovered enough to go home, but his doctors advised him that it would be at least a year before he could resume work. The hospital bills and family expenses during this rehabilitation period left him in a serious financial dilemma, and his attempts to find work once he was mobile again were not successful.

Desperate people do reckless things. The situation quickly deteriorated, and he was literally scraping at the bottom of the barrel when he was approached by an acquaintance, Wolfgang Worz, with a proposition to make good money, quickly and with little effort. The plan was simple: all he had to do was take an all-expenses-paid trip to Bangkok, where he would meet up with a German woman called Michaela Blum. He would be given a number of fraudulent traveller's cheques, and his assignment was to cash them and hand over the proceeds. He would receive 10 per cent of the face value of each cheque he passed, and he would pass at least five each day for a period of ten days, then he would return to Manila. Reinhard accepted the assignment.

He arrived in Bangkok using the passport he had been given by Worz before he left Manila. It was in the name of an Austrian, Erich Klug, but contained a photo of Reinhard. Michaela Blum was waiting for him at the airport. He spent a comfortable night alone at the hotel she delivered him to, and at around 11 a.m. the following morning Blum returned and handed him four Bank of America traveller's cheques, each worth US$500. He was also given a purchase receipt and told to sign them all in the name of Klug, exactly as he had signed the passport.

Blum then accompanied him to a bank and instructed him to cash one of the cheques. He did so without incident, then repeated the performance at another bank nearby, which is when things started to go wrong. The bank officials evidently smelled a rat and tried to delay him until the police arrived. He made a hasty exit and returned to Blum's car. Realising that their mistake had been approaching two banks in the same area in short succession, they planned to change tack after a new passport and receipt had been received from Manila.

The following day, Blum came to Reinhard's room to work on a new strategy while they waited for DHL to deliver the new documents. Fifteen minutes after she arrived, there was a knock on the door, and Reinhard opened it to find six Thai police officers and two Westerners, who introduced themselves as an American Secret Service agent and an American Express employee. The Thai police then apprehended them both and conducted a search of the room, finding the used airline ticket in the name of Klug in Reinhard's suitcase and the two remaining traveller's cheques that Reinhard had signed the previous day, along with one DHL receipt in Blum's name, in her purse. On intercepting the DHL parcel, the police found two passports that Blum had apparently acquired since returning to Bangkok and was sending to Worz for modification.

Later, at the house where Blum was staying, they found US$10,000 worth of fraudulent traveller's cheques and numerous purchase receipts, along with a passport sporting a photograph of her under a different name. Both suspects were then taken to a police station, where they were held for several days while their statements were taken, translated into Thai and finally signed in the presence of a consul from the German Embassy.

Mikhail Ringl, another member of the gang, arrived in Bangkok soon after and was arrested with Blum's help. In his possession was one Turkish passport that had a photo of Reinhard affixed but no signature. They also found US$4,300 worth of dodgy Visa traveller's cheques with matching unsigned purchase receipts.

Eventually, after the standard several months of nonsense, the accused faced the courts. By that time, Reinhard was being detained at The Prem. He accepted the fact that he had been caught almost red-handed, and although he had none of the evidence, apart from the airline ticket, actually in his possession when he was arrested, he decided to plead guilty and take his punishment undisputed, reasoning that his signed confession was unchallengeable because the German consul had been witness to it. Both Blum and Ringl, however, decided that they would fight the case against them.

It was during the first couple of months of the prosecution case that Mikhail Rhonald approached Reinhard and suggested that as he was going to plead guilty, it would be in his best interests if he simply put everything down on paper and request that he be sentenced immediately. Rhonald assured him that if he did this, the court would be lenient, and he would get no more than three years, calculated from the day of his arrest, and would probably be released in two.

Reinhard agreed, and Rhonald, with the assistance of one of his Thai hangers-on, prepared the document for a 4,000-baht fee and had it typed up in Thai ready for submission to the court. When completed, Reinhard was called to the guard's office to check that it said what he wanted it to say before signing it. As he could not speak Thai, he asked three of the foreign inmates who did to accompany him to the office to witness the proceedings. Although I wasn't too well acquainted with him at that stage, I was one of them.

A Thai prisoner read the document out loud, first in Thai and then translated into English. I was the only foreigner present who was able to actually read Thai, and I inspected the two-page document and confirmed that what had been read was what was represented in the text. Reinhard signed the original and one copy, witnessed by the garden officer and the deputy building chief. Rhonald then told Reinhard that both copies of the document had to be sent to the court so that the next time he appeared it would already be there on file.

Several months later, when the accused were at court to hear the verdict, Reinhard received the shock of his life. Though Blum and Ringl both had legal representation, Reinhard had neither lawyer nor translator, and up to that point had no idea at all what had been said during the trial. But having no reason to be suspicious, he believed that his compatriot Rhonald had handled things in his favour.

The documents he had signed were produced and read by the judge. Several minutes later, Reinhard was told that he had been sentenced to nine years in prison, that he had pleaded guilty to all of the offences himself and had exonerated the others of any involvement in the crimes. He hadn't realised until it was too late that the documents sent in by Rhonald now comprised three pages not two.

Gobsmacked, he tried vainly to object, saying in English that he had plead guilty only to being in possession of the two cheques and the one passport, but he was silenced by the judge, and the proceedings were finalised. Blum and Ringl were released that same day.

When Reinhard confronted Rhonald in the presence of several other inmates the following morning, Rhonald's arrogant response was, 'Tough luck, sucker.' I was adamant, when Reinhard asked me later, that there was no mention whatsoever in those original documents of an all-encompassing acceptance of guilt or anything to exonerate his co-accused.

As soon as he could, and with my help, Reinhard appealed to the court to re-evaluate the case, explaining that he had been tricked. He expected to be taken back to the court, with me to assist him as a translator, so he could put the record straight, but he waited for six months and heard nothing. He then wrote to the court to ask when the appeal would be heard but received no response. About 12 months after he was sentenced, I arranged, with some outside help, to find out exactly when his case would be brought before the Appeal Court. We were both once again stunned to be informed that the appeal had been withdrawn, supposedly at Reinhard's request, about a week after he had submitted it. As a result, there remained no possible avenue for redress open to him.

It became painfully obvious that money had changed hands: to Rhonald, for preparing the false document, and to the arresting police, to encourage them to change their story. Reinhard repeatedly requested a copy of the case file from the court during the following years of his detention but all requests were ignored, and to this day he still has no idea what they contained. A royal amnesty reduced his sentence to four years, and he returned to Manila a wiser, but very ill man, vowing never to return to the Land of Smiles.

It was just two weeks after Reinhard had experienced the unbelievable neglect, inefficiency, brutality and corruption while he was trying to stay alive at the hospital that the simmering pot boiled over in Section 2.

The mail situation had become intolerable. Neither Reinhard nor I were now receiving any mail at all, and none of the mail we were sending was getting out of the prison, apart from what was being channelled for me via a Thai conduit. Complaining to the building chief was a waste of energy without evidence to back up the accusations, but something had to be done urgently. My case depended very heavily on my ability to communicate with Brent and my lawyer and various other contacts on the outside and in the UK, and though I had made the arrangement to send some of my post outside the normal channels some time before, it was not possible to use this method exclusively.

Matti Anderson was a Swiss national from Geneva, travelling under that assumed name, which appeared on the fake Irish passport that he was using when he was arrested.

He was a grotesque slob of a man, about five-foot-six and around ninety kilograms in weight, most of which was situated around his gut, hips and backside. His chest – supported by narrow shoulders that were permanently bent forward and slightly stooped – was small and lacked masculine definition. The two protruding blobs of sagging mammary fat certainly emphasised his repulsive appearance. His upper torso sloped from his collar bone to his stomach and hips, and then turned to slope sharply in the opposite direction just below the navel. Although he, of course, must have had a chin, it was almost undetectable in the fold of fat that seemed to start just below his lower lip and slope almost without sign of the existence of a neck to join his torso at the collar bone. He kept his head shaved completely bald and polished to a shine with oil or wax, covering part of it with a small artist's beret, usually slightly tilted towards the front and to one side. His legs were quite thick at the top but tapered from the thigh to the ankles, displaying very little evidence of calf muscles or knee joints. All in all, he was a very oddly shaped person who looked like a combination of a spinning top and a bowling pin joined at the middle.

Matti spent much of his time smoking a pipe, or at least with one hanging from his mouth. Whether this was because he enjoyed smoking or was using his pipe as a shield to hide behind – as psychologists might suggest – is debatable. Whatever the case, he liked to think he was an artist and donned all the stereotypical regalia: the silk open-necked shirts, the billowing silk pyjama-type trousers, the beret, the slippers and so on. Though no Michelangelo, he thought he was exceptionally talented, and, in fact, he could paint a reasonable picture, often indulging his narcissism in his spare time. One thing about Matti that no one could argue about, however, was that he was as camp as a row of tents. He simply oozed homosexuality. His passion for the game that he evidently enjoyed playing so much with very young boys was the reason he was resident at The Prem.

Mikhail Rhonald, for reasons that are not entirely clear, recruited Matti to be a member of his team: maybe it was a marriage of convenience; maybe it was because he was fluent in several languages, including French, English, Dutch and German, and was useful to Rhonald. Whatever the reason, they were closely allied. Matti shared Rhonald's house in the garden, and although he did not share his cell at night, he did have one of the refurbished cells nearby. Rhonald and Matti also shared a couple of effeminate young Thai boys, whom Rhonald had purchased and deliberately got hooked on heroin. His reason – characteristic of his totally selfish personality – was simply to make them dependent on him and consequently under his control. They had no money of their own, and the daily fixes and food he provided them with were their recompense for the daily services that they had to endure, or enjoy, whatever the case might have been.

Little did Rhonald or Matti know, however, that both of these toy boys were also trading their favours for small amounts of heroin with other inmates when Rhonald and Matti weren't around to keep an eye on them. One of their regular providers was an Australian man who spent a little time at least once or twice each week with one or both of them. That in itself was not especially significant, but the fact that, unbeknownst to all but a very few, the Australian was HIV positive and refused to use condoms was. After Rhonald was released from Klong Prem and returned to Germany under transfer, at least one of those boys died from AIDS-related complications. Accordingly, it is quite possible that either Rhonald or Matti, or even both, are now reaping the harvest of the seeds they had sown, a harvest that they would both surely richly deserve.

Wolfgang, although Rhonald's case partner, had no time for him at all. He had not forgiven Rhonald for the deception that had resulted in their mutual arrest and imprisonment, and was often heard to declare that one day he would even the score, though he would never elaborate on the actual circumstances or nature of this deception. Wolfgang, however, was a reasonably decent sort of fellow. He kept mainly to himself, didn't do drugs, didn't bother anyone, was friendly and congenial to most of the other inmates, and was on good terms with me and Reinhard. He was also as disgusted as most of the other non-junkie inmates with Rhonald's failed attempt to railroad my case and to have me lumbered with an inside charge of drug possession and trading. It is not surprising, in that case, that he was eager to participate when I approached him and asked him for assistance in getting evidence against Rhonald for mail interception and theft so that I could force the building chief to take some action.

In his position as foreigners' mail monitor, Rhonald had recruited Matti as his assistant and mail censor, supposedly because of his multilingual talents. In hindsight, it was not long after his appointment that the mail troubles began in Section 2, and Reinhard and I were not the only inmates to experience the irritation and inconvenience, not to mention problems, that were caused when mail didn't get through. Many of the others, particularly the Africans, also regularly complained that their mail went astray or arrived opened and with items missing.

Between the three of us – Wolfgang, Reinhard and me – we devised a plan to catch the thieves in the act and shortly after enlisted two cooperative and reasonably intelligent but inconspicuous-looking Thai inmates as our deputies. Both Thais worked as domestic help for several of the foreigners and already had passes for the garden area – as such, they could enter without restriction. I reasoned that because they were familiar faces there they would be less likely to be noticed while putting our strategy into gear.

The plan was simple enough: we would all take turns unobtrusively watching and monitoring the movements of the three suspects, Rhonald, Matti and a Thai inmate named Jackapoo who helped them in the office. After four days of observation, we were sure that we had sufficient evidence to spring the trap and force the building chief to take the germane action.

It was during the latter hours of the fourth day that the five of us met in front of the building chief's office with what we believed was the proof needed to push the issue right out in the open and have Rhonald transferred from the section. Each of us had seen Matti taking letters each day from the office and locking them in a cabinet inside Rhonald's house, and the two Thais confirmed that they had both witnessed him putting quite a large pile of letters into the locker just an hour or so earlier that afternoon.

I went directly into the building chief's office without knocking and made a verbal complaint, insisting that the locker be searched immediately. Typically, and not entirely unexpectedly, the chief began to berate and threaten me, and told me to leave and not come back. I stood my ground, refusing to budge until my complaints were taken seriously and something was done. My insolence raised more than a little blood to the fat-bloated jowls shaking in rage and contempt before me, but I didn't give a shit.

One of the Nigerians – let's call him Ken – who had also been affected, heard the threats and abuse being directed at me, and ran into the garden gibbering in high octave and looking very much like he could quite easily blow the house down. Within no more than two minutes, he returned with a number of white foreigners and at least fifty of the giant Africans, all yelling and stomping their feet and clapping their hands. I called it the 'Klong Prem War Dance'. It had happened before and had elicited similar results as it was destined to do that day.

There ensued a full-scale and very truculent confrontation with the chief, who was by this time visibly unnerved. With no more than ten guards in the near proximity, there would have been very little he could have done if he'd allowed the situation to escalate into violence. These men were angry and getting angrier by the minute, and the way the Africans in particular were warming up to the possibility of an all-out battle meant there was little he could do other than to try to quell the unrest by yielding to the pressure. He ordered one of the guards to go with me, Wolfgang, Reinhard and several of the other irate protesters to check the locker and then to bring Rhonald and Matti back to his office. Had he shit in his pants? Well there was no way to be certain, but he refused to budge from his seat.

Both Rhonald and Matti were sitting in their house when we arrived and were shocked that they were being ordered to open the locker in front of all of these mere mortals. 'Fuck off. Go and see the chief,' Rhonald yelled. 'What do you think you're doing ordering me around? I'll have . . .'

He didn't get the chance to finish. All of the agitators were yelling at him in unison, 'Open the fucking locker, shit-head, or else we'll open you.'

Now, being what he considered to be a very intelligent person, Rhonald realised that this was probably not an overly congenial exchange, and wishing to avoid the inconvenience of having to replace his intestines himself, being as how he was the only 'dokitor' in the house and all, he reluctantly withdrew a key from his pocket and pulled the door to the cabinet open.

The guard pulled out a handful of envelopes, seven of which were letters that had been posted that morning by Nigerian inmates to their families back home. All of them had the stamps removed. Five of the letters were incoming mail for me, one of them from Brent and another from Jennie, one of the girls who had been raped by the 'enforcers of the law' at the lock-up on the second night of my detention all those months before and with whom I had been communicating since my transfer to The Prem. That letter referred to several other mailings from her, which she said had included various items of stationery and lists of contacts in the UK. I had never received them. Two letters that I had posted that morning were there too, slit open and minus the stamps. There were at least six other incoming letters addressed to other inmates, and they too had all been opened.

With evidence in hand, we went back to the chief's office with Rhonald in tow. Reinhard and I listened in astonishment as Rhonald began to explain to him that my mail was being intercepted because it contained references to drug deals and accusations against the chief medical doctor at the hospital, along with numerous other incriminating matters, and that he intended to send them all to the Thai police. He neglected to enlighten those present, however, as to who had given him the authority to intercept and confiscate other people's mail – a crime that merits a heavy penalty in most countries, including Thailand. Almost as inconceivable, though, the chief appeared to believe him.

I wasn't going to stand and listen to this nonsense. Determined to expose Rhonald, I immediately insisted on having all of my mail translated to Thai right there and then in front of the 60 or more witnesses. One of the Thai inmates could read a little English, and he did a reasonably accurate job. But even after it was obvious that nothing conspiratorial or illegal in nature was included in the contents, Rhonald still insisted that there was suspicion of a hidden agenda. He refused to answer any queries from the crowd in relation to the other mail that had been discovered in his locker.

I remained insistent and with the continued support of the men behind me, who were growing more hostile, asked the chief to call in one of the English-speaking guards to do the translations accurately and in writing. Squirming in his no-doubt increasingly damp underwear, the chief called in an officer from an adjoining section. His name was

Tawichat, a reasonably well-educated man who could speak and write English fluently. He didn't know me, Rhonald or Matti, or any of the other white inmates who were standing in and around the small office, nor did he know any of the Africans. He was asked by the building chief, without being given the reason for the request, to do a complete and impartial translation of all of my letters and to submit the written report to him personally. Then the party was over, at least for the present, and the crowd dispersed, no doubt much to the relief of the chief.

The following day, Tawichat came back to Section 2, where he sought me out and talked to me privately. Not being privy to the circumstances surrounding the disturbance, he was puzzled, because all of the letters that he had translated were quite clearly of a non-offensive and personal nature and contained nothing that could be considered of interest to the Corrections Department. I then explained the situation in detail, giving names of other inmates in Section 2 who had been similarly affected by Rhonald and Matti. Tawichat checked with several of them and then made his report, sending one copy to the Section 2 building chief and another copy to the prison director.

That same day, Rhonald and Matti were taken off the mail desk and allowed no further contact with it, other than to submit their own outgoing and to collect their own incoming mail. Another chip had been honed from the Rhonald block of power, and I vowed to continue the offensive.

I personally didn't give a damn about the junkies or the heroin trade inside the prison, as long as it never in any way interfered with or influenced my own day-to-day business. I could have at any time named at least 50 inmates who relied on Rhonald for their fix but had never considered doing so. If they wanted to turn themselves into cabbage, that was their own affair; but if they screwed around with me, there would be retaliation. Rhonald was learning this the hard way.

There was also a recommendation in Tawichat's report that Rhonald be transferred to another section and disciplined for his thuggery. However, remaining true to form, he had averted this repercussion – perhaps another dinner for two at the Shangri-La Hotel, with the building chief of Section 2 the guest of honour and a pretty young paramour with a thick envelope the hostess.

Even so, Rhonald was losing his control. His influence was being eroded, and it was costing him dearly to keep his little underworld functioning. The building chief had that day shown his true colours and could not be relied on to save him when the chips were down. But what else could he have done? He knew the score. Along with all of the other officers in the loop, he didn't give a hoot in hell about Rhonald as a person. He was only a stupid farang criminal after all and just another cow to be milked. They played his game and allowed him to continue to deceive himself with the belief that he was untouchable, but heaven help him if ever a situation developed where it became them or him.

Rhonald also began to realise that the minute he stopped feeding these hungry rodents whom he believed he had tamed and trained, and with whom he shared a warren – the warren he had dug himself – they would turn on him and eat his conniving arse off. He now had no choice: keep them fed or be fed on.

This time his prevaricating mouth had saved him – yet again. But maybe his luck was running out.

# CHAPTER 15

‖‖‖‖‖‖‖‖‖‖‖‖‖‖‖‖‖‖‖‖‖‖‖‖‖‖‖‖‖‖‖‖‖‖‖‖‖‖‖‖‖‖‖‖‖‖‖‖‖‖‖‖‖‖‖‖‖‖‖‖‖‖‖‖‖‖‖‖‖

# Snakes and Ladders

THE CASE FOR MY DEFENCE BEGAN A BIT MORE THAN ONE YEAR
after my arrest, though no sooner had it begun than it was adjourned
– something that was to happen regularly. This was mainly because the
lawyer Jaidow had appointed was an incompetent fool and because
of the difficulties of arranging witnesses and evidence from inside
a Thai prison. The only contact I had with the outside was through
visitors and mail, and the visit area, apart from having a two-metre
space between the fences that separated the visitor from the inmate,
was almost always crammed with hundreds of people straining their
vocal chords to be heard.

Though at that time I was able to receive visitors any weekday except
holidays, there were very few who made the effort. Om was one of the
exceptions, and she always came to see me at least once each week.
The burden of chasing around, talking to prospective witnesses and
tracking down evidence had by that time fallen almost exclusively on
her shoulders. Even though she had to work for a living, she managed
to handle it pretty well. Writing to the lawyer, however, was a waste
of ink and stamps. He wasn't particularly well versed in English, and
even when I wrote in Thai he never responded.

With the help of another inmate, whom I'm going to call John Lewis – an African American of about 45 who was fluent in several languages, including spoken and written Thai – I translated all of the court transcripts relating to the prosecution case as I received them after each hearing, and we were both amazed at the amount of fabrication and perjury that they revealed.

During that period, I wrote to the lawyer before each hearing, detailing the inconsistencies and obvious lies in the previous testimony, but because he was either too lazy or too afraid to take the risk of showing the police witnesses to be bullshitting, he almost completely ignored what I pointed out and asked him to concentrate on during his cross-examinations.

He had, in fact, been a constant pain in my arse from day one, and, as far as I was concerned, he was making a right cock-up of his rebuttals. Jaidow gave him a retainer of 250,000 baht before the trial started, but, despite that, every time we went to court he would ask for more – 30,000 for this, 50,000 for that. He told us very little about what was happening during the proceedings, and, apart from briefings by Jaidow after each hearing in the very restrictive atmosphere of the prison visit area, I only discovered what had actually been said after I had translated the transcripts. To make matters worse, he never once came to get instructions or to discuss the case before a hearing date. The best he ever managed was a brief discussion for only a few minutes in the courtroom before the judge came into the room.

A month after the defence case started, he came to see me and demanded an additional two million baht to continue the case. When I didn't agree to give it to him, he spent the next couple of months mucking around and doing more harm than good, and then didn't bother to show up at the court at all. I sought and was granted an adjournment to give me time to find and brief a replacement; however, I had no idea how I was going to go about doing that. The main problem was that I had no money; for all intents and purposes, I was skint.

The last time I saw Jaidow was when she came to visit me on 18 December, just a couple of weeks short of 12 months since my arrest. She told me then that she was going to the British Embassy on the 20th to pick up the papers she needed for the Christmas inside visits – 'contact visits' as they were rather generously referred to – which began on the 21st. I was looking forward to them, as they allowed us more time together and more freedom than usual, and I was fully expecting to be able to spend that first afternoon talking to her in a semblance of comfort while holding her hand over a picnic lunch. She was aware that the embassy inside visit for all British inmates was scheduled for the morning of that same day and assured me that she would be there at 1 p.m. sharp so that we could have the maximum time allowed together, but by closing time at 3 p.m. she still hadn't shown up.

At first, I thought she must have been sick, but when Christmas and New Year passed and she didn't show up for any of the extra visits that were allowed over that period, I started to worry. I even began to suspect that she had become tired of the whole damned business and had done a bunk or had found herself a boyfriend. I had seen that happen often enough with other inmates, but it really didn't seem to fit with Jaidow.

Om came to see me on 7 January, and I asked her to investigate. She returned the following week and told me that she had tried to phone Jaidow on numerous occasions but had not been able to get her. She had then gone to our apartment several times after work, but Jaidow had not been there. She then phoned Jaidow's parents, thinking that she had gone home for the holidays, but her family hadn't seen or heard from her either – at least that's what they said. It was the same with her acquaintances in Phuket.

It then dawned on me that there was good reason to believe that something very sinister might have happened, which really did make me very anxious. I recalled an incident that had happened around seven months before, and it now had me thinking the worst, because it seemed to fit the puzzle pretty well.

On the first day of the trial back in May, during the testimony by the police major who had headed up the arrest team, Jaidow had jumped up in the courtroom and abused him left, right and centre, calling him a liar and perjurer, right there in front of everybody. He was lying through his teeth about a whole host of things relating to my arrest and the circumstances leading up to it. Jaidow, knowing for certain that they were not true, evidently decided, on the spur of the moment, to put the record straight.

To say that the cop was not pleased would be a rather gross understatement. He went purple with suppressed rage. The prosecutor appeared to be equally horrified, and the judge just sat there with his mouth open, staring first at Jaidow as if she had just popped in from another planet, then at the cop, then back at Jaidow again. Everyone else in the courtroom, including me, was stunned at the ferocity of her outburst. I had never seen her so emotional; it just wasn't in her nature.

During a subsequent visit to the prison, she told me that she had been shadowed constantly since that day by two, and sometimes three, men on motorcycles. She confessed then that she was very frightened, but the surveillance didn't last long, and after a couple of weeks she had calmed down and things carried on as usual. However, it wasn't too long after Jaidow had vanished before I discovered that things were not really what they seemed.

Shortly after my arrival at Bombat prison, at the very beginning of my tribulations, I met an American fellow whom I'm going to name Paul Worseluck. Paul had been arrested quite some time before me with 220 grams of heroin that he had tried to ship to Bali in some packages of textile goods, with the intention of selling it to tourists there at a handsome profit in order to extend his stay in the 'City of Angels' (a rather deceptive moniker, all things considered). He confessed to me then that he had developed a craving, bordering on addiction, for the charms of the myriad of pretty young girls with whom he had become intimately acquainted since arriving in Thailand and that the thought of returning to America and his rather less alluring wife brought him out in a cold sweat.

He had initially travelled to Thailand for business purposes, but he was almost finished and knew that he would have to head home in the not-too-distant future. If he didn't, not only would the economic benefits of the trip be lost, but his wife would suspect his ulterior motive, and it would be difficult to convince her that he should repeat the trip. He could get away with a couple more weeks, though, provided the costs were covered without diminishing the business profits. A quick trip to Bali with a few grams of dope seemed like the perfect solution.

Paul was not a particularly bright person, and he had a tendency to talk a little too much about things that would have been better kept to himself. However, because we were in the same section in Bombat and were together at The Prem, we often gas-bagged over a cup of coffee or two. As he usually did most of the talking, I learned quite a lot about him and his family. The truth is that I was not particularly fond of Paul; he just wasn't the type of chap I would normally have bothered with. But, then, things aren't normal when you're stuck in prison.

Nevertheless, my dad had told me many times that listening to someone who talks a lot can often give you an edge that you might not otherwise get, and that guidance has stood me in pretty good stead over the years. So, as I had plenty of time and nowhere to go, I accommodated Paul's passion for it. This, however, was evidently construed by him as us being close friends when, in fact, from my standpoint, we weren't.

It must have been early April, while we were still in Bombat, that Paul first approached me about arranging his acquittal. Of course, I knew that this kind of thing was possible: it was Thailand after all. The only prerequisite was that sufficient cash be handed over to make it possible. Paul told me that he was able and happy to pay for a 'not guilty' fix, together with a guarantee of no appeal by the prosecutor during the Criminal Court stage. I did know someone who could possibly arrange such a fix, and I promised Paul that I would talk to that person and try to find out what could be done and how much it would cost. I didn't mention that it was actually Jaidow's cousin, Surachai, to whom I would be talking.

Inmates at Klong Prem prison, Bangkok, lining up like so many waddling ducks to be served their daily ration of prison fare.

'Trusties' in training at Klong Prem prison. These men are long-term prisoners who are used by the Corrections Department to help warders control other prisoners. They are armed with wooden batons and carry handcuffs. This practice is strictly forbidden under the Universal Declaration of Human Rights, to which Thailand is a signatory.

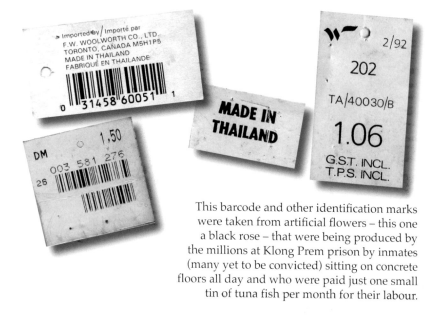

This barcode and other identification marks were taken from artificial flowers – this one a black rose – that were being produced by the millions at Klong Prem prison by inmates (many yet to be convicted) sitting on concrete floors all day and who were paid just one small tin of tuna fish per month for their labour.

Inmates at Bangkwang prison, Nonthaburi, burdened 24 hours a day for years on end with the heavy chains that the Thai authorities have assured the world are no longer used. These ones, though not the largest, would weigh in at around ten kilograms per set.

The execution chamber at Bangkwang prison. The stand in the forefront cradled the rifle that was used to shoot the prisoner in the back; the sandbags against the far wall were covered with plastic sheeting to reduce the clean-up effort; the crosses in front of those are what the prisoner was strapped to, facing the bags; and the screens in front of the crosses, with small targets pinned to them, were to hide the prisoner from view to the rest of the room. The execution process has now been changed to lethal injection.

The 'Ghost Door' in the wall of Section 13, Bangkwang prison, through which the corpses of the executed and otherwise deceased inmates are carried. The small temple enclosure where they are left in a box, out in the elements adjacent to a stinking garbage tip, is directly opposite this door.

A front view of the main office of Bangkwang maximum-security prison.

A side view of the wall between the residential area and Bangkwang prison. This lane leads to the small temple compound beside which the Ghost Door is located.

A view of the sports field located on the outside of the Bangkwang prison walls and which is used by local residents and prison officials. This shot was taken from the small temple compound opposite the Ghost Door.

One of the new small prison vans that replaced the archaic relics that were used up to a couple of years after the beginning of the new millennium. This one is waiting in front of the Criminal Court on Ratchadapisek Road, Bangkok. New rules allow it to carry only the number of prisoners that can be seated. Larger models carry twice as many passengers.

The Criminal Court building in Ratchadapisek Road, Bangkok.

A new sign that was constructed in front of Klong Prem prison
after the Justice Ministry became responsible for the
Corrections Department several years before Sly was released.

The new seven-storey hospital building at Klong Prem prison that replaced the old one to the left.

A couple of weeks later, I discussed the matter with Surachai, and one week after that he visited me in the privacy of the lawyer's room and told me that he had made contact with the appropriate panel judge and that a deal could be made for the small consideration of just 1.5 million baht, at that time the equivalent of about US$60,000. Surachai, of course, was not doing this out of the goodness of his heart – very little is ever done in Thailand out of the goodness of anybody's heart, this particularly the case when officials are involved. He would be adding his fee for making the arrangements. That was understood and accepted without it being spelled out in too many words. The message was passed on to Paul, who accepted the price and immediately sent a letter to his wife in America.

It's best that I don't use the actual name of Paul's wife, but as I don't wish to keep calling her 'wife' or 'bitch' or any of the other names he was calling her by the time she had finished with him, I'm going to call her Lilly Worseluck.

As it turned out – even though he had been kept at Bombat for quite a lot longer than I had – Paul was transferred to The Prem at around the same time I was. A short time later, he received a letter from Lilly to say that she would get the cash organised and come to Thailand as soon as possible. He waited and waited. He wrote more letters. He had nightmares. He consumed the cash reserves he had and waited some more, but she didn't arrive and she didn't write to say when she would arrive. In the interim, Paul was using his lawyer to stall the case in the usual manner, with unnecessary witnesses and adjournment after adjournment, which cost him plenty and which, naturally, the judge, who stood to benefit substantially, went along with for as long as he realistically could.

In August, Paul was told that he had to have the cash in Bangkok within four weeks or he would be convicted and sentenced at the next hearing. He frantically sent yet another letter to Lilly, pleading with her to get there within that time and to bring the necessary cash with her.

Lilly did eventually turn up, late on the Friday just a couple of days before the case was to be determined. She made contact with

Surachai via the phone number that Paul had provided and arranged to meet him, confirming that she had brought sufficient cash with her for the job.

Surachai desperately tried to make contact with the judge, via the customary intermediary, but was eventually informed that he was in Phuket for the weekend and that there were no contact details available. Surachai didn't know his home phone number and the intermediary would have lost his trusted connection to the judge if he had provided it, so contact wasn't made.

On the Monday morning, the session judge was in his courtroom at 9 a.m., having evidently already been given the verdict envelope by the panel judge. It might have been possible for the proceedings to be delayed again for a few days even then, but the intermediary forgot to inform his boss of Lilly's arrival. Consequently, the envelope was opened, and Paul was convicted and sentenced to life in prison.

Paul had no idea that Lilly had arrived, as no visits could be organised over the weekend. He had just assumed that she hadn't made it in time. 'Bitch . . . Fucking bitch.' His vocabulary seemed to be very limited that fateful day.

When he arrived back at The Prem after a torturous day spent in the court holding cells, with nothing to eat and the trauma of the trip back in the cage bus at the end of it all, he was transferred to Bangkwang maximum-security prison to begin what was to be his final couple of years of real life. He was just 25 years of age and was destined to become a human vegetable before he turned 28.

On his arrival at Bangkwang that night, he had about 15 kilograms of rusty chain fitted to steel shackles that were welded around his ankles. He was then put into a cell with 29 other men, all Thai and similarly manacled. Hell had opened its doors and Paul, who, though having experienced the barbaric and inhuman conditions of both Bombat and The Prem, was about to discover a new realm of torment that would have him dreaming of his old cells with fondness and longing.

Newly sentenced prisoners have no privileges at all when they arrive at Bangkwang, and being lumbered with heavy chains for the first 12 months or more is standard practice. That goes for Westerners, too, unless there is a direct request from an embassy to have them removed. Visits are restricted to just once each week for two hours maximum and then only on specified days. It takes at least two but up to six weeks for the prisoner's prison account to be transferred from The Prem or Bombat to Bangkwang, meaning that he has no means of obtaining anything from the welfare shop and is forced to eat what the prison provides. That alone is almost sufficient reason for ending it all at one's own hands.

The water for bathing and washing clothes is not the clean town supply water that is available at The Prem, but the filthy and heavily polluted water pumped directly from the Chao Praya River – the so-called River of Kings – which is one of the most contaminated rivers in the world. Drinking water does, however, come direct from the town supply. The prison authorities provide nothing at all in the way of blankets, mattresses, toiletries or clothes, meaning that the cement floor is the only bed to sleep on.

Most foreigners aren't aware of this, however, expecting that they will be provided with clothes, bedding and other essentials for the duration of their stay at Bangkwang. Paul was one of these naive souls who had nothing when he arrived at the prison, apart from his few changes of clothes and some toiletries.

The cell in which he was placed was the standard seven metres by four and was crammed with so many men that all the bodies seemed to become one during the night, each pressing against the other like sardines in a tin. Hundreds of pigeons and sparrows lived above the ceiling boards, and the remnants of their nests constantly rained down on the occupants below. This combined with the high level of humidity generally prevalent in Bangkok and the fact that there was very little ventilation made for a noxious, suffocating atmosphere, quite sufficient to drive a man to madness. Paul was understandably not the slightest bit happy with his wife.

It was Thursday before Lilly was able to call him out for a visit, and by this time he was positively livid, blaming her entirely for his having had to suffer such degrading, torturous circumstances, and for no other reason than she had left it too late to make her trip to effect his rescue. Had she done what he had asked, he would have been drinking beer and eating hamburgers and fries – with lots of ketchup. He might even have had an opportunity to sneak out for one or two final pokes at the local talent while her back was turned before having to return with her to the drudgery of life in the USA. Therefore, instead of calming smiles and words of comfort that might have been valuable therapy for them both, the visit area rang with the thunder of their loud abuse, blame, accusations and threats of all kinds of violence that each would rain on the other if there ever came a time when they were close enough to effect them . . . not the least bit constructive.

By the end of the visit, though, Lilly had agreed to stay on in Bangkok for a while to see what could be done to ensure that the Appeal Court would find it advantageous to overturn the guilty verdict and acquit Paul. She arranged a meeting with Surachai at his home the following day, during which he managed to convince her to hand over a little deposit to enable him to arrange for her to have a chat with the appropriate judge's go-between. Lilly advanced him 500,000 baht, and it was subsequently agreed that all could be made to smell like roses for just one million baht cash, plus 500,000 baht bail. The bail would, of course, be forfeited when Paul hit the track, leaving Thailand for good. That figure didn't include the fees for the intermediary and Surachai, who would share the 500,000 baht deposit. Without their involvement, however, Paul would rot away for many years to come. Their help was worth ten times what they had asked.

The plan was simple, as most plans in Thailand are. (Cynics might say that they have to be.) The Appeal Court would overturn the Criminal Court verdict, but the prosecutor would appeal the decision, meaning that the case would have to go to the Supreme Court. The Appeal Court would then order that the defendant be held in custody but would not oppose bail, which would be set at 500,000 baht. When the bail was put up, Paul would be released pending the Supreme Court hearing, during which time he would get the hell out of there. The tracks would be covered nicely. No one would be seen to be taking a bribe, and the case would be closed for lack of a bad guy to convict.

The good news was relayed to Paul the following Thursday when Lilly visited him again, and he was confident that all would be well eventually. However, there was to be a wait of six months for the Appeal Court decision. It was not possible to have it appear too quickly after the Criminal Court case without looking suspicious. But six months was insignificant compared to a life sentence. Lilly was required to show the judge's agent that she had the necessary cash but was not required to hand it over to him at that time. Instead, she was told to put it safely into a bank account, which Surachai and Jaidow would help her arrange, so that it would be available at 48 hours' notice.

About a week after she had been to see the agent, Lilly and Jaidow came to The Prem to visit me. Lilly had opened the bank account as suggested by the agent and had deposited most of the required cash, but as it was such a long time before she had to hand it all over, she had decided to make the balance do some work by using it to start a small enterprise with Jaidow, exporting artificial flowers to the USA. Jaidow would take 25 per cent of the profits for being the Thai connection.

Shortly afterwards, Lilly returned to the USA, taking a consignment of flowers and the merchandise that Paul had accumulated prior to his arrest with her. She also left arrangements for Jaidow to send her more once it was all sold.

It was just a couple of months later that Jaidow disappeared, and I guess it's not surprising to learn that the loot in the bank account, which Jaidow had been given access to, had also disappeared. It would be some time before I was made aware of this fact, however.

After repeated efforts to locate Jaidow or to ascertain what had happened to her without success, and after being told by Om that she had contacted Jaidow's family in Roi Et quite a few more times with the same result, I firmly began to believe that Jaidow had been done away with for her verbal attack on the cop in court. As such, I reasoned that I probably wouldn't be seeing her again. Now, as disturbing as that was for me, it also presented a major problem for Paul. The funds for his liberation were being held by Jaidow and had to be available with just 48 hours' notice. I wrote a short note and informed Paul of the situation. I didn't have any information concerning the bank account but assumed that Lilly would have and suggested that he contact her.

It didn't make sense that she would not have included a safety valve when setting up the account, allowing her to make arrangements for withdrawal of the necessary funds when the time came. That time was rapidly approaching. I knew that if the promised remittance was not forthcoming, the Appeal Court would simply uphold the Criminal Court verdict. And that would be the end of Paul's chance of escape.

I had assisted Paul up to this point without any expectation of personal gain. I was not getting any commission or sharing what Surachai or the judges were charging. Jaidow's compensation for her involvement was the share of profits on consignments for the USA, and her efforts to date had been minimal in any event. It therefore came as a shock when I received a terse note from Paul in reply just a few weeks later, in which he accused me and Jaidow of stealing two million baht from his wife's account.

Naturally, I responded immediately, denouncing the charge as ridiculous. How could I steal anything from the account? I had not moved from Klong Prem prison since being transferred there, and Jaidow had vanished. Even her parents didn't know what had happened to her – at least that's what I had been led to believe at that time. I remained confident that she would not have done anything like that and that the funds were still in place. Furthermore, how had two million baht entered the picture when I had been told that 500,000 baht had already been paid to Surachai and the agent and that Lilly had used part of the remaining 1.5 million to purchase flowers to take home with her?

It was only because of Jaidow's disappearance that I had become concerned and made contact with Paul, reasoning that if he remained in the dark and nothing was done to remedy the situation, he would almost certainly be convicted again come the Appeal Court hearing. I was more than a little annoyed that after having tried so hard to help this ungrateful fellow, he was now accusing me of doing something that I had absolutely no knowledge of – being blamed for doing things that I hadn't done was becoming rather irritating.

Nevertheless, I had to make absolutely certain that my assumptions were on target. The fastest and easiest way to proceed, I thought, was to get Om to ask Surachai to investigate. He would know at which bank and branch the account was established – he had assisted in its establishment – and would know how to get a credit balance statement from the manager, even though that is supposed to be confidential information, available only to the account holder . . . but this was Thailand.

Two weeks later, Om came to visit and gave me some disheartening news. Evidently, my faith in Jaidow's virtue had been a little on the optimistic side. The credit balance was only sufficient to keep the account alive – 200 baht. Needless to say, the end result was that the Appeal Court upheld the Criminal Court verdict. And that was that: checkmate. There was no possibility of Paul being able to influence the Supreme Court, unless, of course, he could provide substantially more incentive. A minimum of eight years now had to be served before he could request a transfer back to the USA. He had nowhere to go and no way to get there until those eight years had passed.

I will probably never know what actually happened or how Jaidow fitted into the picture, but Surachai told me some time later that Lilly had paid him 500,000 baht in cash. He did not pay the agent his share of that because it was conditional on the acquittal being handed down, and he had not considered it his place to return it to Lilly or Paul. After all, he had done his part, even if no one else had. Lilly had then used another 500,000 baht to buy the consignment of flowers. Surachai told me that Jaidow had arranged the deal and had made herself a nice little profit on it without Lilly's knowledge. The other one million remained in the account until early December when it was withdrawn in one transaction. Jaidow had then vanished, and Surachai said that he didn't know where she was. And I believed him – silly me.

I didn't tell Paul the truth of the matter, however. How could I? Instead, I maintained that Jaidow had simply vanished and that I was almost certain she had been murdered. I said that I had no idea whether or not the money remained in the account because I had no connection to that side of things and that he should get Lilly to check herself and take the appropriate steps to ensure it was available when needed. I also said that I was, from that point on, out of the loop and wanted no further involvement.

Paul was, of course, terribly frustrated and very cranky with Lilly for cocking things up at what was essentially the 11th hour – probably deliberately, as I learned later. He wrote her a scathing note, calling her all the ungodly things that he could imagine for being so stupid as to have put her trust in someone she barely knew and ordering her to get her arse into gear and get things sorted out real fast. Not surprisingly, he received no reply.

After his conviction had been upheld, with still no word from Lilly, he sat day in and day out seething with resentment and bitterness, vowing that he would use Lilly's guts for garters if ever he saw her again in the flesh. Naturally, he never once considered the fact that it was his own stupidity and lust that had landed him in the chilli soup in the first place – a common enough occurrence in prisons throughout the world, I guess. There will always be a percentage of inmates who blame the victims of their crimes, or the witnesses who testified against them, or the judges who sentenced them, or their childhood, or their parents, for the predicaments they find themselves in – I have met quite a few people like that during my various stints of confinement.

It didn't end there for me, however, because Paul was still convinced that Jaidow and I had stolen the money that would have freed him, and he was out for revenge. Approximately six months after the Appeal Court verdict, Paul's sister came to Thailand to visit him. After he had confirmed to her the story that she had already heard from Lilly, she came to visit me at The Prem. Brent and Om happened to be visiting me at the time and were both taken aback when this woman, in typical American fashion, muscled her way to the front of the line and began to verbally abuse me at peak decibels, using all kinds of profanities to describe the way she felt about me right there in front of everyone. Brent and Om stood speechless as she screamed that the money had been provided by her father to secure Paul's release and that she wanted it returned.

I allowed the woman to wear herself down to the point of exhaustion, then calmly explained the situation as it had actually unfolded, albeit sticking to the story that I was certain Jaidow had been murdered by the cops and suggesting that they had probably been the ones to empty the bank account. I also said that Lilly could quite easily have made an arrangement whilst setting up the account whereby she would be able to access the account from abroad – perhaps she had stolen the money. Whatever the case, Jaidow had vanished from the face of the earth, and I had no way of knowing for sure what had happened to her or the money.

Surprised but chastened to a degree, she apologised for her unwarranted outburst and informed me that Lilly – whom she seemed to have a certain antipathy towards anyway, wincing when I mentioned the 500,000 baht worth of flowers that her sister-in-law had taken with her on departure – was planning to come back to Bangkok. She then asked me if I would help her to recover the money that had gone missing.

Several months later, Lilly did return and visited me. She began in a bluster of accusation and profanity that mimicked her sister-in-law, trying desperately to cast the shadow of guilt over me for pinching her money. I reminded her that it wasn't hers to start with and that she was just as likely to have pinched it herself. At the same time, I revealed what I knew of the flower consignment, among other things, which silenced her. She sat there with her mouth agape, staring at me like she'd just shit her pants.

It was several months after Lilly had returned to the USA that I received a letter from Paul telling me that she was divorcing him. He apologised for accusing me and Jaidow of stealing the money and confessed that he now believed that it was his wife who was the culprit. He said he believed that she had deliberately ruined his chances of freedom because she had become embroiled in an affair with a young man.

In this same letter, he mentioned that he wanted Om to visit him at Bangkwang prison because he had just discovered some very important and sensitive information that would help me tremendously with my case. I could not imagine what information he could possibly have but thought it might have something to do with Fahad and his boys. Perhaps there were other prisoners in Bangkwang who had been duped in a similar way to me. One could be sharing a cell with me and I wouldn't necessarily be aware of it.

I decided to ask Brent to visit Paul and find out what it was that was of such importance. They had never met before, because Paul had been transferred to Bangkwang before Brent arrived at The Prem. I counselled Brent to take careful notes of everything that was said. He met Paul the following Monday morning, introducing himself as a friend of mine who was stopping over for a week or two from Singapore. He said that I had asked for full particulars of this sensitive information, which, it seemed, could not be sent via mail. He sat stunned while he listened to Paul tell him that he didn't actually have anything of the kind. He had made contact with several very well-connected buyers from the USA and England who wanted large quantities of heroin and that he wanted me to arrange a secure source for them in Bangkok. My commission would be 10 per cent of sale price, paid directly into any bank account I wished, anywhere in the world.

Brent handled the matter with admirable aplomb and encouraged Paul to spill as much of his guts as he wanted. Paul raved on for about 40 minutes about how he had managed to get these contacts and how he was certain that they were safe and genuine and so on. The meeting ended with Brent assuring him that he would relay the message and call again the following month when everything was arranged. Paul was delighted.

Needless to say, when I was informed the following day, I was far from delighted. What kind of fool was he taking me for? What kind of fool was he himself? That afternoon I wrote a very strongly worded letter telling him never to waste my time or that of my friends and associates again, and to cease all communications forthwith.

I later mentioned this stupidity to several of the Americans sharing Section 2 with me at the time and enquired if any of them had ever had any similar experiences involving Paul. One, a heavily built, loud and jovial character whom I'll name Wayne, told me that he had known Paul's wife in San Francisco well before he was arrested in Bangkok. He said she was involved with a cocaine dealer there, and that after her bloke had been arrested and sentenced to 20 years, she had managed to swipe all of his possessions and hit the track, later taking up residence with Paul.

According to Wayne, Lilly was a veritable calamity with legs. He also said that Paul was suspected by all of the other American inmates at The Prem of being an informer for the Bangkok DEA office. As his father was an ex-FBI agent, they believed that a deal had been cut that would result in his release once he was transferred back to the USA, if he assisted the DEA while in prison. For this reason, Paul had been ostracised by all of them during his stay at The Prem.

I was already aware that Paul's father was ex-FBI, because Paul had told me so right at the beginning of our association, confiding that daddy was particularly upset with him, because having been a head dick at the San Francisco FBI office just prior to his retirement, he was terribly embarrassed that his own son had been arrested on a drugs charge. However, now that I had been informed of Lilly's connection to drug dealers prior to her involvement with his son, it occurred to me that one doesn't need to be real smart to be an FBI chief.

Wayne was very anti-DEA – nothing unusual about that under the circumstances, I guess. He had been sentenced to 15 years for his involvement in a shipment of marijuana that was intercepted and seized about 500 miles off the Thai coast. The ship, which was carrying around 100 tonnes of the stuff, was actually in international waters and as such was well out of legal DEA jurisdiction. Nevertheless, it was seized, and Wayne was guilty of trying to get the shipment to the USA, so he accepted his fate. He was eligible for transfer back to the USA after serving four years in Thailand, whereas the minimum for maximum-security convictions – 35 years or more – is eight years. However, the local DEA office kept blocking Wayne's transfer applications. They gave him an ultimatum: 'Assist us and name names or rot in The Prem for 15 years.' He chose to rot in The Prem, at the same time enlisting the help of a senator back home. Eventually, after eight years, he did get his transfer.

It was four months after Brent's visit to Paul that I was at the Klong Prem hospital on a routine visit. A trusty walked by me pushing a wheelchair in which sat none other than Paul Worseluck. He appeared to be completely paralysed. His face drooped, his mouth was open and dribbling saliva, and his eyes stared vacantly. I stopped the trusty, initially intending to interrogate him, assuming Paul would not be capable of providing an explanation personally, but he recognised me and spoke, his speech slow and slurred but nevertheless understandable. He once again apologised to me for being such an arsehole and asked to be forgiven.

Well, I could hardly slap him, which is what I might have done under different circumstances, so instead I asked the trusty to leave us for 30 minutes while we had a talk. The trusty pushed the chair into a shady spot by a bench and left. Paul then made the following confession, and as I listened in astonishment, my anger slowly transformed to sympathy for this wasted man.

He told me that he had been extremely angry when his wife had failed to secure his release. She had written to him several times from the USA telling him that it was my and Jaidow's fault that he was still in prison, and she had reiterated this claim when she'd returned to Bangkok after his conviction. He had believed her and thus began to plot his revenge. Every minute spent with all of those sweating, stinking bodies, with the lice and the dirt and the stale air in that sweltering filthy cell that was to be his home for years, increased his resolve to make me pay for what I was supposed to have done.

After a couple of months of this torment and the resulting build-up of stress and bitterness, he had written a letter to the British Embassy in Bangkok, advising them that he could provide very incriminating information in relation to my case and wanted to talk privately to someone in authority for that purpose. One week later, he was called to a private room in the front office of the prison where he met a woman who introduced herself as being connected to the British police department. Paul told her that Jaidow and I had stolen two million baht of his money and offered to assist the British authorities if they were ever interested in taking advantage of his position. He told her that I was indeed a drug dealer, having personally admitted as much to him, and that he would be willing to work with her to make sure I was not acquitted. He also said that he had been in touch with his father in the USA and that his father had made arrangements with the DEA office to employ him as an inside informer in exchange for certain benefits once he was returned to his homeland.

This woman was extremely interested and told him that it would overcome a lot of problems if it could be shown that I was guilty as charged and that I was conspiring with others to commit similar offences. She then made several suggestions as to how he should proceed and told him that she would return to talk to him after she had made certain arrangements herself. Then she left.

She returned a short time later and gave him instructions, saying she would arrange for DEA people to be the buyers of the dope that he was supposed to get me to broker. This conversation resulted in Paul contacting me and Brent's subsequent visit to meet him. When I put paid to their evil little scheme by failing to be lured into the trap, Paul had then concentrated on other avenues to secure his early release. The deal had been made for him to become a bona fide DEA informer, and as such he set about his next big assignment. The problem was that he was way out of his depth, and all those James Bond movies he'd watched didn't help him a bit. His next and final mistake was to accept as his target a group of Thai inmates who had been sentenced in the Criminal Court for drug dealing in Chiang Mai Province, and who appeared to have a good chance of being acquitted at the appeal stage. This target had been chosen for him by his new bosses.

He set about becoming friendly with these fellows, and after a suitable period made his proposal. He told them that he had an American friend who wanted to buy ten kilograms of top-grade pure heroin but that he was afraid to buy from anyone unless he was sure that they weren't police informants. Paul mentioned that the buyer was willing to pay well above the price that heroin could be purchased for locally for a secure consignment, meaning that there would be a pretty good surplus that could be split between them if they could make satisfactory arrangements for a safe purchase.

The Thais agreed to an initial meeting with this buyer and said that they would have one of their friends visit them at the same time so that introductions could be made and another meeting scheduled. Paul was once again delighted – it wasn't difficult to delight Paul – and he passed the message along. The Thais, though, were not so delighted and, smelling a very big rat, made arrangements for this meeting to be set up using a ringer, with several other associates observing from a distance.

The meeting day arrived, and the ringer did an admirable job of pretending to be a link to the seller as he had been coached. The Americans – there were three of them – were apparently duped into believing that he was genuine and agreed to a follow-up meeting. When they left the prison visit area, however, one of the observers followed them, and when he reached the road in front of the prison, he signalled to several associates who were waiting nearby on their motorcycles. They followed the Americans as they drove to their home base, which was located in Soi 15, Sukhumvit Road, Prakanong, Bangkok, and which they knew – as any self-respecting drug dealer would – was the safe house of the Nana DEA Unit . . . Paul had boiled the soup that was about to cook his goose.

The intended victims had the report within days. They were not in the slightest bit impressed, but what to do? Ignore Paul and warn all others in the prison about him? Smack him around a bit? Or just kill the fucker and be done with it? It was unfortunate for Paul that 'kill the fucker and be done with it' won the vote. The challenge, however, was to accomplish this without being adversely affected themselves. They were still fighting their cases and had no desire to jeopardise their chances of release by having the additional charge of 'killing fuckers' on their slate.

It was more than a little unfortunate for Paul that they had already forged a strong friendship with several inmates who came from the hill tribes of the Thai/Burmese border – people who are renowned for their intimate knowledge of the jungle and what it has to offer – because one week later, Paul had been reduced to a dribbling, slurring and almost completely dysfunctional vegetable. The tiny sprinkle of powder that had been put in his soup was responsible for this virtually instantaneous transformation. It had been meant to kill him, but because the person who had administered the dose was not from the hills, he had mistakenly sprinkled it into the soup rather than on the solid part of his meal. Paul had taken just one mouthful and collapsed, much of his nervous system paralysed. Had the powder not been diluted, he would have been rendered lifeless in less than a heartbeat.

The drug, or poison, or whatever it is – like the one that had propelled Slim into orbit – is said to be undetectable after death, even via autopsy, but is so potent that in minute quantities it can kill a human without actually being ingested. Simply exposing sensitive skin to it will cause death as it is absorbed into the body. It somehow stops or interferes with nerve function and usually induces a deadly seizure.

Although Paul confessed much of the above to me while we talked that day, it was from his intended victims that I learned most of the nitty-gritty much later. I made a point of talking to them at length after being transferred to Section 1 at Bangkwang – one of them actually shared my cell for a while. Because I had been a death-row resident myself for some years, and as I too had been one of Paul's intended victims and had no axe to grind with them, they were happy to relate the story to me. Many people in the section knew who was responsible for what had happened to Paul in any event, and most of them thought that he had been given precisely what he deserved. Prisoners the world over don't usually take kindly to snitches or police informers sharing their space. If discovered, they invariably end up with major problems in one form or another.

Eventually, Paul was repatriated to the USA on medical grounds. Whether or not he is still alive, I do not know. If he is, he will no doubt be less inclined to allow that troublesome appendage of his to rule his brain, or what remains of it.

I never did see or hear from Jaidow again, not that it would have made any difference if I had. But to satisfy my own curiosity, just prior to my release, some 16 years after she had deserted me, I asked a friend and former cellmate to check the relevant government database. His report was not all that surprising when all is said and done. She was still alive and kicking, and still living at the same Roi Et address that she had lived in when I married her.

# PART 4

# Unchallenged Official Abuse of Power and Authority Is a Recipe for Tyranny

*Une injustice faite à un seul est une menace faite à tous.*
(An injustice done to an individual is a threat to everyone.)

*Baron Montesquieu, 1689–1755*

# CHAPTER 16

‖‖‖‖‖‖‖‖‖‖‖‖‖‖‖‖‖‖‖‖‖‖‖‖‖‖‖‖‖‖‖‖‖‖‖‖‖‖‖‖‖‖‖‖‖‖‖‖‖‖‖‖‖‖‖‖‖‖‖‖‖‖‖‖‖‖‖‖‖‖‖‖‖‖‖‖‖

# And What of Time, My Friends?

BRENT AND I HAD BEEN GIVING EACH OTHER PRACTICAL AND MORAL support since soon after his arrival at Klong Prem. We'd spent a lot of time trying to fathom the Thai judicial and penal system that was restricting us in so many ways from putting up a decent defence and at times made it downright impossible.

Brent's own trial was being dragged out by the prosecution, with adjournment after adjournment, none of which he was made aware of until he was actually at the court on the day of the hearing. This meant that he had to suffer the ordeal of getting there and back only to sit chained and stressed in the holding cell all day. When there was an actual session before a judge, it involved, in most instances, just one witness, with testimony that sometimes lasted no more than 30 minutes.

Like me, he had no interpreter apart from his lawyer. Even though this lawyer could speak English quite well, very little of what was said was ever translated for Brent, leaving him ignorant of what was happening.

We had both long since discovered that everything seemed to be stacked against the defendant. Most of the time it is impossible to converse with visitors or witnesses coherently because of the way the prison visit areas are set up. The greater percentage of Thai lawyers are generally far from adventurous when it comes to tackling the absurdity that often makes up police testimony in a Criminal Court, mainly because most are terrified to expose wrongdoing and corruption within the police force and the powers that be. They know only too well that it is not uncommon for those who follow this path to find themselves fertilising someone's mango trees or appeasing the appetite of a hungry crocodile or two.

Most spend very little time preparing a case, nearly always leaving everything until the few minutes before the start of the hearing, and they devote very little time to consultation with their clients prior to that. The majority of defendants are denied competent legal representation by virtue of the fact that competent legal representation is a very scarce and expensive commodity in Thailand, and there is no such thing as Legal Aid. There is also the risk that an appointed lawyer will simply swipe the advance or retainer and not show up at the court at all. That happens all too often, particularly where the defendant is a foreigner.

Additionally, although the criminal code stipulates that a defendant's innocence is to be presumed until proven otherwise by the prosecutor, it seems in reality that the opposite is the case: all defendants are presumed guilty *until* they can prove their own innocence, and in most cases that is made almost impossible for them to achieve.

As well as this, consider the manner in which remand prisoners are treated for many months before being officially charged: some are locked up in chains in terrible conditions for twenty-four hours a day and given access to the visit area for just ten minutes per week, almost completely denying them contact with loved ones or witnesses, as was the case with Brent; detainees are often mercilessly beaten, in many instances unto death, during the course of their trial; and the manner in which defendants are transported to and from the courts when the trial is in progress was horrendous.

Furthermore, though the law dictates that foreign defendants must be provided with competent translators for the duration of their trial, at no cost to themselves, this is very rarely the case. There are very few translators who work to a sufficiently high standard to begin with, and those who do can demand high fees in the private sector so have no interest in working for the pittance that the courts pay them. Foreign defendants can employ a translation service if they have sufficient funds; however, this is extremely difficult to arrange when the defendant has no one on the outside to assist in that appointment. There are no directories within the prisons – not in any language – that list such useful information, and it is a breach of the prison rules for inmates to have newspapers that might be useful in this regard. Then there's the disorder and inadequacies of the antiquated transcript-recording process.

A trial in a Thai criminal court cannot in any way be compared to one in the UK, Australia or America, where a jury decides the fate of the defendant and everything that is said by all participants is recorded verbatim. There is no jury, and very little of what is actually spoken is recorded. What happens instead is that the presiding judge, who in the Criminal Court is more likely than not to be very young and inexperienced, listens to the testimony and decides, as it is being given, what he or she thinks is relevant, recording this in his or her own words into a tape recorder with a hand-held mike. Questions and other dialogue form no part of the transcript; only the interpretation of the answers is recorded. About every 30 minutes, the tape is replaced and a stenographer types up the judge's words in quadruplicate, in Thai, on legal-size sheets of court-headed paper. At the end of the session, the prosecutor, the defendant (together with his or her attorney) and the judge are required to sign these typed sheets. If the defendant is a foreigner who is unable to read Thai, well that's just tough. The deliberation of the case is carried out by a panel of three judges, none of whom have actually seen or heard the testimony being given. They read the transcripts, look at the exhibits and make a decision based on what is there.

A couple of classic examples of the problems that can be caused because of this incredibly archaic and inadequate procedure, which hasn't been changed since its inception a century or more ago, were plain enough to see in the transcripts of my trial. The head cop of the arresting team testified that his officers were in certain locations at specific times at the bank during the operation. He went into a lot of detail about the movements of the accused during the same period and how he employed the assistance of bank staff to record the entire arrest.

Now, quite a bit of this testimony was refutable, because it didn't happen the way it had been described and there was, in the witness's own admission, video evidence that could have been used by the defence to prove that. However, instead of recording each statement individually, the judge simply summarised the entire segment, saying, 'The witness describes the movements of Mr Hansel and his friend in the head office of the Bangkok Bank on the date in question. The witness describes how he asked the security staff of the bank to cooperate with the police and to allow the video cameras in the area in question to be used to record the movements of all the people in that area.' The ten minutes of testimony was reduced to about thirty seconds. How could large chunks of testimony be condensed into a single word and still allow the panel to understand what the witness has said and what actually happened? It is what the witness is *describing* here that is vital as far as the defence is concerned. We were not where this cop and others who followed said we were, and the videos would have revealed that.

Then there was Hansel's testimony during the defence case. Altogether, he was on the stand for around two hours, but during that period the judge, who spent a lot of that time talking to another judge who just popped in for a chat and ignored the proceedings altogether, recorded less than ten minutes of what was said. The transcripts prove that. The judgement document even went so far as to say that he didn't testify at all.

This is what the Thais call a justice system, and it is this system, according to the nationally televised confessions of Pramarn Chansue, who was the Supreme Court president at the time of my trial, that results in, on average, around 65,000 innocent people being condemned to the purgatories of Thai prisons at any given time.

\* \* \*

It was a Sunday morning in May or June not too long before Brent was released that he and I sat together in the shade of the workshop in Section 2, away from the noise and interruptions of the community hut. We had prepared ourselves for a long discussion with a flask of hot coffee and a couple of cushions to sit on. I wanted to go over the transcripts I had translated of the prosecution case, witness by witness, pointing out every lie and inconsistency and getting Brent's opinion of my analysis.

But it was just another day in Klong Prem for most of the other foreign prisoners there. As usual, it was at least 36 degrees Celsius in the shade of the grass roof of the community hut in the garden, with 10 a.m. still 20 minutes away.

It was a little different for the African population, however. For them, Sunday was special. By 9 a.m., they were congregated in their shelter for their weekly devotions. The speaker of the day had begun preaching a sermon with the customary passion and obvious conviction. Not in the American TV Evangelist style, with all that rah-rah and hoopla, but by addressing those present in a simple, strong and purposeful tone as he shared his belief in the Almighty with his fellow devotees. This was soon followed by prayers and hymns, sung in a distinctive, perfectly harmonious and powerful blend of deep baritone and tenor, with a touch of contralto thrown in at precisely the right moment, a marvellous fusion of tones and qualities that are characteristic of African choirs. The temporary release of their frustrations, regret, guilt, claustrophobia, loneliness and all of the other emotions felt as a result of being indefinitely separated by thousands of miles from loved ones and familiar surroundings all flowed out of their tormented hearts and filled the air like an almost tangible hand reaching out to their God for forgiveness and mercy and the strength to carry on.

Although they welcomed participation by any of the inmates, including the Thais, it was rare that anyone took advantage of the opportunity, choosing instead to either ignore the proceedings or to sit back in their own little world and listen. Some people enjoyed the music, some loathed and complained about it and others simply didn't even notice it, being too spaced out on the heroin that was freely available to anyone with the necessary exchange and desire to acquire it.

Although I never personally attended the services, I often sat nearby and listened. Apart from the soothing and meditative quality of it all, I enjoyed the atmosphere it created among the participants. The end of the sessions always intrigued me, too. As they filed out of their prayer hut, embracing each other and giggling and laughing boisterously, all of them looked happy and to a great extent relieved of the tensions and stresses that had built up during the week. It was as if there had been a collective freeing of the soul from the bonds of reality, even if only temporarily. It was a freedom that had become almost addictive to them, and the Sunday services were something that each and every one of them looked forward to with enthusiasm and exhilaration.

I had by now finished translating all of the prosecution case transcripts of my own trial, and Brent was as astounded as I had been by what they contained. However, because there was such a huge amount of obvious misrepresentation and inconsistency, it would have been asking a little too much for my lawyer to link it all together coherently and launch an effective defence unless it was summarised. I reasoned, though, that I needed to keep it as simple as possible by cutting out most of the formal court language. Instead, I would just present the facts, showing in my own words the fabrications and how the various testimonies contradicted each other.

Once I had it laid out like this, it was easy to see that the police had absolutely no credible evidence at all – nothing. I had counted an unbelievable one hundred and fifty instances of inconsistency and obvious perjury in the testimony of the five officers – an average of thirty per witness! The only exhibits tendered by the police were the suitcase, supposedly from the boot of my car, and the key that could open it, along with some photographic evidence, which was later shown to be fabricated and proved nothing other than that the police were abusing their station and breaching the very laws that they were supposed to be enforcing.

It was abundantly clear to me that there was only ever one motivation for my arrest, and that was blackmail and reward money. Fahad and the officers were obviously a well-oiled group of extortionists using seemingly genuine business transactions and their official positions as a way to get millions of baht from their victims, not to mention the additional rewards from the DEA. At the time, though, I was confident the judges would see the scam for what it was.

Though it would make fascinating reading, it would be impractical to cover the trial in full here, mainly because of the sheer volume of testimony and rebuttal that was involved in the final analysis, but to provide some understanding of just how preposterous things can get in a Thai courtroom, I'll highlight a few of the more bizarre happenings.

First, the very fundamental issue of why we were arrested was contradicted throughout the proceedings: at one time we were *buying* the drugs from the cops and later we were *selling*. In fact, in one account we had already sold the consignment to them, even though no money or any other form of conveyance had changed hands. This absurdity was taken to the extreme when the actual judgment handed down four years later mentioned both as being the crime that we had been convicted for.

The cop who was supposed to have been working with the informer to entrap us could not remember a single date, time or place that the five meetings between us all were supposed to have taken place, and he kept absolutely no records. Neither did his boss or any of the other officers involved. He did remember, though, and repeated it several times in answer to several different questions, that the heroin deal had been discussed at each of those meetings while he was present. Then, during cross-examination, he reversed this assertion completely and said that at no point had he ever discussed anything about dealing in heroin with the accused.

They had plans in place to arrest us days before a crime had even been committed. They had cops being briefed about an arrest at the bank and how they would position themselves and at what time before I even knew myself that I would be at the bank that day. They also testified that they had seen a car being driven by me to the bank nearly a month before I had purchased it. That testimony was reversed when they discovered their blunder. They then said that they didn't know what car I had driven the first time I'd gone to the bank.

They said that a huge pile of cash money – more than could be comfortably carried in the arms of a single person – had been handed over and counted right out in the banking hall of the busiest bank in the country in front of a horde of other customers. They even had us doing that counting before the money was supposed to have been withdrawn and, more surprisingly, after the time that several witnesses had testified we had left the bank. What's more, they provided photographic evidence of this stupidity, with the exact time imprinted on the frames, no money in evidence, no cop involved in the supposed transaction and so on, all proving conclusively that they had all lied to the court numerous times.

There were four contradicting reasons given for us not being arrested on the first occasion we visited the bank, all of which stretched the imagination to the limit. One version had the heroin in the car but no arrest because the cops were afraid to go and take a look; another had no drugs in the car; one had drugs in the car but said that it wasn't real heroin; and one account had us with no heroin at all, instead maintaining that we simply wanted to pinch the money that was supposed to be used by the cops to pay for it. All of this testimony was spewed from one officer – the one who was supposed to have been the informer's partner – at a single hearing.

The suitcase that was tendered as an exhibit and the key that was able to open it was supposed to be the one that they had found in my car, but a photo taken by one of the journalists present at the initial press conference, and which was printed in the magazine he represented, proved that both were ringers. The case wasn't even the same colour as the one that was shown at the conference.

The authorities also refused to comply with a court order – requested by the defence – to tender the original video tapes from which the still frames that had been presented had been taken. These tapes would have proven that the testimony that had been given in relation to them was false, but the court allowed the police to remain in contempt of that order for the duration of the trial, right through to the Supreme Court hearing.

There was a lot more, and most of it was just as outlandish, but that'll suffice for now. Let's not forget, however, that I was eventually convicted and sentenced to death on the strength of this insanity.

By the time I had covered it all, Brent was sitting, mouth agape, like a stunned mullet, and the African preacher was reaching the end of his sermon: 'And what of time, my friends? We are all here today transfixed with tormented hearts – on the time we have lost and the time we will lose – and we try to measure the immeasurable, where instead we must adjust our attitude according to the hours that we spend and the seasons we will travel through. We must take this time and make it a stream upon whose banks we sit with comfort and contentment and watch its flowing. We must accept that all of our yesterdays are but today's memories, and all of our tomorrows are but today's dreams. We must make time our friend and not our foe. We must embrace it and not fear it.

'So, my brothers, let today embrace the past with remembrance and the future with longing and anticipation, and let us use the free time, of which we presently have an abundance, to cleanse our spirit and prepare for rebirth . . . The rivers eventually reach the sea, my brothers, as the winds eventually break the calm, and the tides eventually turn, and the storm eventually blows itself asunder, and the fire eventually turns to embers, and the boy eventually becomes a man, and the rose bud eventually blossoms to reveal God's creation in all its magnificence.

'Be assured, friends, that this darkness we find ourselves in now will eventually become the dawning of a new day . . . Be patient. Patience is all you need to get you through the night; patience is the wise man's most valuable possession; patience and faith in Almighty God will bring you to a new horizon. Go now in peace and love for one another with a lightened load and a gladdened heart, and God willing we will again come together in harmony to stretch our hands to the heavens and give praise and song and thanks unto our Lord and protector. Amen.'

Brent and I packed up and headed towards the community area, watching the 90 or so Africans as they left their hut, laughing, chatting and hugging one another and quite evidently uplifted from their touch of heaven and prepared to face another week of hell. For me and Brent, it was time for lunch.

Shortly after this, Brent was acquitted and released. It took him a few weeks to get his shattered nerves and health back on the right track and then, along with another Australian – a good friend of his whom I've named Willie McDonald – he came to visit me at least once each week. They helped me with my case, taking a lot of the pressure off Om and getting things organised in a far more professional manner in the process. Willie was a bit of whiz-kid on his computer, and from then on he prepared all that was needed in printed form. Over the following years, he provided invaluable assistance with formalising the translations of transcripts, appeal and pardon submissions, and many of my communications, among a host of other things, making life a lot easier for me.

# CHAPTER 17

## Love Is Blinding

MANY OF THE GIRLS WHO EXHIBIT THE PRECIOUS GIFTS THAT MOTHER nature has been so generous in bestowing upon them and who rent their talents by the hour, or the day, in the numerous red-light areas of Thailand, are simply so beautiful, gentle and endlessly accommodating that falling head over heels in love with them is often a sticky web that is all too easy for foreign men, and women, to become entangled in. Actually, it is not necessarily always a trap from which they want to escape, and it has been known to have a blissfully happy ending for all concerned. Such a union often fills a void and, provided the leeches and parasites are kept at a safe distance, life can take on a new dimension.

Steven Harrard – that's the name I'll give him – was not a drug dealer and never had been. He was not a drug user, either. He had travelled to Bangkok from Nottingham with the intention of expanding his horizons and in so doing seeing at first hand some of the many supposedly unique attractions that are so often grossly exaggerated in tourist magazine promotions.

A rather handsome fellow in his early 30s, of average height and with an easy-going nature, he had his own void to fill after the failure of various romantic attachments back home. Having heard so much of what Thailand had to offer in that regard, Steven figured that he could do worse with his savings and time, so he decided to give it a try.

Though not a fool, he was an inexperienced traveller and was naive when it came to the treachery that is so often shrouded by friendliness and captivating smiles, not only on the part of the locals, but also the ever-lurking, ever-vigilant foreign vermin who infest the areas most popular with tourists.

Steven's first stop on his first night out in Bangkok was the world-famous Soi Patpong, between Silom Road and Suriwongse Road in Bangkok. A glittering red-light area of hundreds of bars, clubs, brothels, street vendors and restaurants that caters to a mostly foreign clientele, almost anything that is naughty can be found there: gay bars where females are not permitted; lesbian bars where males are not permitted; Japanese bars where, apart from the staff, only wealthy Japanese men are permitted; anything-goes bars where anything and everything is permitted; explicit sex shows of almost every imaginable variety; and lots more. There is only one rule in Patpong, and it is that money is spent, and lots of it. Handsome, pretty, ugly, grotesque, tall, short, clean, dirty, smelling like a rose or stinking like a skunk's fart: it's all the same to those who ply their trade in Patpong. The only conditions that are not acceptable are: broke, stingy and frugal. 'Budget travel' is a four-letter word in Patpong, and those existing on a shoestring simply aren't welcome.

As is the case in the majority of such locations throughout the country, one doesn't need to go looking for a short-term companion because they are for hire by the thousands and approach one after the other, vying for an opportunity to demonstrate their expertise. The rates might vary depending on the bargaining skills of the target, but the services don't vary too much. Regular visitors who have a reputation for generosity are literally swarmed by beautiful young hopefuls, all with only one thing on their mind: extracting some cash from his or her wallet. That a reported average of 70 per cent of these eager beavers is HIV positive doesn't seem to dampen the enthusiasm of those people willing to take the risk.

Steven paid a cover charge to a snappily dressed man standing at a door at street level, walked up a narrow flight of stairs and, after a guarded security door at the top was opened for him, entered a smoky and dimly lit go-go bar. The entire centre of the large room was taken up by an oblong counter that circled a raised platform on which vertical chrome poles about five or six centimetres in diameter were spaced about one-and-a-half metres apart around the circumference. Attached to each was a beautiful and totally naked young girl, performing all manner of erotic gyrations in time to the sometimes low and seductive, sometimes loud and pulsating music, occasionally assaulting the polished pole in simulated sexual bliss, while the patrons – both male and female, but mostly Westerners – who sat on the stools around the perimeter, drank and smoked and cheered, or just ogled at the spectacle.

Steven was almost immediately approached by three beautiful, scantily clad hostesses, who sat one on either side of him and one on his lap. He bought each of them a drink (a small glass of cola) and a beer for himself, and they talked in broken English and made suggestive advances for about ten minutes before a bell sounded and they rushed off, removing the few items of flimsy silk clothing they were wearing as they went, to take their turn on stage.

The performer who had been making love to the silver pole directly in front of him now approached Steven, wearing – apart from a delightfully seductive smile – an almost see-through silk blouse tied in a knot at the front and a very brief pair of bikini bottoms. She told Steven that her name was Ruth and that she was 18 years old. Standing tall, the top of her head reached almost to his shoulder, and with a body that Aphrodite herself would be proud to call her own, she was the most exquisite creature that Steven had ever set eyes on. When she reached for him and asked if he would like to make wild and passionate love to her for the rest of the night, he became instantly entangled in her web. He paid the bar fee to secure her release and took her to his hotel room, where they stayed until early the following afternoon.

Ruth had worked in Patpong for almost two years, and during that time she had learned to speak English quite well. She supported her grandmother and one younger sister, who were both still living in her home town of Chiang Mai. Her mother had died not too long after her father had left the family and went to live with one of his minor wives six or seven years earlier, and she and her sister had been taken in by their maternal grandmother.

Several months before her final exams at school, she was approached by a woman and asked if she would like to work as an entertainer in Bangkok. What 'entertainer' meant in the broader sense was clearly explained to her, as was what her income would be if she performed well. Pole dancing was the basic requirement, while performing on stage in all kinds of explicit sex shows would increase her income. Providing customers with in-house sex services in the small rooms above the bar would increase them yet again, and out-of-house or long-term sex assignments would be a bonus, because apart from receiving a better percentage of the take, she would generally get to stay in good-quality accommodation, be well fed at no cost to herself and not have to suffer the monotony of the pole dancing and sex routines in the stinking bar. Also, if she was lucky, she would be taken shopping by her more appreciative clients. Having no other prospects for a reasonable income, she had accepted the offer and was given the two months' advance retainer by the agent to give to her grandmother. After her school closed for the summer break, she'd left for Bangkok.

She didn't ask Steven for money that first night, nor at any time thereafter. She just wanted to be like a normal girl for once, and there had been something about Steven that had attracted her as soon as she saw him enter the bar. She also noticed that he didn't grope and maul the three girls who had forced their attentions on him, as almost all other male patrons would have done, and that appealed to her.

They returned together to the bar each night for the next week, and Ruth performed her go-go routine but asked the manager to be replaced in the sex-shows, saying that she had her period. When she danced, she positioned herself at the pole directly in front of where Steven sat and performed for him alone. When it was closing time they left together. At the end of the month, after collecting her dues, she told the manager that she needed a holiday and wouldn't be back for a while.

By then, Steven had fallen hopelessly in love with her and asked her if she would stay with him on a permanent basis, telling her that he had decided to extend his stay in Thailand and wanted to take her back to the UK with him at some time in the future. Ruth had a strong desire to abandon her past and start a new life with a good man who would take care of her and treat her like a real person, instead of a toy to be played with for a while and then discarded. She had saved quite a bit of her earnings over the years, and as her exceptional beauty enabled her to charge more than her less fortunate peers, she had accumulated sufficient wealth to feel comfortable about meeting her obligations to her family without relying on what Steven might provide.

After a month of staying at the hotel with Ruth as his constant companion, Steven decided to rent a nice apartment and to set up house with her. When everything is taken into account, this might have been too hasty a decision, but falling in love is no crime. Steven had found his dream girl, and he wanted to stay in Thailand with her. However, he needed a sustainable income to be able to do so.

A month later, while sitting in a café not too far from his apartment, he was still pondering the possibilities when an Australian fellow he knew, who went by the name Ray Stevens, came over and joined him. They had spoken one night in the bar in Patpong and had exchanged phone numbers. Unbeknownst to Steven, Ray was a felon who had escaped custody in Australia a number of years before whilst on bail awaiting appeal after being convicted of murder and drug trafficking there and had been living in Bangkok, as an illegal immigrant, ever since.

As is the case with a significant number of foreigners living in Thailand illegally, Ray was in the clutches of Justice Incorporated and as such was protected by a certain faction of the Royal Thai Police Force, at least for as long as he was useful to them. His main role was as an informer and lackey who would do their bidding for a cut of the proceeds.

One of the many tricks that Ray's employers had taught him was to ferret out foreigners who had gone to Thailand initially as tourists but who had run out of money or overstayed their visas. This was not a terribly difficult undertaking, particularly in the Khaosan Road and other low-rent areas of Bangkok. Once he identified a suitable target, he'd spend a little time befriending them and gaining their confidence. Then, at an opportune moment, he'd propose they courier a little dope out of the country, guaranteeing that there would be absolutely no risk whatsoever because some of the Customs people at the airport were involved in the gang and would ensure safe passage. And there would be no problem as far as the expired visa was concerned – that would be taken care of at the check-in desk. The promise of a nice cash reward and a return ticket was often all that was needed to convince the desperado to go along for the ride.

However, a pleasant and tranquil trip is not in the script. Airport Customs officers approach the target after a tip-off by the police and the drugs are discovered. The arrest is conducted in such a way that it causes a lot of disruption at the check-in counters. While all of this confusion and excitement is taking place, several other couriers who have larger and more valuable cargoes slip through unnoticed.

Steven, however, didn't fall into this category. He was considered a little too upmarket and could be used to far greater benefit and profit. After being invited to join him for a cup of coffee that fateful morning, Ray propositioned him with a potentially very lucrative yet relatively simple and legal business venture, whereby they would jointly import used Mercedes Benz cars from the UK and sell them in Bangkok for considerably more than they paid for them. Ray led Steven to believe that a good clean car could fetch as much as four times what it could be purchased for in the UK, after taking into consideration all of the costs at the Thai end.

Steven was delighted. It was precisely what he had been looking for: a simple, legal and profitable business that would allow him to stay in Thailand with the beautiful creature who had captured his heart. Ray convinced him that, as a long-term resident, he had all the local smarts in his pocket and could arrange unrestricted passage through Customs, the registration of the car, the sale and all other contingencies. However, he had no money to contribute as working capital and as such Steven would have to fund the first deal. They would then share the cost of future shipments. Steven was happy to put up his cash.

Not long afterwards, the first car was purchased in the UK. On the evening that it arrived in Bangkok and was cleared through Customs, Ray arrived at Steven and Ruth's apartment loaded up with food and suggested a small celebration. Steven happily agreed, and Ruth, though she had been sceptical initially, was also pleased that things had worked out so well for them. All that remained was to sell the car and they would be set to do the same thing again. Steven could see himself clearing a couple of hundred thousand pounds in the first year and had already made plans to take Ruth to England for an extended visit after that.

As he had no alcohol in the apartment, apart from a few cans of beer, Ray volunteered to pop out to get some. He left the apartment, saying he would be back in a few minutes, leaving the shoulder bag that he had been carrying when he arrived behind a lounge chair. Five minutes after he departed, there was a knock on the door. When Steven opened it, assuming it was Ray returning, five police officers rushed in. They grabbed Steven then searched the room and found what they knew would be there: two kilograms of first-grade heroin in the shoulder bag behind the chair. Ray never returned.

It is the classic set-up: Ray gets a share of the rewards from the cops for his trouble and is allowed to stay in Bangkok unmolested, regardless of his illegal status. Additionally, he also has the Mercedes Benz, which the cops know nothing about, which he acquired at no cost to himself and which will net him a substantial return.

Steven was eventually sentenced to 30 years in prison and was held at Klong Prem. To have found his Shangri-La and then to have it plucked from him was more than he could handle. His trial was a farce – as most Thai trials are – and he had absolutely no way to reverse the verdict, because there was no way for him to prove his innocence or, as was really the case, to disprove his guilt: the dope was found in his room; the arresting cops were evidently in on the scam; and Ruth's testimony would have been worthless, even if she had been permitted to testify, which she wasn't. She was instead advised to go back to work and to forget Steven. And though she did not forget, self-preservation dictated that she heed this advice and not get involved.

I talked to Steven often initially, but he became increasingly depressed as time went on, and though Ruth visited him regularly and provided him with more than sufficient funds to keep him in reasonable comfort, she and her dedication were, in fact, the cause of his further decline. He ached to be with her, and every time he saw her his frustration and despair deepened.

It was on a Thursday afternoon after her weekly visit and almost one year after his arrest, while he sat silently crying in the grass hut he shared with another inmate, that Mikhail Rhonald approached and offered Steven and his shattered emotions the sanctuary of substance oblivion. 'You have sufficient money, Steven. Use a little of it and escape for a while. It will do you more good than harm, believe me, my friend.'

Up to that time, Steven also shared a first-class cell in the confinement building with two Japanese men, one of whom had spent time with Brent in the 'hell cell' at Mahachai prison. These Japanese men had paid quite a lot of money to have their cell renovated and had initially invited Steven to be their cellmate because of his quiet and conciliatory nature. However, once the inevitable happened and he became hooked on Rhonald's remedy, they insisted that he be transferred and asked Brent to take his place.

It wasn't long before Steven had developed a serious drug addiction, and the more money that Ruth provided, the more he gave to Rhonald to cater for it. Both Brent and I had been extremely sympathetic towards him to begin with and had tried to lift him out of the bog he was slipping deeper and deeper into. He had tried a few times to rally to the challenge, but once he began to get hooked on dope, we distanced ourselves from him, having no desire to be too closely associated with a junkie who wouldn't help himself. We both had enough problems of our own.

Not too long after Brent had been released, he and Willie met Ruth in the visit area. Brent explained to her what was happening to Steven and that her heartfelt weekly financial support was doing more harm than good. She was devastated to think that she might have been responsible, and from that day she sent him only fruit and basic necessities, no cash.

Over the next few months, Willie met Ruth several times, and she confessed that though her dream of a good life had been shattered before, this time it had hurt a little more than usual. She had been fond of Steven. He had been good to her, and a new beginning had appeared to be on the cards. Maybe, given time, she could have even learned to reciprocate the love he had for her. No one will ever know.

She also explained that she had started to work again, but not at the bar in Patpong. The erotic-modelling scene was far more lucrative, and apart from the minimum 20,000 baht per day she received for doing little more than posing, mostly naked, for her employer's Japanese clients, she got to travel all over the country to beautiful and exotic locations, and stayed mostly in five-star accommodation with all of the accompanying luxury.

She did continue to visit Steven occasionally, but the visits became less frequent as time passed, until eventually they stopped altogether. It depressed her to see him wasting away, his eyes filled with longing, hate and despair. The drugs and poor nutrition took their toll, but the main thing that ate deep into his very soul was the knowledge that he had done absolutely nothing to deserve this fate and that he had been abandoned to suffer and waste his short life simply to appease the insatiable appetite of a few corrupt and morally bankrupt swine, who had, no doubt, already splurged their ill-gotten gains on whisky and whores and the good life. The thought of it was more than he could bear.

Just 12 days after the German library episode, Steven was murdered, and my two cellmates, Reinhard and Seth, and I saw it happen.

It was afternoon lock-up time, and the three of us were, as usual, among the first of the foreigners to head up to the cells. When we got to the second floor, we noticed that several Thais were standing around the door of Steven's cell looking in, one of whom was a guard, almost as evil as Tinakorn, I'll name Witchien. He was jumping around and carrying on like he had just bitten his tongue.

As we approached the cell, we looked in through the bars of the door and saw Steven lying on the floor, naked and with a syringe sticking into his arm. He was not moving and looked to be either dead or unconscious. At that moment, we saw Rhonald and a couple of his other guard lackeys, accompanied by two trusties, running down the corridor towards the cell.

Knowing that Steven was heavily into dope by that time and that Rhonald was his provider, the three of us thought he had overdosed. Although that was a terribly sad thing to see, it had happened to many others before him, and there was absolutely nothing that we could do about it. 'If the guy wants to shoot up on dope, that's his concern,' Reinhard observed.

With the situation apparently under control, we walked the ten metres further along the passage to our own cell. I was the last through the door, and as I entered I saw Rhonald shooing away a couple of the curious Thai inmates who had gathered near the cell before he and the guards entered. The two trusties that they had with them waited outside the door looking in.

About ten minutes later, after we had prepared our sleeping mats and had settled in for the night, a Thai inmate from the cell one along from ours popped his head in as he passed and told us that Steven had hanged himself. Reinhard and I looked at each other in astonishment, leaped up and hurried down to Steven's cell to see what the hell was going on. Sure enough, there was Steven, hanging by the neck from the bars, his feet off the ground.

We tried to open the door to get him down, but it was locked. Reinhard yelled at Witchien, who was standing right there outside the cell, 'His legs are moving! He's still alive! Quickly, get this fucking door open! Let us in so we can cut him down!' Witchien refused and screamed at us to return to our cells, threatening us with his baton and blowing his whistle to summon the other guards. Just then,

Steven's bowels and bladder opened and the waste ran down his legs. I figured that if he hadn't been dead when we arrived, he was now, so we went back to our cell. A trusty came along immediately and locked the door.

At about 11 p.m., Steven's body was cut down and removed. The next day, we discovered that the cause of death had been recorded as suicide by hanging. But how could it be? We had all seen him with our own eyes, completely out of it, lying there on the floor. How could he possibly have hanged himself? Particularly when two guards and Rhonald were already right there in the cell with him.

Each floor of the confinement building in Section 2 held two rows of cells, one on each side, which faced each other across an area about eight metres wide, while on the top floor a balcony ringed the drop to the floor below. Each cell was about two by six metres in size, with a barred door, a section at the far end for the toilet and a small barred opening at the top of the wall above that. This arrangement meant that if you were standing by your door, it was possible to see into the cell opposite. With this in mind, the following morning Reinhard and I worked out who stayed in the cell directly opposite Steven's and went to talk to the five occupants – all Thai.

They all told us the same thing. They were already in their cell when Rhonald had come running up the passage, alerted by Witchien's cries. It seemed he had been the first to discover Steven lying there on the floor . . . But why was Witchien calling to Rhonald instead of the other guards?

They said that the Thai spectators who were standing outside Steven's door were told to get to their cells when Rhonald arrived. Rhonald examined Steven for a minute or two, then Witchien spoke to the two trusties who were waiting outside, and they also entered the cell. Clearly following orders, the trusties ripped a strip from a bed sheet and tied one end of it around Steven's neck. Then both of them stood him up and while one of them held him against the bars, the other threaded the rest of the material over the cross member at the top, pulled the material tight as they both lifted him off the floor and then secured it, leaving him hanging there. They all then quickly left the cell, and Rhonald locked the door behind them. Rhonald and one guard then hurried down to the end of the passage and vanished down the steps. Witchien was left to guard the door and make sure that anyone coming to look was moved on quickly.

But why would Rhonald and the guards do this? What did they have to gain by offing this guy or hanging him up if he was already dead? This puzzled us for a while, but eventually we agreed that heroin was definitely invoved and it would cause a problem with the outside authorities if Steven were seen to have overdosed in his cell and before the other prisoners were allowed to enter the building. Too many questions would be too hard to answer. A complete shakedown of the whole section by a team of unfriendlies from another section, or maybe even another prison, might have been required. Such a search could uncover far too much for comfort for Rhonald and his lackeys.

The answer was to make it look like a suicide instead of a dope overdose. Plenty of people get depressed enough to end it all in Thai prisons. There must have been at least ten inmates – both Thai and foreigner – who took that avenue during my first four years of incarceration.

Nevertheless, Reinhard did see Steven's legs moving, which means he was more than probably still alive when they strung him up. That constitutes murder in my book.

That same night, I wrote a report of what had happened and sent it under the table to the British Consul, but it seemed to be ignored, and the official cause of death was registered as 'self-inflicted strangulation'. That's what Steven's parents were told. However it was interpreted, it remained the senseless death of a genuinely innocent man.

When Willie told Ruth of Steven's death not long after learning about it himself, she simply tightened her lips a little, bowed her head slightly and looked down at nothing in particular for a few silent moments, then, nodding slowly but saying nothing, she touched his arm lightly and walked off. There were no tears, just an expression of resignation.

If this story has a moral, it might well be 'Do not trust foreigners, or anyone else for that matter, who might approach you when you visit Thailand and offer you unsolicited help or any kind of deal.' It can be, and very often is, a prelude to a very expensive and traumatic experience.

# CHAPTER 18

‖‖‖‖‖‖‖‖‖‖‖‖‖‖‖‖‖‖‖‖‖‖‖‖‖‖‖‖‖‖‖‖‖‖‖‖‖‖‖‖‖‖‖‖‖‖‖‖‖‖‖‖‖‖‖‖‖‖‖‖‖‖‖‖‖‖‖‖‖‖‖‖

# And the Iniquitous Stand in Judgement

NOTWITHSTANDING THAT MY NEW LAWYER HADN'T BEEN PAID A BEAN since he started work on my case, he was not what one could call a very impressive performer in the courtroom. His presentation lacked conviction and force, and his analytical skills seemed to be very limited.

After evaluating his performance when Fred and Hansel were in the witness stand at the very beginning of the defence case, I decided that I had no option other than to feed him with the questions he should be asking in order to get the answers we needed. I spent many weeks going over my analysis of the prosecution case and preparing my own defence, and then sent numerous letters detailing my requirements to him, with instructions on how I wanted him to handle the examinations.

Rather than cover everything at one time, I decided that it would be better to prepare the question-and-answer sheets in sessions, one for each hearing. I planned to spread my own testimony out over a period of at least several months so as to ensure that I had everything covered adequately. However, even though I had gone to all of these extraordinary lengths to ensure that the case was heard entirely and that nothing was missed out, my lawyer persisted in changing things around to suit himself. With the witnesses for the defence on the stand, and the opportunity to expose the many inconsistencies and obvious fabrications in the prosecution's case before him, he was far too pusillanimous and skirted around almost all of them, leaving our case seriously compromised in the process.

He didn't subpoena any of the police officers for re-examination, even though, with the right approach and because of the obvious inconsistencies in their testimonies, he could have demanded it. Nor was he forceful in his demands for subpoenas for other witnesses I wanted called. However, the most devastating abuse of my legal rights was the court's refusal to enforce its own order for the police to tender the video tapes that had been recorded in the Bangkok bank on the days in question and which would have been sufficient evidence to prove, beyond any shadow of doubt, that the major portion of the prosecution's case was fabricated.

When he complained to the judge that the police would not obey that court order and were refusing to produce the tapes, the judge asked the police the reason for their lack of cooperation. They replied that they 'didn't wish to tender that evidence'. My lawyer then asked the judge to enforce the court's order, but he replied that he wasn't empowered to do so – and did nothing.

The manager of the bank who had agreed to discount the letter of credit was called as one of the defence witnesses, but she stayed very much on the low road as well and conveniently couldn't remember a thing about the transaction. All of this was, of course, a far cry from what I was hoping for.

I was the final witness and gave testimony during seven sessions over a period of eight months, detailing everything as precisely as I could and forcing my lawyer to ask me questions that I wanted him to ask. When those questions were not forthcoming, I simply started to talk and wouldn't stop until he got the message and followed my lead. My answers were sometimes as lengthy as essays, but I took no notice of his impatience and fear, cutting him off if he interrupted before I had said what I wanted to say.

As the prosecution had made so much of the involvement of the Bangkok Bank staff in our arrest, I was keen to have those witnesses brought in to testify. The relevant bank officials were approached and agreed to assist, but when the time came for them to be subpoenaed, my lawyer forgot to serve them, and the witnesses didn't appear. In order not to waste our session entirely – or my nauseating bus trip – my lawyer challenged the court as to why it had not been able to force the police to produce the videotapes. The sitting judge discussed the matter with a colleague and asked to hear what I had to say about it. I took the stand again and explained for what must have been close to an hour what these tapes would reveal and why they were so vitally important to the defence. Why would we want them to be tendered, I asked, if doing so would prove detrimental to our case? And why, if the police had given truthful testimony, were they not willing to hand them over?

The judge recorded none of this testimony, but when I finished and returned to my seat, he adjourned the hearing for 30 minutes and left the courtroom. He returned with the Criminal Court Chief Justice, who told the court that he could not make the police tender the videotapes as evidence for the defence if they did not wish to do so, even though they had been issued with an order to that effect – this little sidestep was a blatant travesty of the judicial process, as the relevant sections of the criminal code prove. He went on to say that as there were no more witnesses to be heard – even though he was informed by my lawyer that this was not the case – the proceedings were to be closed forthwith. The trial was then terminated.

The only thing left was to have one final say with a comprehensive written summing-up statement. As there is no jury in a Thai court and the closing statement is not made directly to the panel deciding the case, the three judges who meet behind the scenes only have what is recorded by the sitting judge on which to deliberate. If the lawyer chose to deliver that statement verbally, it would be made to the young and inexperienced judge hearing the case on that day and, as such, would be superfluous. But a written summing-up statement can be handed directly to the judge and becomes part of the court case file and public record.

Considering the lawyer's performance, I decided a couple of months before the final hearing that there was only one way to do this, and it was for me and Brent to prepare the closing statement ourselves. By the end of August – four years and eight months after my arrest – the job was complete and the summary had been handed to the lawyer with instructions for him to have it tendered immediately.

He didn't. Instead he prepared and submitted a very mild submission of his own, one which would not cause loss of face for anyone or call anyone a perjurer or fabricator. Unfortunately, neither Brent nor I had any inkling that he had done this, and we didn't find out until some time after the verdict and penalty had been handed down.

I lay on the floor of the tiny cell of Section 5 in Klong Prem, staring at the mouldy grey ceiling. Only the dim glow from the small red pilot light above the cell door broke the darkness. The other four occupants were asleep, but for me it was going to be a very long night.

I had returned from the court several hours before in a state of shock and bewilderment. The heavy chains and shackles had not been removed from my legs, as they normally were on arriving back at the section on court day, and they hung heavily against my already bruised and lacerated shins. Hansel and I had been ordered to pack our things and were immediately transferred from Section 2 to Section 5 – otherwise known as the punishment section. My head ached, my throat and mouth were dry from the assault my nerves had suffered earlier, and my back felt as if it had been flogged. It was not an uncommon condition to be in after enduring a day in the filthy holding cells at court and the harrowing bus trip both ways, but things had been more traumatic than usual that day – a lot more traumatic. I had a constant urge to vomit as I lay with my back against the cold concrete floor, contemplating my next move, but I had nothing left to throw up.

That morning, I had been completely confident that I would be liberated. I had even gone so far as to plan what I was going to do after being released. I knew it would probably be late in the night, as was usually the case after an acquittal or bail grant, but that wouldn't stop me. Willie and Brent had agreed to lend me some cash to carry me over until I got myself sorted out, and I had arranged it all with Om that morning at court. As soon as she heard the not-guilty verdict, she was to book me into a nice hotel, buy me a set of decent clothes and make reservations at a good restaurant. After I had restored some of my shattered nerves with the soothing therapy of a long, steaming-hot shower, we were all going to have a lovely relaxing freedom dinner together to celebrate the victory. Then I planned to set the stage to sue the thugs who had put me in my predicament. As I saw it, I had a very good case against them, and I certainly wasn't going to accept lying down the losses I had suffered because of their greed.

It was almost five years since I had been thrown into a seemingly endless tunnel and for no other reason than these defenders and enforcers of law and order, and their accomplice, wanted to fleece me. For the first year, I had walked in darkness with not a speck of light to head towards, while they played out their ridiculous charade. But then the defence case began and the end had been in sight at last. After each hearing, the light became brighter, and that day I thought I was going to take the final step out into the sunshine and never look back.

It was the final day of the Criminal Court case and the day the verdict was to be handed down. I believed with all my heart that there was absolutely no possibility of conviction. There was not one iota of evidence to support the prosecution's claims, and even though my lawyer's handling of the case left a lot to be desired, I still thought that I had an ironclad defence.

Then, at the very last second, an explosion of insanity and confusion and shattered expectations flashed before me and the tunnel once again became a tomb. The liberating light had vanished. Even with all of the proof pointing indisputably towards my innocence, and no evidence at all to point towards my guilt, the court found for the prosecution.

Hansel was lying on the floor at the other end of the cell, apparently asleep. Fred was still in Section 2. He had been acquitted but was being held for a further 30 days to allow the prosecutor to appeal.

I kept asking myself, over and over, how was this possible? How could they possibly convict me and sentence me to death with the mountain of evidence showing my innocence? How was it possible? Where the fuck did the judges come from?

I had spent close to five years in a living hell, a world unimaginable to most people in civilised society, but I had been confident that that night it would be over. However, it was far from over, and that night was, in fact, the beginning of a whole new chapter of my life, one in which I saw and experienced a broad spectrum of degradation, torment and abuse, one that would sap my very essence and leave me clutching to the last thread of my life and existence on this planet.

# *PART 5*

A Vortex of Sludge, Vermin, Blood, Judicial Idiocy and Misery

Within the realms of power and influence,
the Eunuch is King.

*Baron Montesquieu*

# CHAPTER 19

‖‖‖‖‖‖‖‖‖‖‖‖‖‖‖‖‖‖‖‖‖‖‖‖‖‖‖‖‖‖‖‖‖‖‖‖‖‖‖‖‖‖‖‖‖‖‖‖‖‖‖‖‖‖‖‖‖‖‖‖‖‖‖‖‖‖‖‖

# Transferred to Hell

HELL SURELY HATH NO RIVAL BUT DEATH ROW, BANGKWANG maximum-security prison in Nonthaburi Province just north of Bangkok, where I was destined to become a resident, and where, as far as the Thai courts were concerned, I was to spend the remainder of my days – the last home I would ever know.

Both Hansel and I were transferred to Bangkwang six days after the Criminal Court judgment. The small cell that accommodated us in Section 5 till then was identical to the cells that we had left behind, and we shared it with five others – all Thai, each shackled with about ten kilos of chain. That I didn't throttle Hansel during that time remains something I can scarcely believe, because every time I looked at him, every time I heard him speak or even cough, the fire of resentment and loathing that raged within me intensified. I certainly came very close to the edge of my self-control several times, and I believe that it would have taken very little additional aggravation for me to lose it completely. Looking back now, I am quite sure that had we not been let out of that little cell during the day, I would have done something that I would later have regretted.

Hansel seemed to sense that there was a large keg of powder at the end of a very short fuse, and, not wanting it to be ignited, he didn't so much as speak one word to me while we were there. At night when we were locked up together, he made sure he was as far away as it was possible for him to be, ordering the other residents to position themselves between us.

During the day, from around 6 a.m. to 4 p.m., we were free to move around the section, which, unlike Section 2, had nothing more than the confinement building attached to a small, almost triangular concrete exercise yard that was surrounded by a four-metre-high concrete wall with barbed wire and an electric fence on top. There was a coffee shop of sorts, where small bags of prepared food, bread and a range of other items could be purchased, but it was not possible to order anything from the outside. However, because our prison accounts had not been transferred from Section 2 with us, neither of us had any money or credits with which to buy anything.

Hansel ate what the prison provided, but I was a little more fortunate. An Australian – let's call him Peter – with whom I had become quite well acquainted when he was in Section 2 came to my rescue and provided me with sufficient food from the coffee shop to save me from the prison slop. He had been moved to the punishment section a few months before for being a bit of a lad, and although that wasn't much of a blessing for him, it certainly proved to be one for me. I will always be grateful to him for his assistance. He was also well acquainted with Hansel and for that reason gave him a wide berth.

September is into the wet season in Thailand, and in Bangkok in particular when it's not raining it is generally as hot as hell, with humidity you can almost drink. There was no cover outside, and because we were not permitted to go into the cells during the day, we had no alternative other than to spend most of our time on the ground floor of the confinement building, sitting on the concrete, chatting or reading. The natives were employed manufacturing plastic flowers, but for us there was virtually nothing to do.

Brent, Willie and Om had all tried to visit on different days during that period, but as Brent didn't receive my mail for some days after it had been posted, they didn't know I had been moved to Section

5. Because no one took the time to tell any of them, they put in their visit request papers for Section 2. They then sat and waited, and waited some more, and wondered why I didn't show up. When Brent eventually did manage to find out where I was being held, he was told that I was not permitted to have visitors until I had been moved to Bangkwang.

Several British Embassy staff went to visit the British inmates at The Prem three days after I had been transferred to Bangkwang. None of them knew where I was, and they didn't bother to find out. They then deposited my monthly allowance from Prisoners Abroad to my account in Section 2 as usual. It took six weeks for that money to reach my account on death row, during which time I would have been in real trouble had it not initially been for two other inmates. Brent and Om couldn't see me for one week after the transfer, because death-row inmates were permitted just one visit per week, and they missed the first one.

As luck had it, a lifeline in the form of a young Thai fellow, who was about 25 years old – I'm going to refer to him as Tut (pronounced like 'put' not 'cut') – was virtually waiting for me to arrive. Tut was well acquainted with Om, who had written to him the same afternoon the verdict was announced, asking him to do what he could for me if I was sent to the section where he was being held. He had been an employee for about four years at the restaurant in Siam Square where Om worked, and after he had changed his job and become an assistant hairdresser at a beauty salon in Phyathai district, not too far from where Om lived, she had kept in touch with him almost to the day of his arrest and thereafter visited him regularly while he was being held in Bombat and later in Klong Prem.

Another lucky break was that he was being accommodated in Bangkwang's Section 1, which is attached to death row. And yet more luck – I was positively gushing good luck that week – because of his culinary talents, he was appointed as cook for the guards in the section and twice daily prepared food for them.

Tut's story is one that can be told a thousand times in relation to a thousand different people wasting away in Thailand's prisons, in as much as he knowingly committed no crime but was instead one of the many who had been suckered and used by drug traffickers as a diversion so that a large consignment of heroin could slip through the gates at Don Muang Airport on its way to more lucrative destinations.

Tut, an unsuspecting mule for one of the wealthy clients of the beauty salon where he worked, was caught with a specially made suitcase that had been given to him by the real traffickers to carry through the check-in at Don Muang International Airport, and which, unbeknownst to him, had a double-shell casing that was filled with several hundred grams of heroin. He was convicted and sentenced to life, hence his presence when I arrived at Bangkwang. Although he had appealed that verdict, it had been upheld in the Appeal Court, and as his family could not afford the cost of taking the case to the Supreme Court, that's where his chances of vindication ended.

My arrival on death row was yet another shock to my already fragile nervous system. I thought that I'd seen the worst that there was to see after Bombat and Section 5 at The Prem, and I was mentally prepared for no better, but I was not – could not possibly have been – prepared for what greeted me.

It was a little before noon when I was shoved, stumbling over my chains, into a filthy, stinking cell, four metres by seven metres, crammed with twenty-eight men, all of them Thai. The shackles I had been wearing in Klong Prem had been removed and another heavier set welded around my ankles. All of the occupants were similarly manacled and, as I was to soon discover, almost every one of them had been sentenced to death for assassination, brutal murder or for raping and killing children or young women.

I had been subjected to the crowded conditions in Bombat prison, but in the main the cells and the toilets there were kept reasonably clean, the inmates washed often and were not generally violent towards each other, and we enjoyed the privilege of being let out of the cells during the day. The Prem was in comparison quite comfortable. Though the cells were smaller, most of the time I shared mine with just two other inmates. None of that could be compared to this place, though, and I was appalled to see the conditions I was now being forced to live in. The stench was almost overwhelming.

The guards – there were three of them – didn't enter the cell when they pushed me in but rather stood at the door and shouted to the occupants to make room for me somewhere. Most of those inside simply ignored the order and looked at me like I was a roach intruding on their space. A couple started chanting derogatory remarks about me being a filthy farang invading their country and taking their women. Perhaps they were worried that this would create a shortage and that there wouldn't be enough left for them to rape and murder. Who can say?

Eventually, one of them, who was clearly used to being obeyed, calmly instructed some of those closest to the door to move a little to make room for me to sit and put down my meagre belongings. I ended up with an area of bare concrete no more than 45 centimetres wide and just as long as my body to call my own; as far as anyone was concerned, that was all I was going to get for 23 hours per day from then on.

I had no bed roll. When I was taken from Section 5 at The Prem, I was told that I could take only my carry bag with whatever it would hold and nothing else. This meant that I had several changes of clothes, some toiletries, a pair of flip-flops, some writing material, my case files together with a few letters and a few diaries that I had managed to save, and a bottle of drinking water that I had bought before I left.

I hadn't been there for an hour before a vicious verbal conflict erupted between three of the cell's occupants. It escalated shortly thereafter into a full-blown battle, resulting in one man being stabbed to death right before my eyes. I was numbed with the realisation that I was stuck in that cage filled with these wild animals for an indeterminate period, possibly years, and that at any time I could become a victim of something similar myself.

I sat petrified for most of the remainder of that day and night, scarcely noticing the filth or the cloud of mosquitoes as I became acclimatised to the activities and behaviour of this mixed bag of society's rejects. I don't know what happened to the attackers. They were removed with the body, and I never saw them again as long as I was there.

Death row is actually part of Section 1 in Bangkwang, which normally holds a total of one thousand or more inmates at any one time and consists of one main two-storey cell block with several attached factory buildings. The death-row segment is a closed-off area on the ground floor of the rear section of that block, separated from the remainder by a wall of spikes and barbed wire. It houses sixteen identical cells, eight on each side of a three-metre-wide corridor.

Almost all of the inmates are kept in their cells at all times, other than once in the morning and once in the afternoon when they are let out for about 30 minutes to wash themselves and their clothes at the water troughs. When that is done, those with no money collect their twice-daily and unvarying prison ration of boiled red rice and fish soup and take it back to their cells or to the tables in the corridors to eat. Others pick up the food that they have ordered and had sent in from the section coffee shop. The regime is strictly enforced and any who attempt to deviate from it are given a taste of what will be forthcoming if they persist. Those who ignore the warning are mercilessly flogged by the guards with wooden batons, on occasion until they are left with no further concern as to when they will be executed, because they already have been.

Alongside the open toilet block, the rest of the wall is taken up with rows of small lockers, and each inmate is issued with one of these in which to keep his belongings. There is an open concreted space in front of these lockers where the several wooden mess tables with attached benches are located and right beside them is an open sewerage drain that carries the untreated sewage from all of Section 1, as well as several other sections. That, of course, always stinks to the high heavens and harbours a relentless plague of vermin. Strung across between the toilet block and the main building at the end of this area, about six feet from the concrete, are several wires that are used as clotheslines.

Each cell has a small alcove of around two square metres, situated in the corner furthermost from the cell door and separated from the rest of the cell by a two-foot-high plastered brick partition. This is where the squat-type ceramic toilet bowl and a trough for water are located. At the time of my residence, the taps above these troughs had long since clogged with rust and were useless, making it necessary to carry water in from the outside troughs. This was probably the only chore that some of the inmates were prone to fight over; not to get out of it, mind you, but to have the privilege of taking a walk around outside the cell and getting some fresher air and a little exercise.

The only ventilation in the closed-off cell area was one small barred opening at the top of the outer wall and the bars on the cell door. There was no mosquito netting anywhere and no lighting at all. The ceiling fans – one in each cell – had quite obviously been turning for donkey's years without a clean and were thick with the built-up grime of a million smoked cigarettes, combined with the oily pollution and dust that had become an intrinsic component of the atmosphere.

Life had certainly had its cosier moments, but Tut proved to be a godsend right from the moment I arrived. He was working in the area, cooking for the guards, and, being forewarned, he recognised me as I was escorted into the section. That afternoon when I was let out of the cell for the prison-fare dinner, which I was certainly not going to attempt to eat, he came over to me with a big plate of fried rice that included all manner of tasty ingredients, such as shallots, Thai parsley, sausage and ham, a little grilled chicken, and some fried egg. He had cooked more than he knew the guards would eat, and for the next few weeks, he did the same thing at least once each day, and I was the beneficiary. The death-row guards were, without their knowledge, providing me with victuals, and very tasty and well-prepared ones at that. I will be for ever in Tut's debt for doing that, because I'm not sure that I could have survived otherwise.

After we had talked for a few minutes that first afternoon, he rushed off to organise a sleeping mat for me, paying only ten packs of cigarettes – half the normal price – for one about two inches thick. Not long after we had been returned to the cell for the night, he arrived at the door, and the guard allowed him to give it to me.

He also advised another inmate – let's call him Nik – with whom I was well acquainted from The Prem, of my arrival. Nik, an Italian, was serving life for dope trafficking and was being held in the adjacent Section 1. The following day, he saw that I was given the use of his credit at the coffee shop, which allowed me to at least feel a bit more secure in regard to sustenance. Both of these men became close friends of mine over the ensuing years.

Even with the added comfort of the mat, I wasn't able to sleep much that first agonising night, mainly because those lying on either side of me were a little (a lot) on the nose; as there were so many of us, they were actually squashed up against me. Apart from their body heat and odour, the temperature in the room and the September humidity were stifling, and the slow revolutions of the ceiling fan were doing absolutely nothing to mitigate it. I had nothing comfortable to rest my head against – the vinyl carry bag that I was using for a pillow was a poor substitute. In addition, because the occupants were either too lazy or too indifferent to flush it, there was a putrid stink wafting from the toilet from which there was simply no escape.

By morning, I wasn't feeling too cheerful. However, while I was at the wash troughs trying to decide, as evidently a significant number of my cellmates had already, whether I would stay cleaner by not washing than I would by using the filthy water there, I was approached by a Thai man whom I had heard quite a bit about since his arrest, and he managed to brighten me up considerably.

Ben – as I'm going to refer to him – had been sentenced to death for arranging the murder of his wife in what had become a rather sensational case. It had been in the headlines for months on end because his two-year-old daughter had been found in his wife's car, crying and holding on to her mother's decomposing body at least 24 hours after she had been shot. Ben, a doctor at the time of the murder, maintained that he was innocent of the crime, claiming that he was set up to take the rap by several adversaries.

Whether this was truth or fiction, I really cannot say, but one thing I must mention in his favour – he was to save my life twice in Bangkwang, so I owe him this – is that one of the prosecution's few witnesses was the child, still not three years old. I eventually read the transcripts of his trial, and right there in black and white was sufficient evidence, as far as I could determine, to show that his daughter had been coached with the answers to the questions she was asked. One doesn't need to be Einstein to understand that a baby is not capable of providing reliable testimony in a complicated case like this, especially bearing in mind the horrific circumstances and the fact that the trial was held many months after the event. The judge's words, as is the case with all testimony in a Thai court, replaced hers and, as such, were totally out of character. But as ridiculous as it might sound, the little girl's testimony was considered by all three courts as sufficient to hand down, and later uphold, a sentence of death. That's how things are done in Amazing Thailand. Some time later, a royal amnesty commuted his sentence to life in prison, but until then Ben was there with me on death row for close on three years.

From the way he spoke and joked with the guards, it seemed clear to me that he was on reasonably good terms with them and enjoyed privileges that most of the other prisoners didn't enjoy. Death row is no sanctuary from corruption, of course, and Ben had discovered on his arrival that if the right officials were suitably encouraged, certain benefits could be had.

He was, in fact, very pleased to see me arrive; certainly a lot more pleased than I was to be there. Being an intelligent and educated man, he craved the stimulation of sensible conversation, something that he had discovered was a mystery to most of his fellow inmates. My presence, as the only Westerner among the 250 or more prisoners, was also a chance for him to keep his English honed. He told me that he could arrange that I be moved to a slightly more comfortable environment if I wished, and being as how I was indeed wishing something like that at the time, I gratefully accepted the offer.

The following day, I was moved to the cell that Ben and just 12 others occupied. The contrast with my old cell was extreme, and almost immediately my taut and tormented nerves began to relax, albeit just a little. Although the cell was identical in size to the one I had just left, the space allowed for each of the occupants was considerably larger, about two square metres per person, and it was also evident that they had taken soap and scrubbing brush to it, because it was relatively clean and didn't stink like the sewer I had just left.

The men in the new cell were all several cuts above those whom I had been thrown amongst on my arrival. They were all clean, quiet and polite. A few were well educated and of sufficient means to allow them to keep their death-row occupancy at a bearable level of comfort. They included two previously high-ranking police officers, Major Pracha and Colonel Niran, who over time became good friends of mine and eventually very productive sources of information.

There was a mixture of crimes represented among them: several were hit men, several were drug traffickers, including one of the aforementioned ex-police officers, and several were murderers, including the other policeman. Then there was a young man who had sprayed a restaurant with M16 bullets to kill a group of people who had repeatedly gang raped him – two of his assailants/victims were cops. He was a little perturbed and repentant at having also inadvertently killed and wounded other innocent people during the attack, but as he explained to me later, he had just slipped off the deep end at that time and didn't care. His only thought was to kill his tormentors before they could attack him again. There was also one Islamic terrorist, who called himself 'the Avenger'.

All in all, they were a lovely group of chaps, and I considered myself fortunate to be now sharing space with them. Although they were probably no less dangerous than any of the other prisoners on death row and mostly deserving of their fates, they didn't appear likely to flare into spontaneous violent rage and start cutting me to shreds. This was some comfort, as over the following months I came to realise that about half of the 250 or so death-row residents were a few marbles short of a full bag and some nothing less than unpredictably vicious and crazy.

Many of the inmates showed little concern for the punishments meted out for any other offences they might commit before they were executed. In reality, there was very little that could be done to them that would be worse than what they were already experiencing, apart from perhaps a period of isolation in the punishment cells. These were just one metre square by one and a half metres high, with no window or light. But when one has been stuck for years in a cell cramped body to body with a bunch of lunatics, even the punishment cells might be considered an improvement, providing a chance to be alone and quiet for a time.

This was death row in all its glory, although that moniker soon took on a completely different meaning from the one intended. It wasn't simply a place to wait to be executed; it was a place where one could die at any moment. It was literally a row of death, and I had, with my transfer there, been catapulted into the most excruciating, inhospitable and inhumane environment that I could ever have contemplated in my wildest imagination.

# CHAPTER 20

|||||||||||||||||||||||||||||||||||||||||||||||||||||||||||||||||||||||||||||||||||||||||||||||||||||||||||||||||||||||||

# The Scabs from
# Society's Wounds

HANSEL, HAVING BEEN GIVEN THE LESSER SENTENCE OF LIFE, HAD been accommodated in Section 2, where he was locked in a cell from late afternoon till early morning only and things were a lot more comfortable. The food provided by the prison for foreigners was also of a slightly higher quality than that fed to the natives but, just the same, was not what those who could afford otherwise would choose to eat. According to the regular reports about him that I received, Hansel, having no reservations at all where food was concerned, ate the free stuff. True to form, though, he became an instant pain in almost everyone's posterior. He hadn't been in Bangkwang for more than three months before a group of Thai inmates who had apparently had quite enough of his nonsense decided to send him a little message.

As with Section 2 at The Prem, there was an open toilet area with low partitions between each of the rows of squat pedestals and small concrete reservoirs that held water for flushing and washing. This group decided one morning not to use the toilet block, but instead to deposit their waste into a bucket for 'recycling'. They also solicited donations from their friends until the bucket was filled. Having, after several days of surveillance, ascertained approximately what time Hansel took his ablutions, they moved into position a little beforehand and waited patiently beside the toilet block for him to make an appearance. He did, of course, and after he had pulled down his shorts to the chains on his ankles and had squatted over the bowl, they moved in from behind with their weapon and, taking care not to splash themselves, inverted it and placed it firmly on his head.

The shock of the attack caused him to stumble over his shorts and chains as he attempted to remove it, and he ended up flat on his back. His head smacked against the partition, and he gasped faeces into his mouth. He spent several minutes after he had managed to stand up desperately trying to cough them back out again.

I guess it's not so difficult to imagine what must have gone on there for a while as Hansel struggled to clear his eyes and nose and wash himself off with what water remained in the reservoir. By all accounts, it seems that he was particularly annoyed – and who wouldn't be? Dozens of inmates, including foreigners, witnessed the incident; however, as amazing as it might sound, nobody saw a damned thing, and not a single person could identify the assailants. The guards, aware that he was a shithead before the bucket landed on him, didn't even bother to investigate after he made his complaints.

Hansel's attitude changed little for the better, though; in fact, he plunged deeper into a chasm of hate and malice. But he did stay well away from the Thais in Section 2 for the remainder of his stay there.

Quite some time prior to leaving The Prem, Hansel had been heard to brag to all and sundry on numerous occasions that when he arrived in Bangkwang he would fake an accident and use his already damaged hip and wobbly legs as an excuse to be returned to Germany. Where he got that idea from, no one seems to know. Maybe someone suggested the idea to him; maybe it was nothing more than a product of his own imagination. I really have no idea, but he did mention it on several occasions while we were at The Prem, and I heard that not too long after the bucket episode, he had done exactly as he'd said he would.

\* \* \*

It didn't take me long to realise that death row was a 24-hour-a-day nightmare. The truth is that in the early days, after being let out for meals, bathing and so on, I was pleased to be locked back into the relative safety of the cell. There were a couple of other cells that held fewer than 20 privileged occupants, and they too seemed to remain virtually problem free, but the others were madhouses, where minor conflicts regularly erupted without preamble into all-out battles to the death. Almost daily, men were pulled out of cells and thrown into the back of pickup trucks to be disposed of or left in the corpse yard outside Building 13 for relatives to collect. Most died of injuries, many died from disease, some just gave up and killed themselves, while others were beaten into oblivion by the guards. Unlike Bombat, where inmates were flogged to death to satisfy maniac guards' sadistic urges, this usually only happened when there was reasonable justification for intervention. The guards on death row usually didn't enter cells to break up fights; instead, they left the inmates to continue to the end and then took the appropriate disciplinary action.

It was not uncommon for brawls to start outside of the cells during meal and wash periods as well, and that's mainly why I didn't feel too comfortable to be out and about with these renegades let loose.

At times, some of those in the privileged cells were permitted to stay out longer than normal, sometimes even up to a couple of hours, and on occasion I was given a little unsolicited favouritism in this regard by a couple of the guards. I don't really know why, but being the only Westerner there at the time probably had something to do with it. Whatever the reason, when it happened, and once all of the other inmates were safely locked up after their break, I usually sat at the tables to write letters and prepare things for my appeal.

One morning after breakfast, not more than three months after my arrival, I was doing just that – on this occasion, I had started before everyone had returned to their cells – when two men came over to where I was sitting. They weren't interested in me, however, or in what I was doing. They were there to kill another chap who was sitting beside me finishing off his meal.

With a viciousness that left me completely staggered, they hacked him to death with pieces of metal they had sharpened into blades, stabbing him repeatedly in the back and throat, his blood covering me and the letter I was writing to Brent. Several guards rushed up when they heard the guy's screams, and after one had used a cattle prod on the two offenders to slow them down, they pulverised them with their batons and boots right there and then. I sat in stunned, petrified silence, not able to move a muscle until it was all over. When the guards retreated, without a second glance in my direction, I slowly collected my belongings and moved cautiously around the three bodies and over to my cell, where a trusty with whom I was on pretty good terms, mainly due to Tut's influence, held them for me while I went to the water troughs to wash myself and the clothes I was wearing. When I returned, he unlocked the door to my cell and let me in.

Some time later, Ben told me that the prison authorities deliberately created this tense and murderous atmosphere, not merely to make life as unpleasant as possible for us, but to encourage the killing of one inmate by another. That was why those convicted of the worst and most heinous crimes were squashed together in conditions that could only result in conflict among them.

'It serves a purpose,' he said, 'and that is to get rid of some of the trash at the hands of other trash and so avoid the controversy and complications that generally surround executions. That is also the reason why there is no segregation of AIDS or TB sufferers on death row and why there is such a high infection rate and resulting death toll. It is also the reason why medical attention is virtually non-existent. Very few inmates are taken to the hospital section until they have to be taken there on a wheelbarrow, and by that time they are too sick to respond to the inadequate and amateurish treatment provided and rarely return.'

From what I was witnessing, Ben's claims all made perfect sense. Such a strategy might even be considered by some to be the perfect solution of eliminating those who are too dangerous to ever be returned to normal society.

Living in such a closed community as death row, and having two former police officers sharing my space for most of my time there, it didn't take long before I knew quite a lot about the crimes that many of the inmates had committed. Time was all we had – there was simply nothing else – so talking and sharing experiences and stories helped to pass the time and to keep the boredom under some semblance of control.

Most of the inmates who had already exhausted all means of appeal and were on the execution waiting list seemed to gain some satisfaction or enjoyment from bragging about their criminal and demonic accomplishments, so there were few secrets. It was actually a source of stimulation for some of the longer-term residents when a new convict arrived, as there would be something new to talk about.

Though the conditions we were kept under were nothing less than abominable, it became unquestionable in my mind that many of those being detained did indeed deserve to be locked up like the vicious animals they were and never released. One of the men in the cell in which I spent my first night was deserving of no mercy whatsoever. A man of reasonable build, in his late 40s and as ugly as a pug with crooked teeth, he was on his third conviction for raping pre-teen girls. His latest crime was the rape and murder of a two year old. This depraved vermin spent a lot of his time masturbating while looking at fashion magazines and sales brochures that showed pictures of young girls in swimsuits and underwear and talking about how much he relished his conquests.

Another fellow sharing the same cell had raped and murdered numerous teenage girls and young women and then dismembered them. 'I just love to see them all in little bits,' he'd say when asked why he cut up his victims. He admitted these crimes and frequently relived the experiences while his hand pumped in his lap.

Then there were the professional assassins, including two in my new cell, all once again admitting guilt; some, in fact, still soliciting business for when, *if ever*, they were released. These hit men sold their talents to some of the most highly placed people in the country. I was given the names of several of those customers, but even though many

Thais would not be surprised to see them, it wouldn't be prudent of me to include them here. It is more than a trifle sickening that those customers are still enjoying their 100,000-baht bottles of wine with their meals each day, while the assassins – the dispensable patsies – are on death row waiting to be executed for carrying out their orders. These illustrious clients are just as deserving but will never face the punishment for their own involvement.

There were also several vicious robbers who never failed to murder their victims so that there were no witnesses to point a finger at them. They too were happy to brag about their exploits, and few people would argue that they did not deserve to be removed from society, one way or another.

Another was a fisherman who owned a trawler and used it to smuggle Burmese workers from mainland Burma to a coastal region in southern Thailand. He was caught by the Thai Coast Guard and subsequently sentenced to five years in prison. He actually served just two years and six months. A few days after his release, he fired up his trusty old fishing boat again and began to do exactly the same thing, this time, however, with a very slight modification. He took recruitment fees from the workers, but instead of delivering them to Thailand, he killed them and fed them to the sharks in the Andaman Sea, stealing their belongings as a bonus. He admitted to fellow prisoners that he had murdered more than 50 Burmese men and women this way, adding with a laugh, and to lascivious exclamations from most of his audience, 'Naturally, I raped the women before I threw them overboard.'

He was now on death row because he was a little drunker than normal when he shot his victims one night. One, a young man, was only wounded and was strong enough – and lucky enough – to swim to shore without becoming a meal and subsequently made a report to the police. The fisherman was initially sentenced to death in the Criminal Court, but this sentence was later reduced to life in prison in the Appeal Court. He eventually had his sentence cut by royal amnesty and was released.

Another inmate who admitted his guilt was a man who simply could not be told what to do and resented it when his boss had the audacity to expect him to actually earn his wages. One day, after being scolded for his insubordination and incompetence, he went home and collected a hand grenade (one that he had saved from his previous military service, possibly for just such an occasion) and returned to the company office, which he proceeded to blow apart while his boss and three young female secretaries were still inside.

Then there was the unrepentant chap who was initially sentenced to 15 years in prison for raping a woman in Chonburi Province. He had his sentence reduced by several royal amnesties and spent just six years in jail. On his release, he went directly back to Chonburi Province, where he kidnapped, raped and murdered the 14-year-old daughter of the judge who had convicted him. This man spent a lot of his time telling those around him that he was glad that he had done what he had and if released would do the same thing to other young girls. In all likelihood, he *would* commit those or similar crimes if ever he were to be released. Few people would argue in his favour, and society will be a safer place if he remains where he is, there is no doubt about that.

There are, no doubt, those who would conclude that there is a certain justification for exterminating the vilest of the rats that plague our communities. However, I have never been an advocate of the death sentence, and even after several years on death row, living among scum that ought never to be allowed back into society, I still don't believe that it should be an option open to any judiciary. My reasons, however, influenced as they are by what I have learned of the judicial system in Thailand and other nations where corruption is rife, are probably at variance with those of other opponents of capital punishment.

In my own case, I had committed no crime at all – and had always been able to prove as much – but had ended up on death row simply because I had not been willing to hand over sufficient cash to Justice Incorporated to ensure that I received a fair and just hearing. While I was on death row and later in Section 1, I met quite a few others who had also been sentenced to death without committing any crime. Some, like me eventually, had their sentences commuted to life; others weren't so fortunate.

# CHAPTER 21

# Scapegoats Are Cheap Today, Cheaper than Yesterday

PROMART LEUMSAI WAS EXECUTED IN JANUARY, ALMOST EXACTLY SIX years after my arrest. Though I had seen him numerous times since arriving on death row, I first met him the day he was transferred to the cell I had by this time been occupying for about a year. One of my fellow inmates had won his appeal and been released, and Promart was quick to arrange sufficient incentive to be permitted to take his place in the cell.

I was initially surprised to discover that he could speak reasonably good English, and my Thai was coming on, so we were able to communicate very well. Over the following months, and probably due to our mutual need for some semblance of moral support, we became amigos and discussed our respective cases at length on many occasions. During these conversations, Promart related the circumstances surrounding his arrest and conviction, and it was as clear to me, and my two ex-cop buddies, that influential figures had played an iniquitous role. However, because of who and what they were, trying to expose them was never going to be possible, at least not in his own lifetime, which he expected to end in the very near future.

He told me that because the man a lot of people referred to as the 'Poison Dwarf' had been elected and become prime minister, he expected to be executed in the not-too-distant future. The Poison Dwarf, he said, was rather good buddies with the Kamnan, a powerful Mafia godfather who at the time controlled the whole of the eastern seaboard, including Chonburi Province and the sin-city of Pattaya, and the Kamnan wanted Promart dead.

Promart had been found guilty of two murders, and he believed that were it not for the Kamnan, he would not have been convicted. He admitted to me that he had carried out both killings, but he considered the second to have been self-defence, or at the very most manslaughter. He also professed that there was no evidence to link him to the first crime, though that had not stopped the police from tendering a false exhibit, in the form of a weapon, and a fabricated forensic report in relation to it.

The press in Thailand is frequently used by officials to hoodwink the public with misinformation, and, to give a good example of that, although drug trafficking did not form any part of Promart's charge, it was reported in one of the English-language newspapers to have been an associated crime. This additional offence materialised out of nowhere, evidently to add to the legitimacy of having the man executed.

Promart was the nephew of a respected (by some) MP – I'll call him Uthai. Uthai had been elected some years before to represent a district in Chonburi Province, where the Kamnan was the kingpin. However, Uthai decided some time after taking the reins that he was not happy to play the game the Kamnan's way. I'm not suggesting for a moment that he was totally incorruptible, mind you. With the reputation that Thai politicians have managed to make for themselves, it would be perhaps a little naive to go so far as that, but he was not prepared do what the Kamnan expected of him and refused to cooperate. There is little doubt that Uthai would have realised that the ramification of such impertinence could quite easily be assassination, something that wouldn't have been difficult for the Kamnan to arrange. And he soon did.

The hired killer, however, failed in his assignment, and Uthai lived to tell Promart that he had recognised his attacker as being one of the Kamnan's goons. Promart then took it upon himself to *hit* the hit man before he had another opportunity to strike. Though it wouldn't keep his uncle entirely safe, he reasoned that decisive retaliation would at least show the Kamnan that Uthai was no pushover. After all, who was the MP here?

One night, Promart ambushed his target in the garden of the hit man's home in the Chachoengsao Province, shooting him dead. There were no witnesses. He then dumped the murder weapon in the nearby river – where it is presumably still rusting to this day – to ensure that no evidence could ever be produced to connect him to the crime.

Several months later, Promart was at one of the many illegal gambling casinos in the Chonburi Province, playing cards, when there was a staged raid by off-duty police officers in plain clothes. They had evidently decided to make themselves a little extra pocket money the easy way. After all, who would complain?

Promart managed to wrap the tablecloth around the pot of about 300,000 baht in cash that was on the table and escape with it through a back door. He was pursued by one of the invading officers but managed to stay well ahead. After about two kilometres, the officer began to run out of steam and, unable to gain on Promart, pulled his gun and started to fire. Promart, not a bit pleased about this, pulled out his own gun and returned fire. Unfortunately for them both, he was a better marksman, and his first shot succeeded in blowing a nasty little hole in the cop's head. A rather unexpected turn of events, and one which rendered the poor fellow instantly lifeless.

The resulting investigation saw Promart arrested and charged with murder. Shortly afterwards, he was charged with the murder of the hit man, too. During the trial, the police tendered forensic evidence to prove that both victims had been killed with the same gun. Of course, it was useless for Promart to contest this, even though he did try to do so. It was his word against that of the police forensic scientists – conveniently the only variety of forensic scientists in the country at that time – and as such the odds were stacked against him. Also, he could hardly tell the court that this evidence could not possibly be genuine because he had dumped the gun he'd used to kill the first guy in a river. That wouldn't have helped at all.

The one redeeming factor was that the dead police officer had been off duty, and the mandatory death penalty for that crime was therefore avoided. However, as Promart had pleaded not guilty to the murder of the hit man, together with the fact that a totally fabricated charge of robbery whilst committing that crime was slipped in by the police, he was sentenced to death. Armed robbery resulting in a fatality is punishable by the death penalty, whereas murder alone carries the lesser penalty of life in prison.

In any event, he finished the day with one death sentence and one life sentence. I'm not sure if they were to be served concurrently or not. Nevertheless, he took the verdicts to the Appeal Court and then on to the Supreme Court, but in each case they were upheld. Promart was convinced that the Kamnan had an influence in all of these decisions.

So the wheels turn, the sun rises and sets, the seasons change, and the powers that be who wield the influence and dictate the terms move in and out of their respective positions. The Poison Dwarf became prime minister, and a couple of his more colourful associates became interior minister and justice minister. Not long afterwards, Promart was executed for his crimes. His appeal to the king for clemency had been railroaded and was never processed past the very initial stages. Both of the Kamnan's cherished sons were at the time members of the Poison Dwarf's political party, which was being sponsored heavily by the Kamnan.

Even though there were hundreds of prisoners on death row – many of them languishing there for a lot longer than Promart had – no one had actually been executed in eight years. It was, therefore, necessary to make Promart's execution appear to be justified in the eyes of the public. Bumping off another hit man wasn't really a good enough reason to have someone strapped to a cross and shot in the back.

The answer was simple: just get a few officials to say that he had been found guilty of viciously gunning down a police officer in cold blood and was being executed for that crime. Few people in Thailand would dispute the legitimacy of his being done away with on that basis – after all, it was the mandatory penalty. The media made a big noise about how he had been convicted and sentenced to death for murdering the cop, as well as drug trafficking, but this was bollocks. It was a whitewash, a smokescreen. He had been sentenced to *life* for killing the cop and to *death* for killing the hit man, and there were no drugs involved. Also, the second sentence could be commuted to life imprisonment on application to the king for clemency. Promart had duly made that application within the time limit, but it was clear that it was being deliberately held up. Two life sentences served concurrently would have meant spending around ten years in prison before being eligible for release on parole. Death was just a little more permanent.

At 4 p.m. on his final day, after all prisoners on death row were locked up for the night, a group of ten guards came to the cell where we were both resident. One of them called Promart's name, and he stood up. No one else said a word. We knew what was about to happen and that we were powerless to intervene, regardless of the circumstances.

Promart was resigned to his destiny; in fact, he considered it to be his karma. He simply looked over at me with the shadow of a smile, nodded once as a final salute and followed the officers from the room. They cuffed his arms behind his back and escorted him to the north-east corner of the prison compound, appropriately called Section 13, where they entered a small windowless, concrete-walled bunker through a small white door built into the side.

I can imagine him slowly looking around the room as he stepped over the threshold. Not that there was a lot to see, because although things have changed a little now, at that time it was a bare room except for a three-foot-high metal stand designed to secure the .303 calibre rifle that was to be used to end his life, and which was positioned about five feet from the wall at the right-hand end. The only other items that he would have been able to see were at the furthermost end, opposite the rifle stand. Two fabric screens were fitted into movable free-standing timber frames about three feet wide by six feet high. Attached to each of these screens was a small target printed onto a piece of white paper about six inches square. These were attached to the fabric with pins and could be moved as appropriate so as to position them precisely behind the heart of the condemned. To the right of the screens were the two timber crosses, each comprised of a vertical staff approximately six feet high with a crossbar positioned about four and a half feet from the concrete floor and made of three-inch-by-three-inch dressed teak. The upright staff had been concreted into the floor in front of a seven-foot-high stack of hessian bags filled with sand and painted white, which were piled up against the wall so that the executioner's bullets could be absorbed and rendered harmless – once their designated harm had been done.

It would have been only natural for Promart to take this all in as he was ushered towards those bags. It was 4.15 p.m. when one of the officers removed the handcuffs and brought Promart's hands around to his front as he faced one of the crosses with his back to the rifle stand and the sandbags before him.

The process, I later learned, was standard. The condemned's arms were placed over the crossbar so that it was tucked up under the armpits, then his forearms were tightly bound together from wrist to elbow. A lotus blossom and several incense sticks were placed between his palms, which were held in a prayer posture. One of the fabric screens was then pulled into position behind him so that he was not visible from the rifle stand and the target repositioned so that it was directly behind where the victim's heart should be. After all this was done, the prisoner was left alone until the executioner, several Corrections Department officers and a Buddhist monk entered the room with a couple of other officials. All but the monk waited at the rifle end of the room. The executioner then readied his implement of destruction, spending several minutes adjusting and sighting it until he had it aimed precisely at the centre of the small target. Meanwhile, the monk attended to the prisoner and lit the incense sticks he held between his palms. After talking to him and chanting for a few minutes, he slipped a white cloth bag over the victim's head, checked that it covered his eyes and left to return to the nearby temple from whence he had come.

However, this time was atypical. The director general of the Corrections Department arrived as usual to check that everything was as it should be and then waited with everyone else for the obligatory appearance of the Justice Minister and a few other high-ranking witnesses. When they hadn't arrived after about 15 minutes, the director general evidently decided to retreat to the prison director's office to wait in a little more comfort.

Promart would have had no idea when to brace himself for the impact of the bullet that was destined to tear through his body. He could only have assumed that it must come soon, and when it did, it would shatter his heart and end his life. With the hood over his head, he would only have been able to see the floor and, if he tilted his head back, the bottom of the sandbags in front of him. He could only have guessed at what was happening at the other end of the room while he waited. I'm sure he must have prayed to the spirit of the Lord Buddha to ask for forgiveness for his many sins and that his family be kept safe from the devils who controlled his country. I'm also sure that the tension would have been unbearable, but he had no option but to wait, as did the executioner and other officers.

It is an essential ingredient in any execution in Thailand that representatives of the Ministry of the Interior and the Justice Ministry, among others, be present to witness a prisoner's final moment and thereafter make the necessary reports. These ministerial representatives knew that they had to attend the execution, and they knew that it was scheduled for 4.30 p.m. that day. However, they didn't arrive at that time. In fact, it was not until after 8 p.m. that they *did* arrive, and slightly under the weather to boot. They had been delayed, they said, because they had had to attend a meeting and then have dinner after that. It's not nice to have to witness an execution on an empty stomach, after all.

Promart was left standing at that cross behind the black screen, holding a lotus blossom and the remnants of several incense sticks that had been destined to die before him, his arms no doubt turning numb and then black from lack of circulation, not knowing what was happening and not being told. Every agonising second, he must have been expecting to hear the report of the rifle and to feel, if just for an instant, the fire in his lungs. He was tortured in this way for nearly four hours. At times, he might even have thought that he was not going to die after all. It would be a natural reaction in such a circumstance to think that there might have been a last-minute reprieve. Of course, he had no way of knowing that glasses of fine wine and other culinary delights were considered to be of more importance than his suffering or the ending of his life.

With the exception of one man, a sensible and decent chap who I was to converse with often over the following years and who went to talk to Promart on several occasions that night, none of the officers spoke to him. He was a dead man as far as they were concerned, and they were of the opinion that one does not talk to dead men. Besides, they had nothing to tell him. They wouldn't have known themselves why the ministers were late. They simply had to do what Promart was doing: wait.

At 8.16 p.m., his heart beat for the final time when, without warning, the explosion of the cordite in the .303 cartridge propelled the small hollow-point projectile that pierced his back and carried most of it through the front of his chest.

After the execution, the officers and the ministers left the room, and Promart's lifeless body was left hanging on the cross. The following morning, several prison trusties were charged with cutting it down and putting it into a plain plywood coffin. Two of these trusties were friends of Tut's from Section 1, and they later told me how they had to chase dozens of rats away from the body before they could cut the ropes from around Promart's forearms. However, the body had been left in the gloomy confines of the execution chamber for more than ten hours, and the rats had already partially devoured him. The trusties put what remained of Promart in the box and carried it out of the room through Section 13 to a small red door in the prison wall that the Thais call 'Pratu Phii', meaning 'the Ghost Door', and out into the lane that led to a Buddhist temple nearby. They walked across the lane and into a fenced-off area with a small crypt-type building, which was part of the temple complex, and into the yard behind. There they put the coffin out in the open, where it was exposed to the elements, on the concrete floor against a two-feet-high concrete fence that surrounded the yard before returning through the Ghost Door to the confines of the prison.

Promart's family would have had to collect his remains within seven days. If they didn't, the box would be taken to the nearby temple and incinerated in the cremation chamber there. In such a case, the immediate family would be billed for the service. If they had lived in China, they would also have had to pay for the bullet that killed him. This additional humiliation, though, hasn't been introduced in Thailand – at least not yet.

As a final insult, and almost as disgusting, right there beside the small, sun-drenched yard, and in an area of about twenty square metres, fenced off on two of the remaining sides with a two-feet-high concrete wall, is a stinking fly-, cockroach- and rat-infested garbage dump, where all of the refuse from the prison and the adjacent village is kept until it can be collected by the sanitation authorities.

His family did collect the body that same day, and he was given a decent funeral. What was left of him was cremated, as is the Thai custom, several weeks later . . . Rest in peace, Promart.

A total of 170,000 heinous crimes were committed in Thailand during the fiscal year of Promart's execution – a 400 per cent increase on the same period 15 years before – and many people would say that there is a strong argument in favour of having the death penalty at the disposal of the authorities. However, there is no getting away from the fact that innocent people, me included, are sentenced to death and that some are executed. It can only be hoped that sometime in the near future the entire Thai judiciary will be streamlined and that the authorities will ensure investigations are carried out more thoroughly, with more cross-checks and balances, before any 'final solution' action is taken.

The execution at the same prison of Bunchote Pongprahom the

year after Promart's was, as far as I could see, the murder of a totally innocent man. He had been inequitably convicted through the three courts of Thailand – mainly as a result of fabricated evidence that was tendered by the police – and sentenced to death.

Bunchote was a married man with three young children who lived with his family, including his aged mother and father, on a small farm in the south of Thailand. Besides working on the farm, he earned extra income in the early hours of the day tapping rubber at a local plantation. A sober and decent man, he was well liked and respected in his village and had many friends there. It therefore came as a shock to these people when he was arrested and charged with the rape and murder of one of the teenage children from the village.

As is the case in small villages the world over, very little can be done without others becoming aware of it, and news always spreads like a locust plague. As such, it wasn't long before the identity of the real perpetrator of the crime was revealed as being not Bunchote, but the son of a high-ranking local police officer. On learning of this development, the villagers rallied behind Bunchote and protested that he was an innocent man who was being framed. His wife swore, too, that he couldn't possibly be the murderer because he was with her and the family at the time the crime was supposed to have been committed.

Unfortunately for Bunchote, the uneducated and illiterate in Thailand are often used as scapegoats when influential people and their families wish to avoid the consequences of their criminal activities being exposed. Daddy cop needed one of those to save his brat's arse and the family name from tarnish, and to that end evidence was produced by the police to show that Bunchote was the bad guy. The witness to the crime was silenced by threats of retaliation against him and his family – but only after he had already made the whole village aware of what had actually happened.

Bunchote was sentenced to death in the Criminal Court, and the decision was upheld in the Appeal Court and Supreme Court. This whole process took less than 18 months, whereas under normal circumstances it would have taken several years, particularly because the death penalty was involved. In my own case, it took five years to get past the Criminal Court.

By the time this drama had started, the government had changed leadership and a rather famous ex-cop now held the post of deputy in one of the most powerful ministries. He was also purported to be a close friend of the father of the murderer. Having a few spoiled-brat sons himself, who were continuously in trouble, it seems he must have known how his poor buddy was feeling and offered a helping hand.

If you add two and two together here, you can see how concrete evidence becomes unnecessary: the brotherhood of cop and ex-cop provides the catalyst for solving the problem. But things had to be tidied up quickly. The then government was on shaky ground at the time, and there was every possibility that the ex-cop might not remain in a position to assist for much longer. And move with unjustifiable haste he certainly did; after all, what are friends for?

During the course of the trial, the villagers protested outside the courts and supported Bunchote, appealing for careful consideration of his case, and this attracted quite a lot of media attention. At the time this was happening, however, the real culprit committed suicide, apparently unable to withstand the pressure from his neighbours to confess and save Bunchote from a terrible injustice.

Providence, it seems, was not working in Bunchote's favour, because at almost the same time as the murder that Bunchote had been falsely accused of was committed, another man raped and killed two very young girls. He was arrested, admitted his crimes and was eventually sentenced to death. The Thai public was in uproar, and justifiably so. 'This scum must be eradicated! Hang them! Shoot them! Castrate them!' were the battle cries that drowned out the protests of Bunchote's supporters and denied him his right to a fair and just hearing. He was convicted and sentenced to death, then transferred to Bangkwang, where he initially shared a cell with me. The two of us talked together often, and even after I had been transferred to Section 1, I still saw him regularly when I went to the death row section to access my locker.

After the Supreme Court upheld the verdict and death sentence,

Bunchote's family, supported by many of their friends, submitted a petition for a royal pardon on the grounds that the trial was not fair. Bunchote, they said, was innocent of any wrongdoing and was a scapegoat being sent to slaughter for the crimes of another man. Every one of his supporters expected that this appeal would be successful and that he would be spared the bullet. However, they hadn't factored the deputy minister into the equation. The clemency petition never made it past the first base.

There had recently been a groundswell of protest from the public about the rising crime statistics, which provided an ideal opportunity for the deputy minister to score a few political points and kill two birds with one stone: a strategy that allowed for the genuine child killer to be used as a smokescreen to remove Bunchote from the picture post-haste as well, and with the passionate approval of the general public.

Both men were executed at the same time on the afternoon of 5 November, one of the condemned being 100 per cent guilty and the other 100 per cent innocent.

After the executions, several of the prison guards in Section 1 and on death row took up a collection to which many of the other guards and prisoners contributed. They raised a total of 7,000 baht for Bunchote's wife to help her give her husband a respectable funeral. This unprecedented and genuine gesture clearly said what they all knew full well: that an innocent man had been killed to protect the name of an influential family. It was common knowledge, but no one could do anything to prevent it.

It was early in the morning after both men had been shot through the heart that one of the guards who had been forced to witness the event – the same one who had talked to Promart several times while he was tied to the cross waiting to be shot – came to talk to me. He handed me a photograph of Bunchote's three children, one girl about fifteen years old, another about six and a boy around ten, with an address scribbled in Thai on the back. He told me that Bunchote had given it to him moments before he had been strapped to the cross and asked that it be given to me with a request that I provide them with a little assistance if ever I was released. He was worried that his wife would not be able to earn sufficient money to send them to school and that they would end up being as illiterate as he was at his death. I took the photo but made no promises. That same day, the government collapsed and the deputy minister was out of office.

Bunchote's appeals to the higher courts were both thorough and well put together: they clearly showed the inconsistencies in the prosecution case and provided clear evidence of his innocence, yet they were ignored. His Criminal Court trial finished on 18 June the year before his death, and he was executed – murdered, in fact, for that, in reality, was the case – a year and a half later, ahead of hundreds of others in the queue, some of whom had been waiting in line for up to eight years.

I heard later from another inmate who came from the same province as Bunchote that he had heard that Bunchote's wife had died just three months after her husband had been executed – leaving the children with their elderly grandparents. Evidently, she was unable to come to terms with what had happened and the deep depression that resulted must have sapped her will to carry on.

About 18 months after Bunchote had been shot, a Thai man, Pan Saithong, was arrested for allegedly raping and murdering a five-year-old girl in a school toilet block. He was convicted and sentenced to death. At the time, many people believed that this punishment was entirely appropriate.

However, Pan had the mental capacity of a young child. For this reason, after his conviction he was not sent to death row, but was instead accommodated in the same part of Section 1 as me. During his stay there, he spoke to no one and no one spoke to him. Everybody, including me, assumed that he was as guilty as hell, and he never once defended himself against the charge, mainly, we belatedly discovered, because he was hardly capable of stringing two sentences together. On 21 June 1999, he was taken from his cell at 4 p.m. and escorted to Section 13, where he was strapped to one of the wooden crosses and shot through the heart.

On 14 December 1999, a Buddhist monk from the temple adjoining the same school where the child had so abruptly and brutally lost her precious life was arrested for trying to commit an identical crime in the same toilet block. Fortunately for his victim, the monk's attempts were thwarted by an adult. During interrogation, he confessed to the rape and murder of the first child. Pan Saithong had been nothing more than a convenient scapegoat, thrown to the wolves to appease the fury and lust for revenge of an enraged community, and also, no doubt, to highlight the efficacy with which the police rapidly solved such heinous crimes.

Pan didn't have a lawyer and didn't contest the charges. He simply re-enacted the crime exactly as the police told him to – in an event that was televised for public consumption – and went through the motions of a trial. He didn't testify in his own defence, and nobody testified for him. The poor fellow had absolutely no idea what in hell was happening.

To make it even more unpalatable, the monk wasn't sentenced to death – you can't execute a monk in Buddhist Thailand, after all – regardless that the mandatory penalty for this offence was death and that an innocent man had been shot through the heart for the crime that this monk had committed.

These cases alone, not to mention my own – and they are but the tip of the iceberg – show only too clearly that the present judicial system in Thailand is archaic and is used and abused by influential persons and groups for their own ends. If there is to be any legitimacy at all in having the death penalty as a final solution, this abuse must never be allowed to happen.

However, to add further potency to the arguement against the death penalty, particularly in Thailand, in March 1995, Pramarn Chansue, the recently retired former Supreme Court president, admitted in a nationally televised interview that between 25 and 30 per cent of the inmates in Thai prisons were innocent of the charges for which they had been imprisoned. Even the lower 25 per cent translates to around 60,000 innocent people languishing in Thai prisons at any given time – that's more than all of the people who are imprisoned in Australia and New Zealand combined.

As incredible as these revelations were, they were practically ignored by Thailand's powers that be and the rest of the world. Many of these 60,000 innocent victims of numerous nationalities may never be released; some will be flogged to death by vicious guards; many will die from any of the multitude of diseases that they are exposed to constantly; some will be killed by other prisoners; others will commit suicide, no longer able to tolerate their predicaments; some will be executed; and most will be used as virtual slaves to manufacture products for export or domestic sale.

None of this is a mystery to global organisations such as Amnesty International or the UN or heads of state, but still nothing at all has been done to correct this massive abuse of legal and human rights and absolutely no action has been taken by the international community to force Thailand to initiate appropriate reform. Quite the contrary, many of the so-called civilised nations of the world are still pouring truckloads of cash into Thailand and patting it benevolently on the shoulder.

There is no justice or legitimacy or morality in dragging a case out for years on end and then sentencing a person to death – or handing down any other penalty for that matter – after refusing to allow that person to prove his or her innocence. The death penalty in particular must never be a sentence option to any judge where there is even the remotest possibility of innocence. A defendant must be given the right to discuss, freely and without restriction, anything that he or she wishes to discuss and which could influence the outcome of the trial, prior to the verdict being handed down. The defendant must also be allowed to understand what is being said and done, with expert translations being made available where necessary. That is certainly not the case in Thailand: most foreigners, and many Thais, have absolutely no idea what is being said during their trials.

When a person has strenuously defended his innocence throughout his trial and has detailed exhaustively how he cannot possibly be guilty; when he has shown that there is definite and indisputable evidence of his innocence in the hands of those who are trying to have him convicted and that those same hands have deliberately fabricated the case against him; when he has been thrown into a situation where he is in serious danger of being killed or maimed, a place where it is impossible for him to effectively prepare or organise his defence, being crammed and chained in a cell 23 hours of every day, with just a tiny space to himself, this cannot by any stretch of the imagination be called a legitimate judicial and penal system. It can be called nothing else but an abomination of disorder and abuse, and as such the death penalty must be slashed from the Thai criminal code. The rest of the civilised world must insist on it.

About six years after Pramarn's shocking revelation, while speaking at a party meeting, the then prime minister, Thaksin Shinawatra, confirmed that a large percentage of prisoners in Thai jails were innocent victims of incompetence, corruption and malfeasance. He claimed that he knew with certainty that a minimum of 20 per cent of prison inmates had been wrongly convicted. Once again, this was completely ignored by all international bodies and most of the Thai population.

# PART 6

## Trekking Through the Minefields of My Destiny

I am the monarch of all I survey,
And I don't give a bugger what you say.
Maybe you'll be as good as me some day.

*Anonymous*

# CHAPTER 22

# Reduced to Heroin-laced
# Smoke and Ashes

ONE MONTH AFTER FRED HAD BEEN ACQUITTED, THE PROSECUTOR appealed his not-guilty verdict, and he was ordered to be held in custody until the appeal had been heard. Though he was entitled to be released on bail while he was waiting, he had no money to put up as surety, and the Australian Embassy provided no assistance, so he spent a further ten months in Klong Prem, waiting and praying for the Appeal Court to confirm the verdict.

A short time before the eventual acquittal, Hansel played his disabling-accident card in Section 2 of Bangkwang by pretending to fall down the stairs in the confinement building and rendering himself supposedly incapable of walking. Although I didn't hear about it until some time later, it seems he put on a pretty good performance, because he was transferred to the hospital at The Prem, where he was given a wheelchair to ride around in. However, he had made a lot of enemies while he was at that prison prior to his conviction, and one of them decided to get some revenge. He made arrangements for someone on the outside to communicate with the head doctor at the prison hospital, as well as the German Embassy, with a report that these injuries might well be part of a premeditated plan to deceive the authorities. The good doctor then took a closer look at Hansel and discovered that he was indeed faking. He was immediately kicked out of the hospital, wheelchair and all, and the doctor made sure he was sent once again to Section 5 – one of the worst at The Prem – to await transfer back to Bangkwang.

While he was there, I received a note from two Italians who were also awaiting transfer to Bangkwang. I knew these fellows well from my days at The Prem, and they told me that Hansel was having lots of fun making everyone miserable.

After a few months, and as he was getting nowhere fast with his quest for repatriation to Germany as a fake cripple, Hansel decided on a new tactic and proceeded to have a fake heart attack. Once again, he was taken to The Prem hospital. The doctor, once bitten twice shy, ran several tests and discovered that he was bullshitting again. Now, with something of a reputation as the shepherd boy who cried wolf, back to Section 5 he went.

It was around this time that Mikhail Rhonald began to discover that when the Lord Buddha said 'everything changes and nothing stays the same' he must have known what he was talking about. The corrupt and sadistic animal who was acting first and foremost as his partner in crime and second as the Section 2 building chief was replaced on the order of the new director, who had just weeks before taken over control of The Prem. The new building chief had been hand-picked: he was not corrupt and was fair and considerate but tough on the likes of Rhonald. The change had been initiated by the new director with the specific objective of cleaning up the drug problem in that section, and very shortly after his arrival Rhonald's little house of cards came tumbling down around his ears.

Although he thought he was an expert on the subject, Rhonald really had very little understanding of Thais in general. Because he had dealt solely with the corrupt and decadent element of society whom he invariably managed to manipulate or control, he considered all Thais to be tarred with the same brush. He didn't consider for a moment that there are many very religious and honourable people in all levels of society who are not corruptible, who follow the teachings of a variety of venerated religious figureheads and who adhere to the highest level of moral standards regardless of their station. And he didn't appreciate it one bit when there was a change in the line of command or when the officers he had in his pocket were shuffled around, because every time that happened it cost him money to recruit and train their replacements.

I was later told by someone who was there that Rhonald – being the dumb shit that he was – approached the new building chief to tell him exactly where he stood and what would be expected of him. The new boss let Rhonald talk, nodding and showing a lot of interest in what was being said; however, when Rhonald had finished his spiel and asked the chief if he would like to have dinner with a very pretty young friend of his the following evening, the chief jumped on top of him, punched him in the face and had him put in chains. Soon afterwards, all of Rhonald's little perks were removed: no more newspapers delivered to his door with his morning coffee before the other inmates were let out of their cells; no more being permitted to stay out of his cell at night after all the others were locked up; his two little Thai bum-boys were taken from his cell and replaced with Mattie Anderson, along with a couple of huge Nigerian inmates, which combination made for far less comfortable sleeping conditions; and his private TV was confiscated and given to some of the Africans to use in their community area. Then his garden house was worked over and all of the appliances and conveniences removed. When a five-litre pot of home brew was found there, he immediately received two class cuts from excellent to good (class being the way inmate behaviour is graded). The guards who were discovered to be his confederates were transferred to far less comfortable outpost prisons, and Rhonald became just another criminal inmate with nothing but misery for company. In short – and I was ecstatic to be informed of it – his empire had been destroyed.

The new director had replaced his predecessor for one main reason, and that was to clean up the drug trade and abuse in all sections of Klong Prem, particularly in the foreigners' sections. Several weeks after

Rhonald had been crushed, the director gathered all of the foreigners in Section 2 and told them that he would give them one chance to eliminate the problem themselves. He was no doubt aware that, due to the nature of the material used to build the shacks in the garden, it would be very difficult for him to police it properly himself – there were just so many places where drugs could be hidden. He told the inmates that if they could regulate themselves, they would all be given fair and even preferential treatment. If they could not, he would have no option other than to do it for them, and they would lose all sorts of privileges as well.

All things considered, this was a very realistic approach, but the foreigners didn't see it that way, and, refusing to cooperate, they protested to their respective embassies. Several of the consuls then challenged the director. As a result, a set of conditions were agreed by the inmates and the director:

1. The foreigners' garden could stay open provided the prisoners themselves policed the drug situation and held it in check.

2. If any inmate was found with or using drugs, he would be immediately and permanently moved to the punishment section and put in chains.

3. If the inmates did not clean up the drug problem themselves within three months, he would do it for them, and the garden compound would be closed permanently.

The drug situation did improve temporarily – mainly thanks to unannounced spot urine checks – but it didn't last long. Some of the guards, seeing a fabulous opportunity to fleece their charges, began selling small sample bottles that they had filled with drug-free urine, and for a rather hefty fee would palm one to anyone concerned about a positive reading when tested. Eventually, the urine checks became less frequent, and in a few months it was business as usual.

The core problem, however, was that most of the Westerners stuck in prison in Thailand simply cannot cope with the realities of their situation. Being spaced out on dope is for some the only way they can get through the day. Although Rhonald had been severly chastised, he and his buddies took full advantage of this.

It was a losing battle as far as the new director was concerned, so he decided to tackle the problem the Thai way. Two weeks later, at about 11 p.m., after everyone was locked up and most of the inmates were asleep, the garden was torched: 'spontaneous combustion', they claimed. All of the bamboo buildings and their contents, except the coffee shop and one other alongside the lake, were reduced to heroin-laced smoke and ashes. The director had closed the foreigners' garden, just as he had threatened he would.

Some time later, the buildings were replaced with permanent open structures, but they were not built for the foreigners' benefit. They had had their chance and had blown it. Instead, the space was used far more profitably for additional workshops.

# CHAPTER 23

‖‖‖‖‖‖‖‖‖‖‖‖‖‖‖‖‖‖‖‖‖‖‖‖‖‖‖‖‖‖‖‖‖‖‖‖‖‖‖‖‖‖‖‖‖‖‖‖‖‖‖‖‖‖‖‖‖‖‖‖‖‖‖‖‖‖‖‖‖‖‖‖‖‖‖‖‖‖‖

# Fighting Against the Odds

ALMOST AS SOON AS I HAD BEEN MOVED TO DEATH ROW, I STARTED working on my appeal. It took me a couple of weeks to get myself acclimatised and to send a letter to Brent, asking him to get copies of the judgment from the court for me. I wanted to translate them myself to find out what the hell had happened and why I was not acquitted along with Fred. This was never going to be easy, however, because other than the times I was permitted to use the mess tables, I had to do all my writing in my small allotted space in the cell – with all of the associated disruption from the other occupants. I'd either have to place my pad on my lap or hunch over on my knees, with the shackles digging into my shins and with the pad on the floor.

There were other problems too, one being the noisy conditions in the visit area. Most of the time it was necessary to shout every word slowly, then try to catch the reply with our hands cupped around our ears. All in all, it was a hopeless place to try and arrange the essential matters of defence and appeal, and in reality good for little other than receiving some moral support from the outside.

It was fortunate that we had begun work on the translations and had prepared the summing-up statement for the Criminal Court months previously, before I had been convicted, because it meant Willie already had all of this material stored on his computer, and it was a relatively simple matter to rearrange it and add bits and pieces here and there to point out why the judgment was flawed.

I had also given considerable thought as to how my lawyer had completely cocked up the summing-up statement after we had so meticulously prepared it for him. What he had submitted instead was nothing short of a pathetic grovel that completely ignored all of the false evidence, the frequent perjury and incredible amount of inconsistency that made up the farcical prosecution case. Perry Mason he certainly was not, and it had become painfully obvious to me that I had to prepare the appeal petition myself. This time I would insist that he submit it precisely as he received it, without modification of any nature.

I pointed out to Brent that it was not good enough to say things such as, 'It was *suspicious* that none of the police made a single note all the way through their supposed involvement.' Or pussyfooting around with stupidity such as, 'The Defence has cause to *suspect* that the plaintiff has fabricated some evidence.' For crying out loud, what the hell was the fool talking about? It would have been far better to have said, 'This police witness did not make any notes because he was never there, and as such he is a perjurer. Also, there is definite proof, in the form of the exhibits that the plaintiff has provided, that the case against the accused is fabricated in its entirety and that *all* of the police witnesses have perjured themselves.'

I explained to Brent that we had to call a spade a spade, that there were a hundred or more inconsistencies in the prosecution's case. We had to broach each one and spell them out line by line in as simple a manner as possible: 'This police officer said in his first testimony that he saw the car being driven by accused two [as I was referred to in court] on the first occasion in question at the bank. Then he said in his second testimony that he did not see the car on that day. These two statements contradict each other and cannot both be correct. In the face of the plaintiff's refusal to tender evidence that has been subpoenaed by the court, we must point out that this is a breach of the criminal code, and, that being the case, the plaintiff remains in contempt of the court.'

And I had another reason to be concerned about my lawyer by this time. I had met two other inmates who were being held in Section 1. One was Nigerian and the other Iranian. They told me that my lawyer had acted for them as well and that they had been convicted by the second court because he simply forgot to submit their appeal.

Within a couple of weeks of receiving the draft of my petition, Brent got the word-processed version, together with the translation, back to me. He also sent a supply of medication for the ulcers that had developed on my ankles from the constant irritation of the rusty chains that I was still burdened with.

It had been rough going, but the end result was an excellent petition. It showed why *all* of the reasons given by the Criminal Court judgment for convicting me were refutable and challengeable, and why the guilty verdict was not sound because there could not possibly be 'no doubt of guilt', as the prosecution was obliged to prove. As the Thai criminal code dictates that the benefit of doubt – when there is doubt – must be given to the defendant, it was clear that my conviction and sentence should be overturned and that I should be released without further appeal by the prosecutor.

At the same time we were preparing this, I was attempting to get the British Embassy to organise for the chains to be removed from my legs. Apart from the fact that they were causing me actual injury, it was illegal for the prison authorities to be doing this to me. Not only was this clear from the Thai penal code, it was also covered in the Universal Declaration of Human and Legal Rights, of which the Thai and British governments are signatories.

To relieve a little of the stress and discomfort the chains were causing and to keep them from dragging on the concrete as I walked, I tied a piece of cord around my waist and hung them from the central link so that I ended up with a rather attractive inverted 'V' extending from each ankle and peaking at my crotch – a nice touch and, although a bit rough on the back and the hip joints, it did allow me to get the 'inmate shuffle' perfected after a while. I was also able to add a little colour here and there, with dabs of iodine, aquaflavine, Mercurochrome and a Band-Aid or ten stuck on my ankles and shins in random display, and that did look nice. However, despite extensive efforts, I was stuck with them for more than two years.

Though the petition had been handed over to the lawyer for submission in good time, the Appeal Court was not due to deliberate on it for a few more months, and until then there was little that any of us could do but wait and pray. It was during this waiting period that I was approached by the lawyer who had initially handled my case, and, being not the least bit shy about it, he offered me a quick and certain fix to my torment.

There weren't a lot of surprises in what followed: as an ex-prosecutor who knew all of the judges who would be deliberating on my petition, he assured me that if I paid him two million baht he would see to it that I was acquitted and released. It was a Justice Incorporated manoeuvre that I was fully aware of after my involvement with Paul Worseluck, and it seemed the script hadn't changed a lot: convict in the Criminal Court regardless of evidence and hand down a severe penalty; make it discreetly known in plenty of time through an agent that the verdict will be reversed if a certain incentive is provided; acquit in the Appeal Court; have the prosecutor appeal that decision; allow the accused to put up bail and leave the country before the Supreme Court has heard the appeal.

It probably goes without saying that I would have taken the opportunity if I had had the necessary funds, but unfortunately I didn't. However, believing that my appeal petition was conviction-proof, I was confident that I would be released.

The Appeal Court verdict day arrived, and I was taken to the court to be reunited with Fred. Our lawyer had confirmed when I talked to him two weeks before the hearing that he had submitted the petition precisely as it had been prepared for him but said that he would not be attending the court with us because he had another engagement in the south that day.

Brent, Willie and Om were sitting in the back row as we were ushered into the courtroom. We were all confident that this would be the end of it: the final day, the day of my liberation. As astonishing as it might seem, though, another case was being heard in that courtroom at the same time. Three judges, two male and one female, sat in front of a large mosaic of the scales of justice emblazoned in gold, with large photographs of the Thai king and the queen centred on the wall above. The female judge, who sat on the left as we faced her, and the male beside her were turned towards each other, he whispering seductively into her ear and she giggling in response. The other male judge was listening to one of the lawyers for the defendant in the other case (he had three of them in attendance), who was questioning a uniformed police officer in the witness seat in a very loud, aggressive and intimidating manner. This was unusual to see and had me thinking that I should have employed this fellow myself. The prosecutor for the other case was sitting chatting with the prosecutor for our case in a fenced-off area in front of us, neither paying any heed whatsoever to what was going on.

We waited for approximately five minutes, then abruptly, as if she had just remembered what she was there for, the female judge interrupted her dalliance, turned to face the court and, with a curt snap at the bailiff, had us brought forward to face her. We stood, Fred and I, chained at the legs and handcuffed together, not more than a foot from the bench where she hovered above us, as she rapidly read out, in Thai, from the pages that she held. The shouting from the other lawyers, the witness and occasionally the judge, who was himself cross-examining the cop, continued throughout. Neither Fred nor I understood a single word she said.

After just a few minutes, she brought the gavel down with a 'thwack', dropped the papers on the bench top and, just as abruptly, her judge's scowl vanished as she turned to the object of her affections. Smiling lustily, she resumed her whispers and giggles.

Both Fred and I just stood there astounded; we could barely believe what we had just witnessed and were none the wiser as to whether we were free or not. Even Om, who had been trying to listen over the din of the competing proceedings, didn't know what the verdict had been. We stood there for a few minutes before the bailiff retrieved the judgment documents and, handing one to each of us, took us back to our seats. 'In The Name of His Royal Highness the King of Thailand' was emblazoned on the front page of the document.

'What was that all about?' I asked the bailiff in Thai.

He replied in English, first pointing to Fred, 'You go home' and then to me, 'You death penalty.'

Brent and Willie were standing at my side by this time and when they heard they were as devastated as I was.

'This is just too fucking ridiculous for words. It's insanity. Is this the best these arseholes can manage? What the hell is wrong with these people? Is this what you idiots call a court?' Willie was very agitated, and as we were still in the courtroom, and an outburst of this nature could quite easily have landed him in chains himself, Om took him by the arm and led him outside, desperately trying to get him to lower his voice and to calm down.

Brent gave the bailiff a 100-baht note, and the court official allowed us to sit together on the bench at the back of the room for about 30 minutes before the deputy took Fred and me back to the holding cells. Before we left, Om and Willie returned, Willie still fuming but doing his best to control himself as he watched the continuing testimony of the cop, along with the various other disorders that make up a criminal trial in Thailand. The judge and her beau had departed soon after the verdict had been read.

There is still no logical explanation – in fact, none has ever been sought because it would be superfluous to do so – but the lawyer, once again, and for reasons known only to himself, had prepared his own appeal in which he ignored most of the issues raised by us in the 20-page document that we had so painstakingly prepared. The result was once again a pathetic, confusing and inadequate petition that had been reduced to *four* pages and did not so much as mention any of the most important issues.

The only ray of sunshine was that Fred was released from The Prem that same night – at ten minutes to midnight, believe it or not – though freedom was not yet his to enjoy because he was immediately detained by the Immigration Police and taken to the Immigration Detention Centre in Suan Plu Road. He spent several days of additional torment there before he was released and repatriated to Australia. He had spent almost five and a half years in purgatory and had lost, quite apart from those valuable years of his life, thousands of dollars and everything else he had had with him, all for no other reason than he was at the bank with me that fateful day. But even though the Australian government was fully aware of this, the cost that they incurred to get him home was charged to him, and he had to repay it in instalments over the following months before they would issue him with a new passport.

The great and benevolent Australian government, which had not long before gifted Thailand millions of dollars to build the so-called Friendship Bridge across the Mekong River to Laos, and which provides many more millions in other forms of aid to Thailand every year, and which after the terrible tsunami that swept across the Indian Ocean handed out about a billion bucks, was not able to cover the small cost of repatriating one of its own, an innocent man who had spent almost six years of horror at the hands of these beggars.

Under Thai law, Fred was entitled to be compensated for false arrest and for the time he had spent in prison, so as soon as he arrived home he got in touch with Brent and asked for his help. Within a few days, Brent sent copies of the court judgment and acquittal documents, along with the necessary application forms, to Fred for signature and return.

After Fred returned them, Brent tried but failed to find a lawyer who would take the job on the basis of their fees coming from the proceeds; almost all simply froze when the word 'drugs' was mentioned. Fred then approached the Australian Foreign Office for assistance. He later wrote to Brent to say that, despite his efforts, he was getting nowhere; his requests for help had been denied completely.

The final insult came when Brent, out of frustration, decided to do the whole thing himself. In the company of a translator, he went to talk to the appropriate officials at the court, where he was told that foreigners are not entitled to any compensation at all because they don't work while they are in prison.

Fred had spent four years and nine months in squalor and torment waiting for the end of the Criminal Court hearings then, after being acquitted, he was detained for an additional ten months on a whim of the prosecutor. But because he hadn't worked as a slave, they claimed that they were not obliged to compensate him in any respect. On the contrary, there is no such stipulation enshrined anywhere in Thai law. Legislation states that those acquitted must receive the equivalent of the minimum wage per day for the time they have spent in confinement. For foreigners, that minimum is increased 100 per cent, which meant Fred was entitled to a minimum of 200 baht for every day of his detention. This amounted to around 400,000 baht or, at the exchange rate at the time, A$20,000. Instead, he got zilch.

Still taking up space in Section 5 at The Prem after his fake heart attack backfired, Hansel was ready to get back into the spotlight again. However, had he known the fate of one of his countrymen for doing something similar, he might have thought twice.

Some seven years earlier, another German man had gone to Thailand for a holiday. He was alone, and, as many of the single chaps who visit Bangkok do at some time during their stay, he visited Patpong. However, as he was inexperienced when it came to the tricks and scams that are so prevalent there, he was lured by touts at the base of a long flight of steps to a second-floor bar, with the promise of drinks at just 50 baht each and a fabulously erotic floor show.

When he entered the bar, he found just a few other customers present, only one of whom was not Thai, but there was a naked girl on the stage and she was doing a semi-erotic dance, so he sat and ordered one of the 50-baht glasses of beer. Several minutes later, a large icy one was brought to him by two seductive young girls wearing very little. After handing him his drink, they sat one on either side of him and began to fondle and caress him in a very friendly manner, whilst at the same time asking if he would buy them a drink, too.

Of course, he couldn't refuse such a minor compensation for their rather stimulating hospitality, and one of them rushed off to fetch two tiny glasses of coke. After a while, he ordered another beer and two more minute cokes. The dancer continued to make love to the slippery chrome pole she was holding with both hands, though her performance was not what he would have described as 'fabulously erotic'. After finishing his drink, he decided to leave and take a look behind another green door. He asked for the bill and was astonished to see that it was for 3,000 baht.

He had bought two glasses of beer and four tiny glasses of coke, and his instant mental calculations told him the bill should have been around 300 baht. When he pointed this out, he was informed that the beer was 50 baht per glass, but the drinks for the girls were 500 baht each and the not so fabulously erotic floor show was 900 baht. 'Can't you read the sign?' asked one of the barmen as he pointed towards the entrance. Sure enough, one had miraculously appeared at the top of the stairs.

Needless to say, he wasn't too pleased. He took the cash from his wallet, threw it on the floor and screwed it under the heel of his shoe. Well, that was just being unpleasant, as far as his hosts were concerned, and several particularly aggressive bouncers pounced on him and gave him a thumping. Shortly afterwards, several uniformed subordinates of the high-ranking cop from the Bang-Rak police station who owned the bar arrived, gave him another thumping and arrested him. He went to court in the standard manner after spending seven days at the police station and was finally sentenced to fourteen years in prison for the crime of putting his foot on the image of the king. All Thai currency carries the head of the monarch, and it is a very serious offence to deface it in any way. The offender spent several years regretting his little tantrum before he was transferred back to Germany.

However, even though he had spent many years in Thailand, Hansel was apparently unaware of the law relating to the defacement of the king's image. He was caught by the guards in Section 5 with two five-hundred-baht notes and asked to hand them over, in accordance with prison rules. Instead, he immediately tore them to pieces and threw them on the ground, yelling at the guards that if he couldn't have them, then neither could they.

Of course, this earned him a severe beating, and he was put in chains in solitary confinement while the authorities considered whether to punish him further for this crime. Would he never learn?

The chains on my legs were removed a bit over two years after my initial conviction, and by that time my appeal to the Supreme Court had been through the mill. However, regardless of a superbly prepared second appeal petition, I remained a guest of the Crown on death row. I had raised a total of fifty different issues, in a sixty-page document, that I considered to be indisputable reasons for the verdict of the other two courts to be reversed, but the effort was to no avail.

On the day after May Day, six years after I had been arrested, I arrived at the court, once again with confidence that justice would finally be done. Even being handcuffed together with 14 other defendants and taken into the courtroom like a member of a chain gang did not curb my optimism. Besides, I had become accustomed over the years to the Thai way of doing things.

We stood in a line in front of a female judge who sat on her throne a metre above us and rattled her way through each of our judgments, barely drawing breath between them. Just like the last time, she read at such a pace that even most of the Thais couldn't understand what she was saying. When it came to my turn, she covered the entire appeal document in no more than two minutes, and I had absolutely no idea what she had said until the bailiff came to escort us to the back of the room where Willie and Brent were standing with Om. I was stunned rigid when Om told me that the conviction and death penalty had been upheld.

This was the end of the line as far as the Thai courts were concerned. What more could I do? My only options now were to petition the king to be pardoned – pardoned for something that I had not done – or to apply for a prisoner transfer to the UK after I had served the mandatory eight years in hell. The British Embassy had suggested such a transfer, but there were strings attached – strings that I had no intention of being tied up with.

Exactly one year after the Supreme Court decision, John Major's Conservative government was swept from office on a tidal wave of Labour support, and Tony and Cherie Blair became Britain's first couple. Baroness Elizabeth Symons was immediately appointed parliamentary undersecretary of state at the Foreign Office, with responsibility for consular affairs. She entered the office that was to be hers for the next couple of years with a battle cry that foreign relations from now on would be linked to human rights rather than trade considerations. Human-rights abuses were simply not going be tolerated at all – not a jolly bit of it.

Things were looking up in more ways than one. During the previous year, my sentence had been reduced from death to life by a blanket royal amnesty that also saw my two ex-cop cellmates, Ben and a Canadian fellow who had shared my space on death row for about fifteen months moved to Section 1, where we were all put in a cell together, increasing its occupancy to twenty-eight people. Because of the monthly payment to the building chief there, it had, in fact, been more comfortable for us on death row, where the maximum cell occupancy was 16, but at least now we were only locked up at night.

The occasion of the royal amnesty warranted a small ceremony before we were released from death row. About 100 inmates, all of them in leg chains, lined up to receive the sentence reduction warrants and to have the welded shackles cut away from their ankles. However, as the second shackle on the first man in line was almost severed, the carbon cutting wheel on the electric grinder snapped, and there was not a replacement to be found in the entire prison. It took another two weeks before the chains were removed from everyone else.

Meanwhile, new foreign secretary, Robin Cook, was screaming for the whole world to take notice that China, Burma, old Saddam in Iraq and other terrible abusers of human rights were just going to have to shape up or they would be mighty sorry. There was no mention of Thailand specifically, but it was a sort of blanket warning if you analysed it carefully enough.

Naturally, China began shaking uncontrollably at the knees. Old Saddam, well, he positively shit in his pants. Burma ho-hummed a little and had a 'We've kicked those Limey bastards out once and we can do it again' kind of attitude. It takes a lot to stir those guys, and, anyway, Britain was already supposed to be restricted by UN sanctions from trading with them. Any clandestine trading going on through the Thai back door was going to carry on regardless and was mostly to Britain's benefit anyway. But Cook put on a great performance to 'Bravos!' and pats on the back. He was so convincing that he even managed to raise some tentative hopes in the hearts of yours truly and some of my friends.

'At long last we have a government that respects human rights,' we said, breathing a collective sigh of relief. 'Finally we have someone who will take the bull by the testicles. These guys are afraid of nothing. Once old Robin and the baroness see this incredible and blatant breach of the Universal Declaration of Human Rights by Thailand, they will bring the heavens down to right this terrible wrong. It won't be long, you'll see. God save the Queen!' Even Brent wrote with new-found confidence, 'You'll be home before Xmas, mate.'

In Thailand, of course it was business as usual. Thais are never ones for listening to the advice of the West, therefore it came as no real surprise when they started executing people again, just as Robin was galloping around on his human-rights white stallion. Perhaps to make a point, a total of 25 men were shot at Bangkwang prison that year.

Then – as if to rub salt into the open wounds on my ankles – it wasn't long before we discovered that Cook had hoodwinked us all too, because his human-rights stallion sort of galloped off into the sunset with nothing at all to show for his empty rhetoric. The same went for Baroness Elizabeth.

# CHAPTER 24

# Their Contempt
# Reigned Supreme

NOT TOO LONG AFTER SETTLING INTO MY NEW SURROUNDINGS IN
Section 1, I began to suffer with a severe and persistent gastric infection
that caused me constant discomfort for several weeks. I just couldn't
seem to shake it. Kilos were dropping off me as fast as Monica's
knickers, and I was throwing up everything I ate. The only thing I
could keep down was a little black tea. I had been to the Bangkwang
hospital just once before, whilst on death row, but I had vowed never
to return unless I was going to die regardless. Finally, out of sheer
desperation, I applied for permission to once again see the fellow there
who had the audacity to prefix his name with 'Dr'.

Up to that point, I thought I'd been rendered unshakeable during
my years of confinement in the various prisons I'd called home,
but I was indeed shaken further when I arrived at the hospital
that day. It was then that I discovered the depths of contempt to
which Thailand's persecutors can sink. Their lack of respect for even
the most rudimentary of human rights knows no bounds, and the
absence of empathy shown by some of the Corrections Department
medical staff borders on the satanic.

The scene that greeted me was one that I will never forget. The hospital was populated by dozens of virtual living skeletons who lay on thin, blood-stained fibre mattresses, mouths and eyes gaping, coughing blood, and rasping and groaning with the constant agony of tuberculosis-infected lungs, or melting with the heat of malaria, or suffering from various AIDS-related maladies. Many had festering sores all over their bodies; some had infected eyes; others had bloody saliva dribbling from their mouths; and still others were in the final agonising days, or even hours, of their pathetic lives, struggling to get sufficient oxygen into their systems to keep the flame flickering a little longer. Almost all seemed to be agitated by an itchy rash that covered at least part of their torso, and they scratched relentlessly with filthy fingers to no effect. I saw men so completely devoid of hope, or so deeply depressed, that they lay in their own waste, not even bothering to chase the flies or swat the mosquitoes. And every single one of them, regardless of their condition, was wearing heavy rusty chains that ate into their already ulcerated and bleeding flesh. All of this in barred wards with no mosquito screens, no suitable ventilation and no fans.

This was incredible enough, but the section I was taken to was also full of stinking dark smoke. It was nauseating enough on the ground floor, but it appeared to be filtering down the stairwell from the second floor. It turned out that the incinerator for Section 1 was positioned against the wall adjacent to the hospital building, and the smoke poured into the hospital through the bars at the top of the walls, from where it gradually wafted throughout the building.

I had seen some pretty rough treatment of inmates but was appalled to see how these men were being treated; however, being a death-row inmate and in chains myself at the time, I had been escorted there by a guard, and there was no option for me to return to my cell before seeing the doctor. To make matters worse, because of the stomach disorder I was there to have treated I was obliged to use the toilet while I waited and was escorted upstairs by a trusty. This was a further assault to my already shattered senses: the squat bowls were literally overflowing and no attempt had been made to clean up the mess. I couldn't even imagine what kind of mentality was necessary for someone to leave such foul conditions unattended in a hospital, but there it was.

However, I was now in a terrible condition, so despite my previous resolution while on death row not to return to the hospital, and after paying a fee of 500 baht to the building chief, I was given permission to once again see the fool who liked to be called doctor. My consultation was short. He gave me a very brief once-over and then handed me some tablets in a plastic bag with no label on it, telling me to take three immediately and two more three times each day for the next week.

I returned to Section 1 and sat in the shade of the confinement building watching a one-legged Thai man hop around the exercise yard. His lonesome leg had a shackle welded around his equally lonesome ankle, which was attached to one end of a length of rusty chain, the other end of which he held in his hand. This fellow had been hopping around like this for almost a year by then and caused no end of amusement among some of his fellow inmates, as well as some of the guards. The Thais called him 'Hopalong', the foreigners 'You Poor Bastard'. He was fortunate in one respect, though: it was a whole lot easier for him to take his trousers off than it was for his similarly tethered two-legged companions. But this ridiculous extreme is a clear example of the lack of intelligence that prevails in the Thai prison system.

I took three of the tablets I had been given with a long draw on my water bottle, hoping that they would be effective. My stomach was killing me, and I had had quite enough of running to the toilet every 30 minutes, doubled up with spasms of pain. However, relief was to remain elusive, as my torment and agonies mounted to new heights. Within a couple of hours, I swelled like a toadfish on red alert and blistered as if I had been set alight. My blood pressure went through the roof, and my extremities became so painful and bloated that I could not bear to walk or touch anything. Even my clothes had to be removed.

To add to my quandary, Ben wasn't present: he had been taken to provide medical treatment for one of the guards in another section.

When he returned at lock-up time, he was taken aback to see me sitting naked on the floor, grimacing in agony. Initially, I had sought the sanctuary of my cell and was the sole occupant, but as the cell filled later, I was left with just my one square metre of allocated space as usual. I couldn't even lean against the wall to rest, so sat with my knees bent and my arms held away from my body, the tips of my fingers resting on the floor beside me, unable to bear contact with anything.

He was quick to take action. On inspection, he discovered that the tablets I had been given were a powerful antibiotic, a generic version of the drug Bactrim. I had been prescribed this drug even though my medical file specifically detailed in large red letters that I was never to be given any form of sulphonamide. I was highly allergic to them, and they had the potential to kill me in hours if I took them.

After being told of my allergy, Ben could see the dangers I faced and helped me to drink litres of water over the next few hours to try to flush the poison from my body. During this time, I had to make frequent excruciating visits to the toilet. It was a very long night, and the following day was even longer. Had Ben not been there, I don't know if I would have survived. It took a further six weeks for me to recover fully, the first couple of which I spent in constant agony and mostly sitting in an almost perpetually motionless posture. Luckily, Ben had ordered me some medication after my stomach problem had started, and it arrived a couple of days after I took the antibiotics. The new tablets eventually did the trick, but, even so, it took a couple of weeks before I was confident enough to eat a hearty meal. Even then, my blood pressure remained uncomfortably high, and it wasn't too long before this caused me another serious problem.

Well into the second year after my transfer to Section 1, a Hong Kong inmate – I'll call him Choiching – suffered a stroke in Section 1. I had known him since our time together at The Prem, and we were reasonably good friends. At my request, the British Embassy was notified of his condition by one of the more compassionate guards and advised that Choiching needed urgent medical treatment – and not by the pretend doctor in the Bangkwang prison hospital.

There was not even a murmur from the embassy in response, and Choiching lay on his allocated bit of concrete floor in his cell for five days without medicine and without any medical attention other than that provided by Ben. The embassy was contacted several more times by visitors to other British and Hong Kong inmates, but nothing was done. Late on the fifth day, Choiching was moved to the hospital section, where he was put in leg chains. That same day, he suffered a heart attack; the chains remained in place. Seven days later, he was put into the back of a Toyota pickup truck and taken to the Klong Prem prison hospital. This came after the standard monthly British consular visit to the prison that same day, at which the embassy staff had been severely castigated by me and several of the other appalled inmates. During the journey to Klong Prem, however, Choiching apparently suffered another heart attack and was discovered dead on arrival at the hospital there, still wearing heavy leg chains, of course.

This man was almost 65 years of age and was seriously ill, but instead of medical attention, or even a smidgen of support from those who were charged with monitoring his welfare, he was ignored for five days then chained and kept in squalor for an additional seven days before being thrown into the back of a pickup to be transported through heavy traffic in the blistering sun. You can't get much more contemptible than that. But no one at the embassy uttered a single word of protest.

It was ten in the morning on 5 May, almost exactly one year after Choiching had died, when I collapsed in the exercise yard on my way to the table where I usually sat each day to put in several hours of letter writing and diary updates. I had just an hour before been informed that the British government would not agree to support my first petition for a royal pardon.

Pain seared through my chest, and I fell to the ground. My eyes went out of focus and the left side of my body became numb from my ear to my toes. My scalp tingled, and my head throbbed. My breathing became shallow and laboured. I had no idea what was happening but suspected I was suffering a heart attack. Figuring that this was the end, that the bastards had finally won, I prepared to meet my maker.

As I lay there on the concrete with what I had been carrying in my arms scattered around me, my entire life began to flash before my eyes. That it was a terribly inconvenient time to be dying also entered the spectrum. I still had a thousand things to take care of, a million hopes and dreams unfulfilled. My mind seemed to focus in on segments of thought or memory, and though many of them would have been insignificant a minute before, they now became kaleidoscopes of colour and detail and somehow of great importance. The reality that I had wasted the best part of my adult life behind bars for one reason or another hit me like a train, and a most intense remorse and regret engulfed me.

It seemed as if I had been lying there for hours, battling with my conscience and reeling in the knowledge that if I died in this cesspit, my corpse would be tossed into the back of a pickup without ceremony and carted off like a bag of refuse, but it was in reality just moments before Ben was kneeling beside me. He recognised the symptoms at once and took immediate measures. One of the section guards had also moved in to see what was wrong with me, and Ben ordered him to rush off and get his medical kit – he had to keep it in the building chief's office. The guard, taking no offence at being ordered around, returned in moments with the bag, and Ben washed several tablets down my throat and gently massaged my chest over the heart. The kiss of life was fortunately not necessary, and we were both more than pleased about that.

It wasn't long before the drugs took effect and my breathing got a little stronger. About an hour later, Ben helped me back to the cell and made me as comfortable as he could. He prescribed rest and kept his tablets handy, administering additional doses throughout the next few days until my condition stabilised. My blood pressure on that first day rose to as high as 245/188 and hovered there for some time before falling slightly to the region of 220/160. The entire left side of my body stayed in a semi-paralysed state with my face on that side droopy and numb, leaving me slurring my speech and dribbling when I ate or drank. My left eye also remained out of focus, and I was almost deaf on that side, the combination of which made it quite difficult for me to coordinate my movements.

I later attributed this attack, at least partly, to something that had happened a couple of days beforehand: one of the Thais in my cell had gone berserk and had started punching me for no apparent reason, necessitating a little defensive action on my part, which included kicking him decisively in the gonads. Several of my cellmates then intervened and finished him off. But though I was not injured, I was indeed shaken up by the incident and reasoned that it could quite conceivably have been a contributing factor.

It was fortunate for me, though, that the guards knew this fellow to be a candidate for the loony bin and didn't penalise me for my part in the confrontation; instead, they moved him out the following morning and put him in a punishment cell for an indeterminate period. There was no such thing as appropriate medical treatment for the mentally unstable at Bangkwang, just more punishment and misery to augment their insanity. However, it would have been the end of me if I had also been put into solitary at that time, of that I am quite certain.

The following day, I scribbled a short note to the British Consul's office, explaining what had happened and informing them that, because Section 1 inmates were not permitted to get sick unless it was a Wednesday, I wouldn't be able to see the pretend doctor at the hospital for a week. I requested that arrangements be made for an outside doctor to be sent in to treat me urgently. Nothing happened. Ben did what he could, and I rested as much as was possible under the circumstances.

Seven days later, I penned another note to the Consul's office, explaining that I had seen 'Doctor Death' – a moniker he had earned – the day before and that he had given me some paracetamol tablets, prescribing two every six hours if I suffered any more chest pains. He had also graciously offered me a bed at the hospital, but I had gracefully declined, the requirement to be shackled not being the least of my concerns. I explained that Ben had diagnosed a stroke, and though he was doing what he could to assist me, the attention he could offer was clearly very limited and his medical supplies insufficient for more than emergency relief. Again, absolutely nothing at all happened.

I wrote again two weeks later then decided not to bother wasting any more stamps. It was not until three months later that two embassy officials arrived at the prison to see all of the British inmates – their first welfare visit since a couple of weeks before my collapse. During that meeting, one of them casually asked me how I was. I replied that I was feeling a little better. I was then asked what had actually been wrong with me. I didn't bother to respond, but just the same she informed us collectively that a doctor was scheduled to visit the prison within two months to give us all a once over. 'Bloody lovely. Just bloody lovely,' was all I could think to offer.

The doctor did arrive in mid-October – almost six months after I had collapsed – and confirmed the stroke, as well as diagnosing hypertension and asthma. He prescribed some medication and left. I sent the prescription off to the embassy that same day so that the medication could be delivered to me via embassy channels to avoid delays and complications. I received it, after several reminder letters and a few phone calls from Brent, on 10 January. Happy New Year! It had taken the embassy all of eight months to address my medical emergency.

In spite of my health problems, I was luckier than some. Just 18 days after the doctor's visit, a series of executions created quite a stir among the inmates at Bangkwang prison. Never before had so many taken the bullet in a single massacre. One of the five to be shot was taken from the cell that I had once occupied on death row; the other four were taken from two adjacent cells. They were cuffed together and escorted, single file, to Section 13, flanked by ten guards.

Although executions were never announced, most of us sensed when they were about to happen. As was the custom, we were all locked up earlier than usual, and the whole place became very quiet. The fellow who occupied the space beside me in Section 1 – a Thai man about 45 years old – knew one of the condemned men very well; they were close friends and case partners. When he heard from a trusty at around 5 p.m. that the five men had been shot, he became intensely agitated, sobbing uncontrollably and tearing at his hair. He then collapsed right there beside me. Ben and I intervened at once, but although we tried desperately to revive him with mouth-to-mouth resuscitation and heart massage, it was too late. He was dead, and there was no bringing him back.

Guards were called, but they did not remove the corpse or even enter the cell to check if the man was in fact dead. Instead, taking Ben's word for it, they left him there stretched out on the floor, face up, a decaying body for me to sleep beside until 6 a.m. the next day. By that time, due to the heat and humidity at that time of the year, the cell had become a very unpleasant place to be, particularly for me, as I was right up against him. But even when the gates were opened and the rest of us were let out, the body was not removed and remained there until just after 3.30 p.m. Needless to say, when we returned that afternoon, about 30 minutes before lock-up time, the cell reeked of death and decay, a stench that lingered throughout the night.

In spite of all of this, I remained hopeful that my own health problems might be deemed by those who were in control of my destiny as me qualifying for 'compelling or compassionate circumstances' status and that the pardon petition I had submitted – without official British government support – would be given a little priority. But that was wishful thinking. Not only was there no support of any nature forthcoming, it seemed clear to me that obstructionism had replaced it.

# CHAPTER 25

‖‖‖‖‖‖‖‖‖‖‖‖‖‖‖‖‖‖‖‖‖‖‖‖‖‖‖‖‖‖‖‖‖‖‖‖‖‖‖‖‖‖‖‖‖‖‖‖‖‖‖‖‖‖‖‖‖‖‖‖‖‖‖‖‖‖‖‖‖‖‖‖‖‖‖

# A Ray of Sunshine

I HAD NOT SEEN NOK SINCE WELL BEFORE JAIDOW'S DISAPPEARANCE.
During her last visit, while I was at The Prem, she had been terribly
appreciative of Jaidow's assistance and support. They had become
friends after Jaidow had plucked her from the meaningless and
hopeless life that she had lived for so many years, initially as a child
sex slave and then for a few more years after her 16th birthday as a
paid prostitute, which was when she had met Hansel.

I had initially considered asking Nok to be a witness for the defence
in the early stages of the trial, believing that her testimony in regard
to Fahad, whom she told me she had seen together with Hansel on
numerous occasions, would have been helpful, but I later decided that
it would not be safe for her or her family if she did so. Considering
the life she had been forced to live up to the time she met Jaidow, I
had no desire to make things any harder for her.

I was therefore surprised and more than delighted when she arrived
with her two daughters just before Christmas one year to visit me at
Bangkwang. She was a ray of sunshine to brighten the days of otherwise
bleak insanity that had become standard fare. It was early on a Monday
morning, and she had been given special permission for an extended

visit period because she had travelled so far. As luck would have it, there were not too many other people in the enclosure at the time, and we were able to converse without the usual constraints. At first, I didn't recognise her, such was her transformation, and I was amazed to see that her eldest daughter was now almost an adolescent, her sister a few years younger, and both as pretty as a picture. They were all beautifully turned out, and the children both had their hair pulled back into half ponytails, with the rest bobbing on their shoulders, and adorned with bows and butterfly clips. They all respectfully *waiied* (the traditional Thai bow) in greeting, the two girls accompanying theirs with a gentle curtsy and captivating smile. Nok and I then sat and talked for almost two hours while the girls quietly chattered together.

Nok recounted what had transpired since Jaidow had disappeared, and I listened in admiration and with a feeling of warmth and respect for this determined young woman who had crawled from the sewer that her mother had thrown her into and demonstrated what was possible given the chance. Though she could not have known it, she gave me something that morning that straightened my back, stoked the furnace and regenerated the inner strength that had been almost exhausted. Her gift was to show me living proof of the power of determination, and that power flowed into me with a potency that enabled me to battle to the bitter end against all those who had tried or were still trying to crush my spirit and destroy me.

Jaidow had assisted her with the establishment of her tiny business and had taught her how to operate it successfully and profitably, introducing her to the textile companies and giving her lessons on negotiating the best prices. Nok had learned quickly and was soon expanding her enterprise and increasing the quantities of her orders. As such, she was able to negotiate even better prices and make additional profits. After the business had begun to flourish, Jaidow had pulled out of the partnership, and Nok had not seen her since. By late 1997, she had six small retailers working for her on a commission basis, and by the end of 1998 eight were selling her wares. She was planning an increase of two that month and was in Bangkok to negotiate a better deal for her stock.

Her mother had died of cervical cancer three years before, and, as the oldest living member of the family, Nok had taken control of the family orchard that now belonged to her and her two younger brothers. She had bought the boys a new pickup on hire purchase, thus reducing the transport costs for moving their produce to market. The farm had almost no debt and, as they were doing most of the manual work now, very little outside help was necessary, giving them a far better return.

She told me that every night and morning she lit candles and incense and she, her daughters and siblings prayed for and paid tribute to Jaidow. She told me that had it not been for Jaidow taking her soiled hand when she needed it most and guiding her from the darkness towards the light, she should surely not have survived, and her own children would have in all probability been sacrificed by her mother, as she had been herself. Jaidow's kindness and goodness, she assured me, had saved not just her life but the lives of her children and brothers also. She pledged that she would give thanks for that deliverance till the day she died.

I only wished I could have said the same thing. Although I recognised that Jaidow had had a charitable heart where Nok was concerned, I could only curse her for abandoning me and tossing me to the wolves.

There were times when the never-ending stupidity, back-stabbing, incompetence, complacency, insensitiveness and deliberate obstructionism in some quarters was just too much for me to handle. At these times, I would seek out a fellow inmate and sit quietly in the shade talking to him. I had met Sompon a few weeks after I had been transferred from death row to Section 1. A smallish Thai man of about 45, he had been afflicted with polio as a child and, as a result, both of his arms were useless, little more than dangling skin and bone with barely enough strength to allow him to raise his food from his plate to his mouth, let alone take care of the other daily essentials of bathing, changing, washing clothes and so on. But it was his inner strength that was a form of therapy to me, and talking to him put some perspective on my own problems and also helped to bolster my determination to keep on going.

I had initially approached Sompon out of curiosity, having spent some time after arriving in Section 1 trying to fathom what crime such a man could have committed to warrant a sentence of life in prison. It took just minutes after our introductions to realise that, although Sompon was uneducated in an academic sense, he was a very intelligent person and astonishingly, under the circumstances, one with a pleasant and friendly personality.

His tale, though, was one of the saddest testimonies of selfishness and corruption that I had ever heard. We sought each other's solace quite frequently, and by the time I was transferred back to The Prem, he had poured out his heart and told me things that he had never felt able to tell anyone else. He related to me a story of loveless victimisation that had begun as early in his life as he could recall. After the debilitating effects of polio became evident when he was about five years old, he had been ostracised to a great extent by his family. His parents had no time for him, and his siblings resented having to take care of him. Although he could grip lightly with his fingers, he was unable to lift anything that weighed more than a few grams. He could not, for example, raise a book to his eyes or carry his own plate of rice. Yet, as unimaginable as it might seem, for the first year of his sentence, he had had heavy chains fitted to his legs.

Sompon had, to all intents and purposes, no arms, yet he had been sentenced to life in prison for shooting a man dead with a .45-calibre pistol. He told me that he could not possibly have done this because he was incapable of lifting a handgun, let alone firing one as well. The police knew who had killed the man, but they had been encouraged to turn the other way while an arrangement was made. Sompon had then actually watched the murderer make a deal with his own family to substitute him as the villain. Converting him to cash evidently made perfect sense to them because for 300,000 baht they had not only agreed to the charge being laid against their kinsman but had also given evidence against him in court.

The judge saw nothing amiss during the trial. The police testified that Sompon had committed the crime, and as this was confirmed by his own family he was convicted of murder and sentenced to life in prison.

Sompon was an alert, bright and intelligent person who fully realised what had been done to him, but, even so, he harboured no resentment towards his family; at least not that I could detect. Instead, he defended their right to make the deal and told me that he understood their motivations and at least now he was contributing a little to his family's well-being for the first time. He did not contest the guilty verdict and did not appeal. In fact, he believed that he was really not that much worse off where he was. His family visited him from time to time, and they saw that he had a little money in his prison account to pay for a personal helper and buy extras such as coffee and sugar. In reality, he had more friends and better companionship in prison than he had ever had at home. Most of his fellow prisoners were gentle and considerate with him, many going out of their way to assist him with the things he found difficult to manage by himself.

'This is my life,' he once said to me, 'and this is what I must suffer.' Like most Thais, he accepted his lot as his karma, believing that the next life would be better because he had manufactured a stockpile of merit in this one by helping his family to enrich themselves. The thing he didn't seem to realise – or maybe he did but simply didn't like to mention it – was that his family would surely have had no compunctions about using him again in a similar manner after his release.

It was yet another classic example of the bottomless chasm of decadence in which Justice Incorporated wallowed.

# CHAPTER 26

# The Pracha Dossier

AFTER SEVERAL ADDITIONAL ROYAL AMNESTIES THAT COLLECTIVELY reduced my sentence to 17 years – calculated from the date of my arrest – it was fast approaching liberation day. By this time, I was resigned to the realisation that I would be serving every last minute of my remaining sentence, quite certain from bitter experience that there would be nothing forthcoming from the British Foreign Office, embassy or the Thai PM's office to bring the release date forward.

At long last, it arrived. Surprisingly, though I initially had a bit of a job to nod off the night before, I slept soundly and woke as usual at 6.00 a.m., had some eggs on bread and a cup of coffee for breakfast, and prepared for the big event. At 7.30 a.m., I was escorted to the central office, where my photograph and fingerprints were recorded and a bit of paperwork was taken care of. I was then returned to my section, where I said goodbye to those I had befriended and even some whom I hadn't. I was certainly feeling pretty chirpy – who wouldn't have been?

One of my most ardent supporters in the UK had sent sufficient funds to cover the cost of my airfare home, with a bit of change left over. Willie had arranged new clothes and essentials to carry me over for a while, along with a suitcase that I could wheel instead of carry, and with locks to prevent anyone from slipping in a few kilos of dope, just for fun. Everything was in order, and there was absolutely nothing that could go wrong now. Or was there?

At around 10 a.m., I was taken by two police officers from the NSD headquarters to the Immigration Detention Centre (IDC), processed and locked in a room with about 200 other men. I was supposed to be leaving on a flight that had already been booked by Willie, at around 8 p.m. that same day. However, due to a lot of additional nonsense, I was kept in those extremely uncomfortable conditions for a further two nights and three days before I was taken by immigration officials to the New Suwanapoom Airport at around 9.00 p.m. But it cost Willie 800 baht in tea money before they would agree to make that little trip in time for my flight. Willie also had to pay an additional 9,000 baht in penalties because the plane tickets had to be changed twice. Eventually, I was taken aboard the plane – last in line – told I was not permitted to drink any alcohol during the flight and departed the Land of Smiles at 2 a.m.

But here's a little something to reflect upon: whilst still at the IDC, I saw at least 30 other British men being held there and took the time to talk to some of them. I was told that the numbers increased at the rate of around five each week. They were almost all there because they had overstayed their tourist visas and had no money to pay for return tickets to the UK. The Prisoners Abroad organisation provided some funds so they could purchase food, but I learned on my return home that this contribution was soon to be terminated because of budget shortfalls.

The British FCO will not even start to consider providing any repatriation costs until after a detainee has stayed at the IDC for at least six months. This decision was taken because around 70 per cent of those classified as distressed people after losing loved ones and everything else they had with them during the tsunami in 2004 and who had been repatriated at government cost hadn't repaid the advances. The British government handed out hundreds of millions of pounds to the native victims of that tragedy without any provision for it being repaid but couldn't provide a tiny bit of help to their own. The UK was the only EU nation to be so heartless and mean-fisted with its nationals.

In contrast, if a Thai whore, a Nigerian drug trafficker or anyone else who has been caught in the UK for being naughty is deported, it is done at the cost of the British taxpayer. As was only too evident in my case, the Thai government doesn't pay so much as the few baht it costs to take a deportee to the airport.

Nevertheless, I was on my way, and I don't have the words to describe just how I felt the moment I boarded the plane, knowing it was the end. It was over, and I was at long last FREE. Free to get my train back on the tracks and to look forward to the challenges of beginning a new life and all that lay ahead. And apart from the multitude of conflicting emotions – tremendous relief, anger, surging anticipation, growing optimism, gut-wrenching disgust, gratitude to some, humiliation, cautious excitement, nagging fear, an almost debilitating weariness and, yes, a certain degree of bitterness, too – I can say with certainty that it felt pretty damned good.

During my years of confinement and association with Major Pracha – the ex-cop with whom I shared a cell – I was entrusted with disclosures of numerous horrors that he told me were commonplace in Thailand and which – in many cases – radiated from the very top of the ladder of power and influence. Pracha had been popping over from Section 3, where he was resident, almost daily to see me and his friend Colonel Niran, and we had spent countless hours talking about all manner of terrible things that go on in Thailand. It was, therefore, a sad day for Niran and me when we learned that he had died of a heart attack.

Just two days before he departed this world, perhaps realising that the end was very near, he gave me a key to a safe-deposit box, along with a handwritten and signed letter addressed to the guardian of it. This letter said that I or my trusted agent should be permitted access to the box in private and that I was authorised to take possession of all that it contained. Pracha explained the significance of its contents to me and stressed the dangers associated with possessing it and made me promise that I would make all haste to have it taken out of the country and revealed one day for the world to see.

'That,' he whispered, 'is to be my legacy, my bequest to those who have betrayed me and to those who allowed me to pay with my own life for their crimes.' He told me that because he had accumulated a massive karma debt during his present life, he had no desire to be reincarnated and risk returning as a camel or a goat or something just as unappealing. My promise, if kept, would allow his spirit to just drift around and rest in peace for all eternity.

I kept that promise. The guardian of the safe-deposit box was met by someone whom I trusted implicity, and that person was provided access. Inside was a ten-inch-thick dossier dating back some thirty years. It revealed, in Pracha's characteristic precision, and among hundreds of other almost inconceivable perversions, his membership of the Wen Asawin (Knights of the Ring), a super-secret group of specialists that even the CIA or MI6 would be proud to boast as its own. A platinum or silver ring – which I had seen often enough – with a kind of head design and a sparkling white faceted diamond of at least one carat in the centre was their badge.

The dossier reveals a huge amount of detail about those who had employed Pracha to do their dirty work for them: the assassination of rivals, enemies, adversaries and associates; the blackmail of scores of people; and the fabrication of evidence against hundreds of others. Also meticulously recorded are details of the drug, sex and slave trades and the worlds of gambling and oil-smuggling, and how these activities are almost entirely controlled by high-ranking police officers, politicians and military officials. It goes even further back in some sections to disclose events of over 50 years past that were then, and remain today, simply too taboo to ever mention in Thai society. Dates, times, names, events, details, figures: they are all there in that one huge file.

As promised, it all went immediately into safe keeping far from its roots, and there it shall remain until the time comes for 'the Pracha Dossier' to be published in a manner that will allow my promise to him to be fulfilled.

The guardian of the security box wanted to know nothing, wanted to see nothing, wanted to hear nothing. He was terrified to be in the same room when the box was opened, and his relief was almost tangible when he saw the dossier being carried away. The key was tossed to him, and he was told to relax, our paths would never cross again, his name was already forgotten.

# Epilogue

HOW DID I FEEL TO BE REUNITED WITH THE REAL WORLD? WELL, I was hugely apprehensive, of course. Yes, I had been removed from society on a number of previous occasions, but those periods of isolation had been short-lived in comparison, and there had been no major complications in regards to re-entering society on my release. However, being locked up in a terribly cramped, structured and totally controlled environment with all manner of terrible things going on around me for more than 17 years had made an indelible impression on my subconscious, which I knew wouldn't be easily shaken. I was not going to slip back into what had become a strange new world of mobile phones, the Internet, smart buildings, smart cards, smart cars, smart passports, smart shopping and so on without a period of considerable readjustment and adaptation.

For the final few years that I was in Klong Prem, wondering if I had a hope in hell of ever getting out, things had been fairly comfortable as far as accommodation was concerned. I was afforded the luxury of having just 12 other men to share my sweltering cell, but the thought of actually sleeping alone in a proper bedroom with all of that space to myself, or sitting at a table in the living room to write a letter without a lot of inquisitive chaps popping over to say hello and asking, 'Whatchadoin', Sly?' was a little difficult to imagine.

There had been quite a few changes for the better at The Prem after my return there. The visit areas had been improved considerably, and there was just one partition between inmate and visitor, allowing conversations to be conducted at normal volume. A new seven-storey hospital had replaced the old one, and, though it was mostly used for prison staff and their families, there was a certain comfort in knowing that it was there and that I would be admitted if the need ever arose. New regulations had been introduced governing the transport of inmates to the courts, with new buses replacing the dirty old blue ones and the number of prisoners limited to how many can be seated comfortably during the trip. Chains hadn't been eliminated, however, and inmates continued to be shackled for long periods just as they always had been.

I don't know for sure what happened to Hansel in the end. I heard several times that he had become so gross from eating so much of the rough red rice that the prison provided – actually highly nutritious food – and from scavenging for extra rations that he ended up barely able to move and died lying in his own waste in the hospital at The Prem. But then I heard later that he had gone completely insane whilst at the hospital and had been shipped back to a mental institution in Germany. I personally never laid eyes on him again after we had been sent to Bangkwang.

Ben remained in Bangkwang after my release, amnesties to that date not being sufficient to have him transferred to The Prem. Tut was moved to The Prem before I returned there and shared my cell, my food and my struggle in Section 1 for several years after I arrived. I have not heard from Fred since the day we stood together before the female judge at the Appeal Court hearing, though he did communicate with Brent several times whilst trying for compensation. I received a letter from Bangkwang almost exactly one year before my release to say that my old mate Colonel Niran had joined his friend Major Pracha. Sixty-six years old and apparently fed up with the waiting and the constant disappointments, he had just lain down one morning and died. There was no heart attack, no stroke and no other complications sufficient to cause death. He simply set his soul free.

As if all of this wasn't enough, I received a letter from Phuket several weeks later to inform me that my dear friend Om had also died. She was just 42 years of age, and I had known her for half of her life. She had supported and encouraged me through all the years of my ordeal, literally from day one, even though she was almost perpetually unwell herself. The leukaemia she suffered from won in the end. Although her death wasn't altogether unexpected, it was upsetting to me just the same and depressed me for some time.

I don't know for certain what happened to Jaidow. Her last ID-card update was a couple of years before my release, so she must have still been kicking then, but, frankly, whether or not that is still the case, I couldn't care less.

As for those responsible for the theft – for that is what it was – of those 17 years of my life, should our paths ever cross again, may God have mercy on your conniving souls, because I will give your earthly presence none.